The Psychology of Peace

Recent Titles in Psychological Dimensions to War and Peace

Perpetration-Induced Traumatic Stress: The Psychological Consequences of Killing
Rachel M. MacNair

Memory Perceived: Recalling the Holocaust
Robert N. Kraft

The Psychology of Peace

An Introduction

RACHEL M. MACNAIR

Psychological Dimensions to War and Peace
Harvey J. Langholtz, Series Editor

Westport, Connecticut
London

8.2-2004
WW
$23.95

Library of Congress Cataloging-in-Publication Data

MacNair, Rachel M.
    The psychology of peace : an introduction / Rachel M. MacNair.
        p. cm.—(Psychological dimensions to war and peace)
    Includes bibliographical references and index.
    ISBN 0–275–97855–9 (alk. paper)—ISBN 0–275–97856–7 (pbk.:alk. paper)
        1. Peace.   2. Nonviolence.   3. Peace—Psychological aspects.   I. Title   II. Series.
    JZ5538.M355 2003
    303.6′6—dc21   2002028307

British Library Cataloguing in Publication Data is available.

Copyright © 2003 by Rachel M. MacNair

Library of Congress Catalog Card Number: 2002028307
ISBN: 0–275–97855–9
        0–275–97856–7 (pbk.)

First published in 2003

Praeger Publishers, 88 Post Road West, Westport, CT 06881
An imprint of Greenwood Publishing Group, Inc.
www.praeger.com

Printed in the United States of America

The paper used in this book complies with the
Permanent Paper Standard issued by the National
Information Standards Organization (Z39.48–1984).

10   9   8   7   6   5   4   3   2   1

Every reasonable effort has been made to trace the owners of copyright materials in this
book, but in the case of Richard Gregg this has proven impossible. The author and
publisher will be glad to receive information leading to more complete acknowledgments
in subsequent printings of the book and in the meantime extend their apologies for any
omissions.

Contents

Series Foreword   vii

Introduction   ix

1   Psychological Causes of Violence   1

2   Psychological Effects of Violence   31

3   Psychological Causes of Nonviolence   57

4   Psychological Effects of Nonviolence   87

5   Conflict Resolution   109

6   Nonviolent Struggle and Social Movements   133

7   Public Policy Issues of Violence   161

8   Gentle Lives and Culture   191

A Short Chronology of Peace Psychology   213

References   219

Index   229

Series Foreword

In *The Psychology of Peace: An Introduction,* Rachel MacNair has provided a background for the study of peace psychology, and also a discussion of current issues on the subject, linking personal and individual topics related to peace with broader social concerns. MacNair has addressed both theory and practice, philosophical topics and also practical application.

The concept of peace psychology means different things to different people. Some will disagree with several of the findings and assertions of this book, but peace psychology is a developing field and the author is candid enough to acknowledge we don't have all the answers yet. In this book, MacNair begins with a discussion of the psychological causes and effects of violence, and then addresses the same for nonviolence. She looks at conflict resolution and how nonviolent approaches to social struggles can be adopted, and closes with an examination of both public policy and personal living. Along the way, we are invited to consider nuclear warfare, militarism, abortion, the treatment of animals, TV violence, Greek theatre, and thinkers and writers on peace who include Gandhi, Tutu, and William James.

In the post–September 11 world, we have come to realize the changing nature of warfare and the changing definitions of peace. No longer sufficient are the definitions of war as violence between nations, or peace as an absence of declared war between nations. Violence can come within society, within groups, and within individuals. In modern society, with all its vulnerabilities, the full cruelty of war can be perpetrated by a small group of dedicated terrorists and can be delivered with a speed and efficiency we did not anticipate as possible. Our existing models for war and peace changed on September 11, 2001, and we all realized that the motivations for aggression had to be considered on a different level. Our understandings of war can no longer be only through the fields of international relations and the military. The motivations for today's warfare can often be traced to deep psychological feelings of ethnic identity, animosity, and an acceptance of violence as an effective way for small groups or even individuals to confront what they see as aggressors. In this book, MacNair has conducted a thoughtful but rigorous examination of these issues in an effort to understand some of the psychological causes and effects of both violence and nonviolence at the political and personal levels. It is through this approach that psychologists and other social scientists may help us to better understand—and perhaps even limit or prevent—the use of violence, and replace violence with peace both politically and personally.

Harvey J. Langholtz
Series Editor

Introduction

The subdiscipline of peace psychology grew steadily over the course of the twentieth century. At the beginning of the century, pioneering psychologist William James published his classic essay on the moral equivalent of war. The study of war, aggression, and violence has ever since been accompanied by studies of peacemaking, kindness, and nonviolence. A profusion of ideas have been put forward and tested to account for these from a psychological point of view.

What causes violence, and what can be done to counter it? Since violence wreaks its destruction in nations and in schools, on the street and against businesses, an understanding of what makes the human mind inclined to such behavior is crucial. Even more important, however, is what disposes the human mind to prevent or counter such behavior. Medical doctors whose job is to study physical health actually spend most of their time studying the causes and effects of disease and how to treat it. Peace psychology is analogous for societal health. The first task is to study the cause and effects of that which keeps peace from existing, and then to study what needs to be done to avoid a violent result.

The structure of this book is in four themes in complementary pairs. The first theme is the causes and effects of violence, with the second being the causes and effects of nonviolence. The third theme is problem solving: conflict resolution for those occasions when both parties are willing, and nonviolent struggle or "people power" for when they are not. The final theme is the public and private: public policy first and then peaceful lifestyles and culture.

peace: a positive societal state in which violence, whether direct or structural, is not a likely occurrence, and in which all humans, animals, and ecology are treated with fairness, dignity, and respect.

psychology: the science of individual human and animal behavior and of mental life.

peace psychology: the study of mental processes and behavior that lead to violence, prevent violence, and facilitate nonviolence as well as promoting fairness, respect, and dignity for all, for the purpose of making violence a less likely occurrence and helping to heal its psychological effects.

FURTHER READING

These are overall recommendations. Suggestions for more specific topics follow each chapter.

Chirot, D., & Seligman, M. E. P. (Eds.). (2001). *Ethnopolitical warfare: Causes, consequences, and possible solutions.* Washington, DC: American Psychological Association.

Christie, D. J., Wagner, R. V., & Winter, D. D. (2001). *Peace, conflict, and violence: Peace psychology for the 21st century.* Upper Saddle River, NJ: Prentice-Hall.

Glad, B. (Ed.). (1990). *Psychological dimensions of war.* Newbury Park, CA: Sage Publications.

Kool, V. K. (Ed.). (1993). *Nonviolence: Social and psychological issues.* Lanham, MD: University Press of America.

Peace and Conflict: Journal of Peace Psychology, a quarterly scholarly journal available from: Lawrence Erlbaum Associates, 10 Industrial Avenue, Mahwah, NJ 07430–2262.

ORGANIZATIONS

Peace Psychology Division of the American Psychological Association, Division 48: http://moon.pepperdine.edu/~mstimac/Peace-Psychology.htm.

Psychologists for Social Responsibility: http://www.psysr.com.

Web page with links to an extensive set of peace studies resources on the Internet: http://www.webster.edu/~woolflm/peacelinks.html.

CHAPTER 1

Psychological Causes of Violence

The term "violence" is defined broadly here, as injurious activity that is done directly or socially supported, or inflicted by social institutions in the form of poverty. This book deals with broad concepts, not individual cases in which various circumstances cause violence to happen. Here we consider underlying psychological mechanisms generally applying across a wide range of particulars.

This chapter covers many ideas that have been proposed in psychology. Some ideas contradict others or are controversial, some are well accepted and add understanding to the complexity of the problem, and some are new and still under discussion. None are expected to be the entire cause of violence without taking others into account. The ideas are in categories:

- Disconnects—internal mental processes
- The Power of the Situation—external situations impacting mental processes
- Personality—lifelong personality traits
- Passions of War—society-wide psychological processes and emotions

DISCONNECTS

Moral Disengagement

Bandura and his colleagues argue the most inhumane behavior comes from psychological processes by which original ideas of moral conduct are disengaged. That these mechanisms remove inhibitions has been extensively documented in historical atrocities, and confirmed in laboratory studies of punitive behavior (Bandura, Barbanelli, Caprara, & Pastorelli, 1996).

How to Disengage

Mechanism #1: Change How You Think about It
The cognitive transformation of the reprehensible conduct into good conduct.

This is the most effective, and can be done three ways:

1. moral justifications
2. comparison to worse conduct, making this conduct seem less consequential
3. euphemisms

Mechanism #2: Scapegoating or Deferring to Authority
Displacing or diffusing the responsibility for the conduct or for its detrimental effects.

Mechanism #3: Discounting the Effects
Minimize, ignore, or distort those detrimental effects.

Mechanism #4: Discounting the Victim
Dehumanize or blame the victim.

Semantic Dehumanization

The fourth mechanism, discounting the victim, is shown in detail by William Brennan in a 1995 book called *Dehumanizing the Vulnerable: When Word Games Take Lives*. Brennan believes language profoundly colors understanding of reality. One's perception of an object is often determined not by its nature, but by the words used to describe it.

Brennan gives various categories of "linguistic warfare" that have been used to facilitate violence against people, for instance, people as deficient humans, nonhumans, nonpersons, animals, parasites, diseases, inanimate objects, or waste products. He offers an array of quotations from throughout history to depict these attitudes, which have helped cause much violence against vulnerable groups (see table 1.1). Those able to understand the insults can be badly hurt psychologically by the language alone.

Brennan's point, though, is that these are not mere insults. Rivals might use nothing but words in their conflict, and friends and family give out insults followed by reconciliation. In linguistic warfare, the viciousness of the words serves as support for acts of violence against defenseless groups. The words precede violent action, support action by others, or are essential to long-lasting violence by institutions.

The victim being attacked may also be seen as an enemy, especially in war and other power struggles. Dehumanizing can then be *demonizing* the opposition; they are seen as worthy of attack, monsters, demons, simply

Table 1.1
Examples of Linguistic War

	Non-person	Waste Product	Disease
Native Americans	"An Indian is not a person within the meaning of the Constitution." *George Canfield,* Am. Law Review, *1881*	"[Indians are] the very dregs, garbage...of the earth." *Poet Christopher Brooke, 1622*	"The Iroquois had proved more deadly...than the pestilence." *Historian Francis Parkman, 1902*
African Americans	"In the eyes of the law... the slave is not a person." *Virginia Supreme Court decision, 1858*	"The negro race is...a heritage of organic and psychic debris." *Dr. William English, 1903*	"Free blacks in the country are...a contagion." *American Colonization Society, 1815-30*
Soviet Enemies	"Unpersons who have never existed." *Designation for people purged by the Soviet govt.*	"A foul-smelling heap of human garbage." *Prosecutor Andrei Vyshinski, 1938*	"Every religious idea [is] ...contagion of the most abominable kind." *Lenin, 1913*
European Jews	"The Reichsgericht itself refused to recognize Jews ... as 'persons' in the legal sense." *German Supreme Court decision, 1936*	"What shall we do with this garbage?" *Christian Wirth, extermination expert, 1942*	"Some day Europe will perish of the Jewish disease." *Joseph Goebbels, Nazi propaganda minister, 1939*
Women	"The statutory word 'person' did not in these circumstances include women." *British voting rights case, 1909*	"Emptying refuse into a sewer [the woman's body]." *Author Henry Miller, 1965*	"The worst plague Zeus has made-women." *Ancient Greek poet, Semonides*
Babies	"The word 'person' as used in the 14th Amendment does not include the unborn." *U.S. Supreme Court decision, 1973*	"An aborted baby is just garbage . . . just refuse." *Dr. Martti Kekomaki, 1980*	"Pregnancy when not wanted is a disease...in fact, a venereal disease." *Professor Joseph Fletcher, 1979*
Disabled	"New-born humans are neither persons nor even quasi-persons." *Philosopher Michael Tooley, 1983 (disabled in mind)*	"There's a lot of rubbish [patients] this morning." *ER doctor, 1979*	"The feeble-minded... contaminate posterity... whole nations have partaken of the infection." *Dr. Duncan McKim, 1901*

evil. Evidence that they are real human beings interferes with this understanding, so it is ignored or scoffed at.

Brennan proposes the flip side of this coin is that rehumanizing language can be just as powerful. Language challenging these attitudes also confronts the violence they facilitate.

Distancing

The third mechanism of moral disengagement, discounting the effects, is similar to the concept of *distancing*. To continue violence, one can create mental distance from the reality of what is happening—isolation from the horror, a mental barrier.

One example comes from the war in Vietnam. In the 1970s, peace activist William Sloan Coffin related a story told to him by an American veteran. The veteran's plane was shot down, and he bailed out into a ditch. As he came out, he saw a man pointing a rifle at him, and he slowly put up his arms. Though neither could speak the other's language, the body language was clear, and they went marching through the jungle. At one point, the Viet Cong tripped and fell, and the gun fell out of his hands. The American picked up the gun and handed it back. They went on as before.

At this point in the story, Coffin was startled, and asked if it were not his duty as a soldier to use the gun to shoot the man and escape. "Oh, it wasn't that simple," the veteran said. "I forgot to mention there was a parade of children following. They would have run to the village to tell them, and they would have come after me and captured me, so there was no point."

It had never occurred to him to shoot the children.

Yet, when he was up in his airplane, bombing the villages, he was killing children. From a distance, it was no problem. Close up, it was so horrifying it was not even considered.

Coffin could see this right away, since he was upset about the bombing. He used this story in speeches to show the power of distancing, making it more possible to participate in the horror.

Violence is often made easier when distancing is done physically, as with bombs from airplanes, dangerous working conditions out of view of factory owners, or the Nazi gas chambers. In the case of the Nazis, the original plan was cheap, effective, and efficient: the use of bullets well-aimed at rounded-up Jews. However, this graphic violence was hard on those carrying it out, and the gas chambers were designed to physically separate the killers from their victims.

To keep any horror going, it helps to think of it as numbers and abstract principles on a page. The intrusion of reality must be defended against; if this cannot be done literally, with distance provided by airplanes or words, then it still must be done in the mind.

Mark Twain illustrates this in a short story from 1905 called "The War Prayer" (Anderson, 1972). Amid the excitement, banners flying, and glorious parades preparing for war, the prayer at church asks God to watch over the noble young soldiers and help them crush the foe. Then an aged and mysterious stranger appears to address the congregation, and tells them what they are actually praying for. In graphic terms, he describes the pain of widows and orphans, shrieks of pain, and a homeless icy winter. The final line is: "It was believed this man was a lunatic, since there was no sense in what he said." Mental distancing is complete.

Robert Jay Lifton did extensive interviews with Nazi doctors from the death camps. He proposes a variant on distancing called *doubling*. People in extreme situations create two identities, one that does the killing and the other a good family man. It is something like the difference between Clark Kent and Superman, but more sinister.

A related idea is *compartmentalizing*. People put different parts of their lives into different compartments, sealed off from one another. The Mafia boss ordering a hit or the commanding officer ordering a massacre may still go to church on Sunday, making statements of belief contrary to their own actions. They are not thinking of their actions when they make those statements. Another related idea called *intellectualizing*—especially common among highly educated people—involves a focus on reasoning that allows for violence with a firm avoidance of the accompanying negative emotions.

Operant Conditioning and Desensitization

A psychologist and army lieutenant colonel, Dave Grossman, proposes another psychological mechanism allowing for a disconnection from the situation: the classic concept of *operant conditioning*, a behavior modification technique. It is a procedure of stimulus-response training giving a person the skill to act under stressful conditions.

Grossman argues that the human mind throughout history had a strong resistance to killing. This may seem odd with all the wars there have been, but it is from the wars we get the evidence. S. L. A. Marshall did postcombat interviews during World War II. He reports in his book, *Men against Fire*, that only 15 to 20 percent of the riflemen in World War II fired their weapons at an exposed enemy soldier. Firing would increase greatly if a nearby leader demanded it (as will be further explained by the obedience experiments, below). But when left to their own devices, the great majority of individual combatants appeared to avoid killing. Other studies include French officers in the 1860s, Argentine firing rates in the Falkland War, the Napoleonic wars, American Civil War regiments, and numerous others. Grossman views the history of warfare as a series of successively more effective ways to enable combatants to overcome the inherent psychological resistance to killing. This idea, like many in this chapter, is still controversial.

Grossman says the psychological means to overcome this resistance was deliberately put into practice after World War II. Flying bull's-eye targets are uncommon on the battlefield, so this technique of mere marksmanship was replaced with a realistic man-shaped target, popping up and then falling when hit. This was accompanied by an intricate awards system, in what B. F. Skinner once remarked was a perfect example of operant conditioning.

This conditioning influences behavior when people are frightened. For instance, fire drills condition terrified school children to respond properly during a fire. They go beyond merely giving out information ahead of time, to conditioning the children to behave a certain way when their thought processes are not at their best. With conditioning in flight simulators, frightened pilots can respond reflexively to emergency situations. In the case of war, the application of this technique did increase the rate of Americans firing their weapons in Korea and even more in Vietnam. The British, as opposed to the Argentineans, achieved a high rate of firing during the Falkland War.

In addition to its application in warfare, Grossman worries about current violent video games. He calls them "murder simulation training devices."

Violent media as a whole—movies and television shows with graphic violence, watched while eating popcorn in an entertainment state of mind—can also serve as a form of conditioning in a real-world setting. Historically, the Roman gladiator games, the circus atmosphere around public executions, and similar popular violent entertainment could have served the same function. However, unlike the realistic target practice or video games that develop shooting skills, in this case, only the sight is being conditioned, not the action. This form of conditioning is called *desensitization*. Desensitization to victims can lead to greater ability to commit violence against those victims. At the very least, it can provide social support for violent actions of others.

Beliefs

What people believe about situations affects their behavior. Though individuals do not always act according to their beliefs, those beliefs do have some impact. When there is an ideology, a coherent belief system, which has reasoned violence as necessary to attain important goals, then people who hold that ideology are more likely to commit violence or support others in doing so. This is true for the Nazis, Stalinists, Maoists, and practically every set of soldiers ever assembled.

There are other beliefs serving as cognitive processes that indirectly underlie doing or supporting violence. Some of the major ones include:

The Just World View

Many people do not want to believe that grotesque unfairness happens because they must then fear being the victim of such injustice. However, if these people believe the victims are to blame for their own victimization, they can be more mentally comfortable that they will never be similarly victimized because they are not doing such blameworthy things. The just world view is a psychological attitude whereby people interpret violent and other unfair events in such a way as to maintain a belief that the world operates in a basically fair way. People use the view to protect their minds from the fear that they can become victims.

With direct violence, for example, one can believe a rape victim was asking for it by wearing loose attire and displaying suggestive behavior. Therefore, women who do not dress or act this way believe they are more protected from rape. The idea that such a crime might be arbitrary or due to the actions of men over whom the woman has no control is much more frightening—so it is not believed.

In structural violence, there can be a belief that people enmeshed in poverty are responsible for their own condition by being lazy or unwise in using money. This suggests that those who are not lazy and who save and invest are protected from poverty. It also ignores the fact that some in poverty work hard but are paid inadequately, some had inadequate education due to government policies, and some live in crime-ridden neighborhoods with no means of leaving. Some can never consider saving money because they have far too little money to meet basic needs.

The just world view, a view that the world is just, is a psychological mechanism that helps to maintain the status quo even when the situation is clearly unjust. By reinterpreting unjust situations to make them seem more just, efforts for needed change are avoided.

Realpolitik

Realpolitik is the belief that politics deals entirely with the goal of maximizing power. Security is tied to the ability to use coercive power, and each country is expected to want to achieve as much coercive power as it can. Buildup of the military is therefore the safest course, since others dare not attack when one's own power is so clearly on display.

Machismo

A belief that men should behave in a manly way, and that manly means a blustering display of muscle and intolerance for being insulted, can lead to violent behavior. One common manifestation of this is remarks about how being tested in battle turns boys into men.

Violence Is Inevitable/Human Nature/Killer Instinct

When people hold the belief that violence is in our genes, that we have an instinct for it, and it is in our nature, then the expectation of violence can become a self-fulfilling prophecy.

Retaliation

The belief that suffering violence demands a response in kind can be seen as revenge, or as a matter of justice. Suggestions that violent retaliation is not a good idea are then met with disdain, as coming from people who do not care about justice.

Members of a group that is retaliated against may respond by realizing the errors of their ways and apologizing, but this is not typical. More commonly, they share the philosophy of a response in kind, tending not to perceive the violence of the other side as a retaliation that now balances, but rather as a fresh offense requiring its own retaliation. To do otherwise would be to suggest they were wrong in the first place. A cycle of retaliation then spirals upward. In small cases, this is called a feud, in large cases, a war.

Associated with this is the idea that by being a punishment of others' misbehavior it serves as a deterrent for such actions in the future. In other words, it will "teach them a lesson." This idea is held so strongly that it can be maintained through several years of empirical evidence clearly indicating the contrary. People still refer to retaliation as necessary to their own security, even when events show clearly that retaliation works as provocation rather than deterrent. The belief can be impervious to actual experience.

Violence as Last Resort

Many believe that violence should be avoided under ordinary circumstances, but there are times when it is necessary as a last resort. This is essentially the view of the "just war doctrine." This idea is often presented as being the opposite of pacifism; however, on a continuum that has pacifism on one side and unrestrained brutality on the other, it is actually closest to pacifism—with exceptions. It is the belief that there are situations when injustices are great and therefore violence is justified and necessary. Psychologists vary, as do others, on whether the belief is correct that violence done as a last resort will lessen overall violence by removing an injustice on a given occasion. The scientific point is that this belief does influence behavior.

However, the idea can also have another effect. Once violence is perceived as a last resort, the model in people's minds may be that it is effective in solving problems. In other words, violence is only held back because of ordinary needs for restraint, and it should be used only when the situation is extreme. Therefore, when the situation becomes extreme, violence is expected and the nonuse of violence is seen as immoral. It amounts to announcing that the situation is not so extreme or unjust. The question of whether violence would actually be effective in solving the problem is not asked.

A belief that violence is a "last resort" can interfere in understanding those times when it is not an option at all. It may not actually be a viable alternative. If the various options and their likely consequences were laid out, the violent option might not receive serious consideration as lacking merit. Because of the belief in violence as a last resort, however, this option gets selected anyway—not for its merit as a problem-solver, but because the time for a last resort has arrived.

THE POWER OF THE SITUATION

Destructive Obedience to Authority

In the early 1960s, Stanley Milgram did a series of social psychology laboratory experiments on how willing people are to cause suffering under direction of authority. With the relatively recent Nazi Holocaust in mind, his idea was that he would find low rates of compliance in the United States, and then try the experiment in Germany to find the cultural differences that allowed the Nazis to flourish. He never got to Germany. The compliance rates in the United States were too high.

Milgram's ideas were the first *situational* theory of perpetration behavior. His theory was based on the characteristics of the situation rather than on the characteristics of people coming into the situation. Since people did respond in different ways and the compliance rate was far lower than 100 percent, those previous characteristics are not discounted completely. Nevertheless, Milgram showed how the situation itself exerts power. This was also the opposite of violence caused by frustration, or hatred, or other emotions causing people to do violence on their own initiative. When he allowed people to select level of shock, rather than being ordered, they did choose lower amounts. Therefore, the behavior was caused by outside demands of authority rather than inside emotions.

These experiments are likely to be covered in introductory psychology and social psychology courses. They are among the most known and discussed experiments in psychology. There is even a song by rock musician Peter Gabriel on his 1986 album, *So,* in which, after a short prologue about the experiments, he uses his authority as the singer to get compliance from the audience in singing, with meaning, the repeated chorus, "We do as we're told."

Participants were told this was a learning-memory experiment. It was supposedly randomly decided which of two men would be the "teacher" and which the "learner." As one of many deceptions, however, it was rigged so the participant would always be a teacher; the learner was a confederate of the researcher.

The teacher was instructed to depress a key to give a shock to the learner when the learner got an incorrect answer. This happened constantly. The learner was in another room, but audible. The shocks started at low voltage and went up gradually to higher voltage. After the shocks got up to a certain level, the learner started indicating pain, distress, and demanding to be let out. Of course, the learner was an actor and the shocks were not real, but the teacher/participant believed they were. At higher rates, there was silence—no answers to questions, no distress. Teachers were constantly instructed to go on, with the researcher making authoritative statements like "The experiment requires that you continue." Under this pressure from authority, roughly two out of three men went up to the final shock level. Only about one-third refused to comply at some point. This finding was startling to Milgram.

This initial study was done with men. There have been many replications that show variations. Of the ten studies considering gender differences, nine found none in the rates of how many participants went to the maximum shock. The two studies that considered tension about complying showed women seemed to have more than men.

A look at the replications over twenty-two years, from 1963 to 1985, showed there was no correlation between when it was done and the compliance rates. Time did not make a difference within that span. There were no racial or cultural differences, and rates were similar in different countries.

There was some manipulation of circumstances that did make a difference (see table 1.2).

There is a dramatic drop when the researcher is not present, so "cheating" can be done without the researcher knowing. A similar dramatic drop occurs when the person giving the orders does not have the aura of authority. Even more, authority loses its power dramatically when not united. In the last case, the example of similarly situated people rebelling in full view of the participant provides a very powerful influence on that participant also refusing to comply.

Milgram's theory to explain his experiments is that the nature of authority causes the behavior, not a desire to commit violence. The pressure was practically always against the administration of higher shocks whenever the demands of authority eased up to allow it. Milgram's definition of *authority* is that people share the expectation that one gets to prescribe behavior for the other. This power comes not from personal characteristics, but from the position in the social structure.

In many cases, this is good. A doctor knows more about our medical needs than we do, for example. Legitimate authority is used to ease our lives. However, when it gets to the level of demanding violent behavior that would otherwise not occur, then it is destructive obedience.

Milgram gives two reasons why authority is able to elicit destructive obedience:

1. The authority defines reality and its meaning.

2. The participants shift to a different experiential state.

Table 1.2
Variants on Compliance Rates

Learner has heart condition	no change
Milder-looking experimenter/rougher looking learner	no change
Location less impressive than Yale	no change
Learner is another experimenter rather than another participant	no change
Learner gets contract to be let out on demand, experimenter is breaking contract when insisting on continuing	some drop - 40% compliance
Experimenter by phone, not face-to-face	dramatic drop - 1 in 5 compliance
Another participant, an ordinary man, in the role of insisting on going to higher shocks	dramatic drop - 1 in 5 compliance
Participants free to choose shock level	very dramatic drop - 1 in 40 went to maximum
Role reversal: learner demands shock for manliness, experimenter stops early a second experimenter argues with the first	complete compliance with experimenter - *all* stop by time of or soon after argument
Peer rebellion: two experiments running at same time, in the other one, the teacher rebels.	dramatic drop - 1 in 10 compliance

The different state is called the *agentic state,* in which people relinquish responsibility. The consequence of an *agentic shift* is to feel responsible *to* authority rather than *for* actions.

This can explain the dramatic drops. An ordinary person cannot define the situation nor take responsibility the way an authority can. Two authorities in conflict lose the ability to define the situation. A peer rebellion provides an alternative definition of the situation, as well as an example of someone taking responsibility.

Other variations on these experiments have suggested the two most important parts of authority are its legitimacy and its expertise. Mere ability to provide rewards and punishments is not enough.

Milgram offers three "binding factors" to maintain people in the agentic state: the sequential nature of action, situational obligations, and anxiety.

The Sequential Nature of Action

Only at the beginning is a person asked to do something new. The initial action is mild and relatively unobjectionable. Each time, people are asked to become only a little more extreme than the last. They are not asked to do something qualitatively new, but simply to continue what they did before, only a little more so. To break it off, they would have to justify why they did it up to that point. Therefore, people continue up to a 450-volt shock, which they never would have done had they been asked to do so at the beginning. In the context of violence, this is commonly called a *slippery slope*. For example, the Nazis did not begin with death camps. They started out carefully with laws that took rights and property away from Jews. Each successive step was only an escalation over the previous one, until the death camps were established.

Situational Obligations

Since a promise was made to help in an experiment, breaking it off would mean reneging. A consensus was set up in advance, with an agreed-upon set of rules. Repudiating this is not done lightly; even those who did refuse generally did so with politeness and apologies. No refuser actually released the learner, but only declined to go on with the shocks.

Anxiety

Everyone has internalized rules of social life, including respect for authority. In most cases, these rules are helpful. Traffic flows well, we learn things we would otherwise not know, and so on. There is an emotional barrier to be broken to have noncompliance. The anxiety is caused by the conflict between these internalized rules and those against harming others. The anxiety disappears once a decision to break through that barrier has been made.

The displacement of responsibility Milgram defines in his *agentic state* is the same as Bandura's Mechanism #2 of moral disengagement, discussed above. The use of euphemism in how the authority, and therefore the participant, defines the situation is also prominent. Moral justification, as expected, is also evident.

Others have looked at the experiment participants' patterns of behavior. The dynamics were analyzed from audiotapes of sessions (Blass, 2000, chap. 10). At the start, everyone was eager, helpful, and cooperative. This gradually gave way to a turbulent period of hesitation, vacillation, and stress. Finally, there was usually a more stable mode when tension resolved by capitulation or refusal. All twelve who opposed firmly early, at 150 volts or lower, ended up defiant. Of the fourteen who opposed firmly later in the session, nine ended up defiant—64.3 percent. They were more likely to continue vacillating throughout the session. Of the fourteen who never opposed firmly, there was 100 percent compliance.

One way to see this is that defiance is more likely the earlier dissent begins. People who refuse to go to maximum shock are more likely to have objected earlier. Another viewpoint is that there are three patterns: those who oppose early and defy; those who never oppose and comply; and a group that opposes later, continues vacillating, and can end up either way.

These experiments are no longer being replicated due to new ethical guidelines that came about in part because of them. The deception involved is a matter of concern among psychologists, worried it might imply to the public that participating in experiments means being lied to. There was also clearly much anxiety for participants; follow-up has indicated no damage, but this is still a concern.

There is an ironic twist. Not only the willingness of the participants to go to maximum shock was discovered, but also the willingness of experimenters to be hard-nosed in the face of obvious and very real anxiety. Cold, hard words in writing cannot begin to convey what happened. Viewing a film of the distress can make the distancing caused by cold statistics on a page disappear, yet it did not disappear for the experimenter who was on the scene. The distress to the "learner" was fabricated, but the distress to the people being experimented on was not.

Institutions

The Stanford Prison Experiment of 1971 was a laboratory experiment by Zimbardo and colleagues, a simulated prison designed to last two weeks. In some ways, it was the opposite of the Milgram experiments. Instead of the experimenters encouraging more aggression, they tried to hold it in check. There was no deception, as participants were accurately informed. An institution rather than an individual was the authority.

The study had to be called off after just six days. Even though all participants were college students, screened to be within normal psychological parameters, and assignment to being prisoners or guards was random, vast personality changes developed in the situation. Those playing the role of guards became cruel. Those playing prisoners became inordinately depressed. Even the experimenters got sucked into the requirements of a prison institution. A consultant who had been a former prisoner found himself saying the same things while playing a parole officer that he had hated when he had been on the receiving end.

The "terminator" of the experiment was a late entrant, an outsider. Christina Maslach was the soon-to-be fiancée of Zimbardo, the head experimenter. She was a trained psychologist herself, busy with other projects. She never experienced the escalation that gave appearance of normalcy. Invited to observe when the simulation had run six days, she was appalled to see how inhumane it had become, a madhouse. The experimenters themselves could not see this. After much argument, they came to understand she was right, and shut down the simulation (Blass, 2000).

Hanna Arendt (1963) wrote a book on "the banality of evil" in which she argued there are some people who follow other people's violent designs for no other motivation than doing a good job in their bureaucratic assignment. She cites the Nazi Adolf Eichmann, who arranged for Jews to be transported to death camps. His idea of a nightmare was the train being off-schedule. If he had been assigned instead to ensure that all Jews got a dozen red roses by noon on their birthdays, he would have done that just as efficiently, and it would have had the same emotional content to him. Within violent institutions, some people may be sadistic, but many are so enmeshed in the expectations of the organization that they do monstrous things they would never consider doing in other contexts.

Groupthink

Another situational pressure is the power of the group in which one is engaged, without having to be a long-standing institution. Groups can sometimes make decisions that are much more irrational than individuals would do on their own. A prime classic example is the decision under the Kennedy administration to invade the Bay of Pigs, believing this would spark an uprising of the Cuban people against Castro. This did not occur, and careful analysis would never have expected it to. It was not just as a matter of hindsight, but foresight as well. The administration blundered into that fiasco because a group decision-making process did not allow individuals to think the matter through, as they would have if it had been their individual responsibility. In other words, shared responsibility slipped up on what individual responsibility would have caught.

Irving Janis introduced this concept in a 1972 book called *Victims of Groupthink*. The Bay of Pigs fiasco was a major illustration. One of the participants explains:

I bitterly reproached myself for having kept so silent during those crucial discussions in the cabinet room. . . . I can only explain my failure to do more than raise a few timid questions by reporting that one's impulse to blow the whistle on this nonsense was simply undone by the circumstances of the discussion . . . Had one senior advisor opposed the adventure, I believe that Kennedy would have canceled it. No one spoke against it. . . . Everyone around him thought he had the Midas touch and could not lose. Despite himself, even this dispassionate and skeptical man may have been affected by the soaring euphoria of the new day. (Schlesinger, 1965)

Symptoms of Groupthink

1. *An illusion of invulnerability*—Shared by most or all group members, this fosters excessive optimism, and encourages taking extreme risks.

2. *An unquestioned belief in the group's inherent morality*—Ethical consequences are ignored.

3. *Collective efforts to rationalize*—Warnings are discounted. Assumptions are justified rather than reconsidered.

4. *An enemy image*—Rivals are stereotyped as too evil for genuine negotiations and/or too weak or stupid.

5. *Self-censorship of deviations from group consensus*—Each member of the group minimizes to himself or herself the importance of doubts or counterarguments.

6. *A shared illusion of unanimity*—Members believe the majority view is unanimous since the self-censorship of those with qualms leads to an assumption that silence means consent.

7. *Pressure against dissent*—Expression of contrary views is not expected of loyal group members.

8. *The emergence of self-appointed mind guards*—Some members protect the group from information that might shatter their complacency about how right and effective their actions are.

What kinds of groups are most likely to fall prey to this? Janis says those cohesive groups are likely to have these structural faults:

- insulation of the group from outside influences
- lack of a tradition of impartial leadership
- lack of norms requiring methodical decision-making procedures
- lack of diversity in social background and ideology among the group

Technology

The technologies of violence—weapons and the bureaucracy that mobilizes people—increase its impact. Though many throughout history had ideologies and genocidal intent similar to the Nazis, the twentieth-century technology of the Nazis enabled them to kill in greater numbers. The extent to which the presence of such technology is a component that causes the initiation of violence, as opposed to merely maximizing its harmful impact, is another area of psychological study.

The technology of better operant conditioning to killing has been covered above. The availability of effective weapons with known effects can also cause the initiation of conflicts decision makers might have chosen to avoid otherwise. A sense of power coming with the presence of weapons can serve as a temptation for use, from individuals with guns to nations with bombers.

The state of mind necessary to create destructive technologies can also be linked to their eventual use. Social arrangements causing such technologies to come into existence are connected to social arrangements employing them. As with various kinds of violence, there is a circular causation: the presence of the technology can cause violence, violence can cause the creation of technology, and mental processes underlying both technology and its use are enmeshed so strongly that the analysis of causation may have trouble separating them. An act of violence that would not have happened if the soldier did not have the grenade in his hand still required more than the presence of a grenade. Grenades can be harmless at times, yet the effort causing the soldier to be in that location with a grenade in his hand also contributes to causing the event.

PERSONALITY

The Authoritarian Personality

In 1950, soon after World War II, an influential concept was introduced in a book called *The Authoritarian Personality*. Researchers thought there is a kind of personality that is prejudiced and follows leaders unthinkingly. To measure this, they developed an "F-scale"—where "F" stands for fascism—which has been used widely to compare different groups of people. (An interactive recent Web-page version can be found at http://www.anesi.com/fscale.htm.)

Traits of the Authoritarian Personality

1. *Rigid, unthinking adherence to conventional ideas of right and wrong*—Important values are obedience, cleanliness, success, inhibition or denial of emotions, firm discipline, honoring parents and leaders, and abhorring immoral sexual feelings.

2. *Respect for and submission to authority*—A desire for a strong leader, with followers revering the leader.

3. *Take anger out on someone safe*—Since the unquestioning follower cannot express anger toward the authority, it is stored up and displaced to an outsider who is different, a scapegoat.

4. *Cannot trust people*—A negative view of people means harsh laws requiring a strong police force or army.

5. *Must have a powerful leader and be part of a powerful group*—They are highly ethnocentric and relish being part of the "strongest nation on earth," the "master race," the "worldwide communist movement," "the wealthiest nation," the best group of any kind.

6. *Oversimplified thinking*—When authority tells us what to do or what the single source of our problems is, we do not have to take responsibility for our own thinking.

7. *Guard against dangerous ideas*—Ideas are already set; new ones are threatening.

8. *"I'm pure, others are evil."*—They repress their aggressive and sexual feelings, and then project those traits onto stereotyped persons in the out-group. The authoritarians feel surrounded by people preoccupied with sex and/or violence.

They become paranoid, believing many people want to hurt them, which justifies aggression.

Sufficient numbers of people with authoritarian personalities can promote social movements leading to violence. Some have suggested that the reactions in Milgram's shock experiments and the Stanford Prison Experiment were due to high portions of people with authoritarian personalities. This is ironic because both Milgram and Zimbardo proposed it was situational *rather than* personality variables involved. However, there was variation within the situation, so there could be an interaction effect, with some causation due to the situation, some to personality.

The Machiavellian Personality

The Machiavellian personality is named from the work of Niccolo Machiavelli, a sixteenth-century political philosopher known for his amoral approach. Christie and Geis introduced the idea in 1970 in their classic book, *Studies in Machiavellianism.* They developed a short scale with a few statements for people to mark numbers indicating the level to which they agree or disagree. The fourth version, the Mach-IV, is the one most commonly used, and has been used in hundreds of studies.

In the Mach-IV scale, the items that score positively for high Machiavellian personality are:

- Never tell anyone the real reason you did something unless it is useful to do so.
- The best way to handle people is to tell them what they want to hear.
- It is safest to assume that all people have a vicious streak and it will come out when they are given a chance.
- Generally speaking, people won't work hard unless they're forced to do so.
- Anyone who completely trusts anyone else is asking for trouble.
- The biggest difference between most criminals and other people is that criminals are stupid enough to get caught.
- It is wise to flatter important people.
- It is hard to get ahead without cutting corners here and there.
- Most people forget more easily the death of their parent than the loss of their property.
- People suffering from incurable diseases should have the choice of being put painlessly to death.

Items that are reverse-scored, being the opposite of Machiavellianism, are:

- One should take action only when sure it is morally right.
- Most people are basically good and kind.

- Honesty is the best policy in all cases.
- There is no excuse for lying to someone else.
- All in all, it is better to be humble and honest than important and dishonest.
- When you ask someone to do something for you, it is best to give the real reasons for wanting it rather than giving reasons that might carry more weight.
- Most people who get ahead in the world lead clean, moral lives.
- Most people are brave.
- It is possible to be good in all respects.
- Barnum was very wrong when he said there's a sucker born every minute.

In addition to favoring dishonesty in the service of manipulation, the Machiavellian personality tends to take a very cynical view of people. It is a consistent philosophy. Because people are all inherently bad, good behavior is unrealistic and manipulation is justified. It is what everyone who gets ahead does. The authoritarian personality also takes a dim view of other people, but primarily those in the out-group. The Machiavellian, to use the old joke, cannot be said to be prejudiced because he or she hates *everyone*. The Machiavellians also take an entirely different view of religion. Inasmuch as they pay any attention at all, it is to manipulate others, such as a businessperson making sales contacts at church.

In both cases of personality type, it makes more sense to refer to people as being on a continuum rather than in strict categories. People are relatively higher or lower in the traits. The high authoritarian is more likely to provide political support for a dictator or violent social policies. The Machiavellian is more likely to supply technical support to a dictator by selling weapons. Violent social policies are supported when the Machiavellian can make a profit from them.

Narcissistic and Antisocial Personalities

The traits of *narcissistic personality* include extreme self-centeredness and being excessively conceited. They can contribute to violent acts in at least three ways:

- An associated lack of empathy and compassion.
- A belief that acts of violence will have much grander consequences than is realistic.
- Grandiosity can allow a person to play God, deciding certain goals are worthy of violence and whose lives are expendable.

For example, Timothy McVeigh believed his bombing of the federal building in Oklahoma City might lead to uprisings against the government. He thought it was "revenge" against the *government*, not innocent individuals.

That the narcissistic personality might underlie some criminal activity is not surprising. It becomes a problem when the society as a whole feeds the grandiose beliefs of such individuals, for example with Adolf Hitler. The question then becomes why the society agreed with the conceited beliefs.

The *antisocial personality* belongs to those who are indifferent to the fate or feelings of other people. Terms such as "psychopath" and "sociopath" have also been used. The grandiosity of the narcissistic personality may be missing, but the lack of empathy and compassion is all the more complete.

This is one area where biological findings are fairly consistent. Studies show that many with this kind of personality have suffered horrific abuse. A constant barrage of stress hormones results, the system becomes exhausted, and the emotions go flat. Missing are the racing heart, the adrenaline rush, and the perspiration that the rest of us have under stress. This is one of the most consistent findings in sadists and cold-blooded killers. Emotional numbing is extreme.

These few individuals are expected to be overrepresented in the population of those who commit violent crimes. Society strongly disapproves and has institutional arrangements to restrain them. There is no controversy over a desire to find the causes and remedy them.

When the society as a whole becomes violent, however, it is not necessarily because its portion of those with these personality traits has grown exponentially. Such people may get events rolling, but they cannot do so unless the societal response allows it. What is the difference between a society that confines its violent people and one that elects them its leaders?

PASSIONS OF WAR

Appeal of War

William James, a pioneer of the science of psychology, was also a pioneer of peace psychology with an essay called "The Moral Equivalent of War." He suggested that war has appeal in meeting certain psychological functions, particularly the need to belong to a group. He put it this way: "All the qualities of a man acquire dignity when he knows that the service of the collectivity that owns him needs them. If proud of the collectivity, his own pride rises in proportion. No collectivity is like an army for nourishing such pride" (James, 1910/1971).

James proposed that to get rid of the scourge of war, society must offer nonviolent alternatives that meet those psychological needs. He identified the following needs as helping make war attractive:

- Pride in one's self by belonging to a greater group, helping achieve its ends. It gives a sense of aliveness as part of the vast undertaking.
- Giving meaning and purpose to an otherwise boring life.
- Projection of self-doubts or self-hatred onto someone else, redirecting anxieties toward a more comfortable target.
- Displacing aggression onto a third party. Group cohesion improves when faced with an external threat. Arguments internal to a group cease when everyone faces a common enemy. When a population is involved in a war, it is unified. When peace returns, so do quarrels. Many people remember the sense of unity with fondness.
- The admirable virtues of discipline, courage, and self-sacrifice for the greater good. People like to think of themselves as having and demonstrating such qualities.
- The anxiety of uncertainty vanishes when war hysteria arrives.

Lawrence LeShan discusses these needs in his book *The Psychology of War: Comprehending Its Mystique and Its Madness*, but adds much more detail about the last item. He starts with the idea that, psychologically, we all have different modes of perceiving reality at different times. We move between these modes easily and automatically. A businessman at work has a construction of reality that goes by his senses—LeShan calls this the *sensory mode*—and the rules involve a realistic understanding of how the world operates. At home, the businessman hears his child crying out fearfully, and as he dashes up the stairs, he says a prayer that the child will be all right. It would never occur to him to pray that way at work. Seeing the child is fine, he holds her and assures her that everything is all right and safe. He would not say this at work either, since it is inaccurate. But he is not lying to his child. The rules of comforting a frightened child are different because the construction of reality is different. The businessman shifts between these different perceptions of reality, with their different rules, without any effort. It seems normal and natural (LeShan, 1992).

In the case of war, LeShan argues, there is usually a shift to a *mythic mode*. The rules of understanding what is going on change, qualitatively and dramatically. Reasons that make so much sense in the sensory mode are quickly forgotten.

The escalation to World War I is a prime example. The level of international travel in Europe was much higher than it had ever been, so that dehumanized views of the enemy were not caused by lack of exposure to other peoples. Many pacifist groups existed, and the international socialist movement was fairly strong. However, once war broke out, the socialist groups shifted to belonging to their own nations and enthusiastically supported the war effort. All the work on explaining what was wrong with war was abandoned, remarkably quickly. LeShan suggests this is because people were no longer in a sensory mode that takes reasoning into account. Large numbers of people shifted to the mythic mode, and the war was on.

The following chart is paraphrased from LeShan's book, explaining the difference between normal peacetime thinking and what has commonly come to be called war hysteria.

To illustrate this with a literary example, consider the classic movie, *The Wizard of Oz.* Kansas, in black and white, is the real world, and things work in sensory mode. Dorothy travels to the mythical land of Oz, a full-color world where the rules have changed, and she kills two women. When the falling house accidentally kills the first woman, the people immediately sing, dance, and throw a party. When the second woman is

Table 1.3
Sensory vs. Mythic Perception of Reality

Peacetime (Sensory Mode)	Wartime (Mythic Mode)
Good and *Evil* have shades of gray. Many groups with different ideas and opinions are legitimate.	*Good* and *Evil* are reduced to *Us* and *Them*, with no bystanders. Opinions on crucial issues are wholly right or wrong.
Now is pretty much like other times - more of some things, less of others, just quantitative differences.	Now is special, qualitatively different from all other times. Everything is cast in the balance. Whoever wins now wins forever.
The great forces of nature, God or human evolution, are not involved in our disputes.	History is on our side. The great motivating forces of the cosmos are for *Us*.
When the present period is over, things will happen pretty much as they have in the past.	When the war is over, everything will be vastly different. Winning or losing will change the meaning of the past and shape of the future.
There are many problems to be solved. Their relative importance varies from day to day. Life is complex, with many foci.	There is only one major problem to be solved. All others are secondary. Life is simple, with one major focus.
All people act from pretty much the same motives.	*They* act from a wish for power. *We* act from self-defense and benevolence.
Problems start on many different levels - economic, political, personal - and must be dealt with on these levels.	The real problem started with an act of will on the part of the enemy and can only be solved by breaking his will or making him helpless.
We are concerned with the causes of the problems we want to solve.	We are not concerned with causes, only with outcomes.
We can talk to those with whom we disagree. Negotiation is possible.	The enemy is evil. It lies. Interaction is not possible. Only force can settle the matter.
All people are fundamentally the same. Differences are quantitative.	*We* and *They* are qualitatively different. The same actions are good when *We* do them, evil when *They* do them.
The people of another country, even one opposing ours, have a variety of views. A report of a decision against our country's interest will say, "The government of X decided this, with the Y party dissenting."	The enemy country is a monolithic nation. Members of this nation are just part of the whole. A report on the enemy nation's decisions will say, "The nation of X did this."
In war, people get killed on both sides. This is sad for both, and a good reason to avoid war when possible.	The heroes kill the villains. *We* are the heroes, and *They* are the villains. If one of them kills one of ours, this breaks the rules and makes us angry.

killed, her guards immediately give Dorothy a cheer. Dorothy maintains her status as heroine because both women are witches, representing evil. They cannot be reasoned with because they are not real people.

Back in Kansas, Miss Gulch is the prototype for the Wicked Witch of the West, played by the same actress. She threatens the life of Dorothy's dog, Toto, causing the girl great grief. The worst that befalls Miss Gulch, however, is that Auntie Em tells her off, and her plot to destroy Toto is foiled when the dog runs away. Both fates are entirely proportionate to her offenses, and can therefore be cheered by the audience.

How would the audience feel if Dorothy had killed Miss Gulch?

Even accidentally, an entirely sinister plot element would have been introduced. Though the sympathies of the audience are against Miss Gulch, this does not mean a killing could be even remotely justifiable. Kansas is the sensory world, the real world. People may be mean, but they are not evil incarnate. Dorothy would no longer be an innocent person.

This shift to mythic mode is a psychological way of referring to war hysteria and describing why it looks like madness when people are back in sensory mode. It could also be called a cartoon mentality, or a fairy-tale view of the world.

This shift starts with a few people and builds. The point at which the mobilization to war becomes strongest is when enough of the population has made this shift that those people who remain in sensory mode are in danger because questioning the rightness of the cause becomes treason. Such people can be imprisoned, killed, or at least ignored. Therefore, many of them keep quiet accordingly, or choose the path of least resistance and join the shift to mythic mode.

The beginning of "The War Prayer," by Mark Twain (Anderson, 1972) describes this shift especially well. The excitement generated by the war, the withdrawal of those who questioned its rightness, and the minister praying for victory are all signs of the shift to a mythic perception of reality. A stranger, still in sensory mode and grounded in factual reality, comes and explains to the people what it was they had actually prayed for. That the congregation remained in mythic mode is shown by the punch line: "It was believed this man was a lunatic, since there was no sense in what he said."

This is not to say all wars are fought with most of the population in mythic mode. The world wars were, but for Americans, the wars in Korea and Vietnam were not. The American population never mobilized for them and had no popular war songs. When factual data from Vietnam came through on television sets, people were still in sensory mode. Accordingly, they were appalled.

War as Pathology

The idea of war as an endemic disease or pathology on the body politic has been suggested many times. Freud proposed there is a "death instinct," called *thanatos*, countered by the "life instinct," *eros*. He believed the death instinct is directed at ourselves, but gets displaced onto other people. This theory has not had much support among scholars, even Freudians, but it is always mentioned in discussions of the history of these ideas.

Also mentioned are the ideas of Konrad Lorenz, an ethologist who believed violence was instinctual. He alleged that there was an "aggressive instinct," urge, or drive, inherent in animals due to the evolutionary past, which must seek release. This idea was popularized in the 1970s, but has not received much support since then. Among other things, the drive to eat and reproduce are clearly universal, but a drive to aggress is only practiced by a small portion of people. Though wars have been common throughout history, as have crime and exploitation, the part of the population actually participating in them has been numerically small.

Sue Mansfield analyzes unconscious motivations to war through a historical approach to gestalt therapy. She considers child-rearing practices under differing circumstances of different historical eras. In the Neolithic period, with the advent of agriculture, changes in child-rearing practices involved earlier weaning, earlier chores, and a requirement of submitting to arbitrary authority. Children were afraid to lash back against their parents for the new frustrations, but as adults the men could displace this aggression onto the enemy in war. The ritual nature of warfare also gave more of a sense of control over dangerous and capricious forces of nature. Wars generally stopped after only one killing. They were psychological rituals rather than means to political ends.

With more advanced civilization and greater social stratification, Mansfield says, war became a means of making changes and imposing control. Parents had less time to nurture children, so children grew up thinking that acquiring material goods was a substitute for love. Greed was more of a motivation for war than before. Battle became, for men, one of the few endeavors where camaraderie, goals, actions, and results were clear in a world that was otherwise loveless, repressed, and frightening.

In the industrial age, by contrast, greed and pragmatism work against war. Wars happen in spite of them rather than because of them. The character of child training shifted from physical abuse to cleanliness and structure. Expectations for performance led to a different kind of self-hatred and powerlessness. This got projected onto people's own sociopolitical group and was felt as vulnerability. According to Mansfield, the major motivation for war throughout the twentieth century has been unconscious fear.

Barbara Ehrenreich (1997) also looked at prehistory and historical processes in a novel theory she puts forward in a book called *Blood Rites: The Origins and Passions of War*. Primates, and therefore early humans, were constantly preyed upon and had much anxiety about predators. Throughout recorded history, fear of being eaten by animals has remained a constant problem. Yet weapons technology enabled people to eventually become predators themselves. What followed was a widespread, close to universal practice of blood sacrifice, ceremonial rituals with a public display of killing humans or animals. In her words:

Rituals of blood sacrifice both celebrate and terrifyingly reenact the human transition from prey to predator, and so, I will argue, does war. Nowhere is this more obvious than in the case of wars undertaken for the stated purpose of initiating young men into the male warrior-predator role—a not uncommon occurrence in traditional cultures. But more important, the anxiety and ultimate thrill of the prey-to-predator transition color the feelings we bring to all wars, and infuse them at least for some of the participants, some of the time, with feelings powerful and uplifting enough to be experienced as "religious." (Ehrenreich, 1997).

She suggests the *Defense Hypothesis:* human achievements like fire, intelligence, and group cohesion were not due to the needs of hunters, but the opposite need, as defense against predators. Separation anxiety by newborn babies, weak enough to be easy prey, comes from the survival value of yelling loud enough to not be left vulnerable outside the group.

The demons felt to be causing problems, such as disease and bad luck, were then treated in the same way as the predatory beast—they were offered a sacrifice. Real predatory beasts leave the rest of the group alone if one member is sacrificed to them. Demons and gods to whom sacrifices were made were commonly patterned after predatory beasts. To this day, nations use such beasts as eagles and bears to symbolize themselves. The sacrifice ritual mimics the crisis of the predator's attack. The demons and gods are in the role of the predator.

In addition to being safe reenactments, there is the thrill of defensive solidarity. There is fear-dissolving strength against the enemy. Group cohesion is strong, and quarrels among the group cease. Blood sacrifice serves this function as well as war does. To Ehrenreich, it is for the same reasons. In war, the enemy is human, but she argues the emotions derive from long experience with a primal battle that over millennia took a large portion of human lives, leaving strong emotional scars. Larger and more vicious animals once outnumbered humans.

Historically, the universality of blood sacrifices declined as new religions opposed them. From Buddhism to Islam, over the course of about one millennium several major religions arose, using different approaches, but all ending the blood sacrifices. These religions also expected ethical behavior, unlike the gods of old, who were not very ethical themselves. The religions tended to condemn war—the Hebrew prophets spoke against it, and there was pacifism in early Buddhism and Christianity. The prohibition of blood sacrifice was most successful; the practice is now uncommon. The forbidding of war, however, has not prevailed as well.

Ehrenreich believes the new religions were successful for three reasons. First, agricultural societies found sacrifices burdensome and were eager for a rationale to stop. Second, a merchant class arose. They engaged in nonviolent acquisition of wealth, which works more efficiently with honesty, reliability, and rational deliberation. This favored the ethical framework in which the new religions flourished. Finally, in complex societies, the lower class was made up of militarily defeated peoples. This was fertile ground for religious movements on behalf of ordinary people, who resent conquerors. A victim-centered religion that makes a virtue of mercy, is inclusive to the lowliest people, and condemns war is appealing to victims.

Of course, such religion is not appealing to warriors. However, they are always in the minority in any society. The warriors fought these religions at first, but because the religions included ideas that allowed them to withstand persecution, the warriors co-opted them instead. From Christian knights to Buddhist samurai, they reinterpreted the religions to suit their agendas. There was the militarization of the religions, and the sacralization of war. War was again made sacred, through a different means than its relation to blood sacrifice. Ehrenreich argues the passions that initially engendered it remain.

Emotions and Drives

Just as beliefs affect behavior, so do emotions. In psychology terms, there are cognitive and affective components. Few people blindly follow emotions without thinking, but emotions can affect both the thinking and the behavior.

Throughout history, philosophers have considered underlying emotions leading people to war and other violence. Any list is bound to bring objections that something important was left out or insufficiently stressed. This discussion has been going on for thousands of years. This is a sampling of what psychological investigation has found.

Frustration

In 1939, a book was published called *Frustration and Aggression* (Dollard, Doob, Miller, Mowrer, & Sears). Its thesis was that a sense of frustration is caused when people or animals are thwarted from attaining an expected goal or satisfaction. This frustration then causes aggression. There may be occasions when it does not, but the authors believed that when aggression occurs, a frustration should be looked for as the cause. If the person or thing causing the obstacle is not available, a substitute is aggressed against instead.

Many laboratory experiments backed up the contention that frustration led to greater aggression, though not all did. For those experiments that took time into account, it seemed frustration is not very long lasting. It can take minutes or even seconds to dissipate, unless maintained by uninterrupted rumination.

The later Milgram experiments also showed greater "aggression," in the form of higher electric shocks, clearly not caused by frustration. Deliberate actions by soldiers in warfare are discouraged from being based on frustration. This lack of professionalism could be dangerous; it is not the way to win battles.

There was a classic study by Hovland and Sears in 1940 suggesting that if the frustration-aggression hypothesis were true, there should be a correlation between lynchings and economic conditions in the South of the United States. They found such a correlation between lynchings and lower cotton prices. Many used this to say economic frustrations lead to violence. However, other studies have not backed this up. Even the classic study falls apart with more modern statistics, or if it is extended beyond the time of 1882–1930. That extension is not minor. A major depression occurred in the 1930s, yet the number of lynchings went down. Using other economic indicators and various hate crimes and other historical periods, the evidence is that frustration alone does not lead to hate crimes (Green, Glaser, & Rich, 1998).

The assertion that frustration must always or even usually lie at the root of all aggression has not held up well under years of scrutiny. Nevertheless, there are occasions in which frustration may be one of the motivating emotions in specific instances, as in domestic abuse or street crime, when an outburst of frustration can be followed by immediate action. Economic downturns do seem to coincide with surges in child abuse (Steinberg, Catalano, & Dooley, 1981).

Catharsis

In the movie *Analyze This*, a psychiatrist says to his gangster client, "You know what I do when I'm angry? I hit a pillow. Try that." This statement shows the producers did *not* consult knowledgeable psychologists to make it realistic. The point was to make a joke, as can be seen by the next action: the gangster pulls out a gun and shoots the pillow. He then announces he feels better. This makes a good joke, but terrible science. Many in the media have clung to the idea that "letting off steam" is a good thing, but the empirical evidence against this is strong.

The first recorded mention of the concept is in Aristotle's *Poetics*. Aristotle proposed that seeing tragic plays gives an emotional catharsis and therefore a beneficial cleansing to the audience. Freud revived the idea. In his hydraulic model of aggressive drives, Freud believed anger builds up, and if not released, can explode into poorly timed, inappropriate actions. If anger were aimed at an inanimate or symbolic target instead, then anger dissipates and the buildup subsides.

This hypothesis has been tested extensively for decades. In scientific evidence, it has long been known there is virtually no support for it; in fact, this letting out of anger consistently *increases* aggression (see reviews: Geen & Quanty, 1977; Warren & Kurlychek, 1981). This aggression was directed not only toward the targets of their anger, but also at innocent third parties, even when people were given media articles promoting catharsis, so they knew it was expected (Bushman, Baumeister, & Stack, 1999).

This makes some sense. Restraints or inhibitions have been removed, and people feel more permission to behave aggressively. They have been primed with thoughts of aggressiveness. It also fits the sequential steps as shown in the Milgram experiments discussed above. Once one step has been taken, it is easier to take another small step as opposed to a larger leap.

The media and pop psychology books may still be wedded to the idea that catharsis helps avoid violence, but they ignore empirical evidence. Throughout this book, many things are offered as possibilities requiring further research before conclusions can be drawn. This is not one of them. The idea has been studied extensively for decades, and the case is strong. By convincing people to engage in aggressive actions against inanimate or symbolic targets, the level of aggression against other people does not decrease, but actually *increases*. Behaving with the concept of catharsis can be regarded as one of the causes of violence.

The term "catharsis," however, can still be used in the original sense of an emotional reaction during drama. Therapists have used the word in the context of a session where repressed emotions become expressed and outbursts of crying may occur; this is immediately followed by discussion to work through the emotions. The idea of "letting off steam" has also been applied to vigorous aerobic exercise, which often does have a stress-reduction effect. In all three cases, however, there is neither a priming of aggressive thoughts nor removal of inhibitions on aggression, so their effects are different than "letting off steam" by aggressing against a symbolic target.

Hatred

A strong emotional desire to harm others can affect behavior to harm others. Hatred can lead to especially foolish decisions in war. When the goal of violence is revenge, then the motivation is hatred by definition.

As with frustration, hatred is an emotion often involved in violence, but not always. When violence is *expressive* rather than *instrumental*, hatred is often what is being expressed. Yet much violence is instrumental, intended to achieve a goal beyond the violence itself. Even expressive violence could be expressing vanity, or result from fear rather than hatred.

Hatred is especially good at sustaining cycles of violence. Because it can be a reaction to violence from others, the violence caused by it can cause a reaction of hatred in the victims, who then retaliate. Long-lasting feuds with strong hatred on all sides can be among the most intractable and difficult problems to solve.

Cognitive Dissonance and Effort Justification

The theory of cognitive dissonance, in simplified form, is that people find it stressful to have two different ideas in conflict with each other, two cognitions that are dissonant. To reduce this tension, they take actions or make arguments that might otherwise seem illogical. Suggestions of a contradiction are then met with belligerency.

For wars, this can additionally take the form of *effort justification*, which is based on the belief that if one has put resources and energy into achieving a certain outcome, that outcome must be valuable. More effort is then required to protect and justify the effort already made. When the only alternative is to admit that all the effort was wasted, especially to admit stupid behavior or poor judgment, then the effort must be continued. The continuation for several years of the American war in Vietnam is one of the most cited examples.

CONCLUSION

Later chapters discuss other aspects of causation of violence. The subject of long-standing animosities between groups is covered under chronic conflicts in chapter 5. Chapter 6 describes how the psychology of power has much to do with causes of violence, but also with explaining how nonviolent counteraction works. The section entitled "Cycles and Goals" in chapter 2 considers how effects of violence can be further causes of violence. Finally, chapter 7 covers applying psychology to specific forms of violence as issues of public policy.

FURTHER READING

General

Chirot, D., & Seligman, M. E. P. (2001). *Ethnopolitical warfare: Causes, consequences, and possible solutions.* Washington, DC: American Psychological Association.

Christie, D. J., Wagner, R. V., & Winter, D. D. (2001). *Peace, conflict, and violence: Peace psychology for the 21st century.* Upper Saddle River, NJ: Prentice-Hall.

Glad, B. (Ed.). (1990). *Psychological dimensions of war.* Newbury Park, CA: Sage Publications.

Disconnects

Bandura, A., Barbanelli, C., Caprara, G. V., & Pastorelli, C. (1996). Mechanisms of moral disengagement in the exercise of moral agency. *Journal of Personality and Social Psychology, 71*, 364–374.

Brennan, W. (1995). *Dehumanizing the vulnerable: When word games take lives*. Chicago: Loyola University Press.

Grossman, D., & Degaetano, G. (1999). *Stop teaching our kids to kill: A call to action against TV, movie and video game violence*. New York: Crown Publishers.

Destructive Obedience and Institutions

Blass, T. (2000). *Obedience to authority: Current perspectives on the Milgram paradigm*. Mahwah, NJ: Lawrence Erlbaum Associates.

Blass Web Site on Milgram: www.stanleymilgram.com.

Janis, I. L. (1972). *Victims of groupthink: A psychological study of foreign-policy decisions and fiascoes*. Boston: Houghton Mifflin.

Kelman, H. C., & Hamilton, V. L. (1989). *Crimes of obedience: Toward a social psychology of authority and responsibility*. New Haven, CT: Yale University Press.

Milgram, S. (1974). *Obedience to authority: An experimental view*. New York: Harper & Row.

Miller, A. G. (1986). *The obedience experiments: A case study of controversy in social science*. New York: Praeger.

Official Web Site for the Stanford Prison Experiment: www.prisonexp.org.

Passions of War

Ehrenreich, B. (1997). *Blood rites: The origins and passions of war*. New York: Henry Holt and Company.

James, W. (1910/1971). *The moral equivalent of war, and other essays; and selections from some problems of philosophy*. New York: Harper & Row.

LeShan, L. (1992). *The psychology of war: Comprehending its mystique and its madness*. Chicago: Noble Press.

Mansfield, S. (1982). *The gestalts of war: An inquiry into its origins and meanings as a social institution*. New York: The Dial Press.

CHAPTER 2

Psychological Effects of Violence

In addition to all the social, economic, physical, and political damage caused by violence, it is usually psychologically traumatic. This chapter covers:

- Effects of Direct Violence on Victims—details of trauma to those subjected to violence by others
- Effects of Direct Violence on Perpetrators—details of trauma to those doing the violence
- Wider Circles of Violence—broadening to structural violence, nuclear weapons, and nonparticipants
- Cycles and Goals—how the effects can become causes, and the effect of means on ends

EFFECTS OF DIRECT VIOLENCE ON VICTIMS

Posttraumatic Stress

Psychological impacts of violence include increased tendency to abuse alcohol or drugs and other stress-related ailments. A major psychological impact of victimization by direct violence is Posttraumatic Stress Disorder (PTSD).

To get PTSD, there must first be a trauma, something so extraordinary it causes an acute reaction. If the event would not bother the ordinary person, the problem is not PTSD. If the event would traumatize anyone but never actually happened, the mental problem is something else. If a person has all the symptoms of PTSD within the first few weeks after the trauma, but they subside over time and he or she gets back to normal, then what happened was an acute reaction. The "post" in PTSD means that the condition is chronic. An acute reaction can be expected, and the way to treat it is to provide tender loving care and let time handle the rest. For people who have PTSD, time has not been a remedy, and more must be done.

The idea of PTSD started with soldiers. In World War I, it was called "shell shock" and thought to be physical in origin. By World War II, it was called "battle fatigue" or "combat fatigue" and understood to be psychological. It became official with veterans of the American war in Vietnam. Many of those who supported the war thought the idea was an antiwar propaganda ploy. Nevertheless, it developed into a psychiatric definition for diagnosis. It then was applied and expanded to various forms of victim groups, even to victims of natural disasters and major injurious accidents. However, it has been clear that the symptoms are much worse, and the disorder more prevalent, when the trauma that causes the condition is of human origin. Victims of intentional direct violence suffer more, and more often.

For a diagnosis of PTSD, there are two major official definitions of the symptoms. One comes from the diagnostic manual of the American Psychiatric Association (1994), and lists a strict set of numbered and lettered symptoms. The other, given below, is from the manual of the World Health Organization:

Arises as a delayed or protracted response to a stressful event or situation (of either brief or long duration) of an exceptionally threatening or catastrophic nature, which is likely to cause pervasive distress in almost anyone. Predisposing factors, such as personality traits (e.g. compulsive, asthenic) or previous history of neurotic illness, may lower the threshold for the development of the syndrome or aggravate its course, but they are neither necessary nor sufficient to explain its occurrence. Typical features include episodes of repeated reliving of the trauma in intrusive memories ("flashbacks"), dreams or nightmares, occurring against the persisting background of a sense of "numbness" and emotional blunting, detachment from other people, unresponsiveness to surroundings, anhedonia, and avoidance of activities and situations reminiscent of the trauma. There is usually a state of autonomic hyperarousal with hypervigilance, an enhanced startle reaction, and insomnia. Anxiety and depression are commonly associated with the above symptoms and signs, and suicidal ideation is not infrequent. The onset follows the trauma with a latency period that may range from a few weeks to months. The course is fluctuating but recovery can be expected in the majority of cases. In a small proportion of cases the condition may follow a chronic course over many years, with eventual transition to an enduring personality change. (World Health Organization, 1992, p. 344)

In many situations, the social circumstances surrounding the trauma cause further problems. People subjected to continuing abuse, as in domestic violence, can suffer a form called Complex PTSD. People subjected to poverty can have additional problems or exacerbation of symptoms due to deprivation. Physical symptoms such as chronic headaches or stomachaches can also be trauma-related.

Many people have some of the symptoms of PTSD, but are at what psychiatrists would call "subclinical levels." People can suffer from some of the symptoms without having a full-fledged diagnosis.

Children

Children subjected to violence are prone to all the above kinds of symptoms, but with additional features simply because children are still developing. An adult who has lived a happy and peaceful childhood but faces horrific violence has mental and emotional resources available that a child has not yet formed. Children may be able to assimilate a large, acute episode, interpret it as an aberration, and continue with their lives as before. However, lengthy and chronic violence is harder to comprehend. Wars, crime-ridden neighborhoods, or domestic abuse are all the more devastating when inflicted on children who have not yet acquired coping skills.

According to Kostelny and Garbarino (2001), problems that occur in small children include:

- regression to previous stages, such as bed-wetting
- more anxious attachment to caretakers
- social withdrawal, less talking, and disruption in peer relations
- cognitive distortions, trouble concentrating, and learning difficulties
- erratic behaviors that go with these cognitive distortions of reality
- body ailments such as headaches, excessive colds, etc.
- increased aggressive activity

These symptoms are also quite common in adolescent and adult victims of chronic violence, but especially pronounced in children because they have little previous experience, less development of coping skills, and an unclear understanding of what is normal and what is unusual.

Adolescents are particularly prone to the increase in aggressive behavior since they have generally grown in physical strength and ability to move around independently. The resulting delinquency and gang membership can be major social problems. In war situations, this may mean more soldiers and more brutal attacks on civilians. The violence impairs moral development that would normally be expected at this developmental stage.

Both young children and adolescents also find the presence of such violence to be models in learning how to deal with the world. They have not yet developed any alternative way of seeing things.

Community-Destroying Extreme Situations

Some violence is so concentrated and all-pervasive that hope for future recovery is dashed. Robert Jay Lifton conducted one major study with the survivors of the atom bomb on Hiroshima. In ordinary large disasters, panic is common, but so is pulling together to help one another. He found a profound difference with the immediate survivors of the nuclear blast, however, who had a sense that everyone was going to die. From their perception, the whole world was ending.

Rather than panic or frenzied activity, things moved in slow motion. They were people who "walked in the realm of dreams" and felt a "paralysis of the mind." They were closing off their minds so that no more horror could enter. Although these people were alert to the environment—they were able to describe it in sharp detail later—their minds and behavior were immobilized or numb at the time. Lifton called this *psychic numbing.*

Psychic numbing is essentially one of the symptoms of PTSD, though the official definition calls it "constricted affect," or blocking of emotions. Extreme situations call for extreme numbing. At Hiroshima, it was close to universal and intense; only after the outside world intervened with assistance could it recede.

This also explains behavior in desperate situations such as the Nazi concentration camps. A scene in the movie *Schindler's List* shows a man simply walking on and focusing his eyes straight ahead while another man was being shot. There was nothing the first man could do to help the other; any reaction would only endanger himself. He was saturated with constant murders in that location. Psychic numbing would be the expected response.

EFFECTS OF DIRECT VIOLENCE ON PERPETRATORS

Perpetration-Induced Traumatic Stress

Despite the explosion of interest in studying PTSD, only a small number have considered the impact of being active in causing the traumatic situation, in being a perpetrator rather than a victim. Even in the case of the combat veteran, focus was on how the soldier had been afraid of being shot, or angered and grieved at seeing a friend shot. Few studies have looked at the effect of shooting.

Part of this is due to the thinking that there needs to be a lack of control in the situation, or a reaction of horror or fear. Another reason is sympathy for veterans, and not wanting to appear to be making accusations. This thinking could be based either on the idea that the war was right, or that it was wrong but it was the government's fault and not the soldier's. An assumption is prevalent that the veteran's suffering is due to the enemy rather than to what the soldier was expected to do. Admitting that someone has psychological consequences from killing means admitting that this, in fact, is what he was doing. Issues of guilt then also arise, not just for the veteran, but also for the society that sent him into combat. The official government study on Vietnam veterans is a very extensive set of questions, but affirming a sense of guilt was never one of them. There was only one question in which veterans were asked if they affirmed a lack of guilt.

There have been people who have noticed the PTSD symptoms and ascribed it to killing. At the beginning of the twentieth century, for example, sociologist/social worker Jane Addams interviewed European soldiers during World War I. She wrote, "We heard from . . . hospital nurses who said that delirious soldiers are again and again possessed by the same hallucination—that they are in the act of pulling their bayonets out of the bodies of men they have killed" (Johnson, 1960, p. 273). This describes the symptom of flashbacks, and is at the end of a discussion of negative feelings about killing.

More currently, some researchers have noticed PTSD symptoms resulting from killing or injuring others. Every time the question has been considered, it appears that PTSD is *more severe* in those who kill than in those for whom the trauma is unavoidable (MacNair, 2002). The form of PTSD in which committing violence is the trauma that causes the pattern of symptoms is called Perpetration-Induced Traumatic Stress (PITS).

In the case of war, it seems that there should be a connection between engaging in killing and the intensity of the battle. It would stand to reason that the intensity of battle should be related to the severity of later PTSD symptoms. If PTSD is caused by trauma, then the greater the trauma, the greater the PTSD. However, analysis of U.S. government data shows that even taking this into account, killing still leads to more severe symptoms. Those who killed in what they remembered and assessed as light combat had higher PTSD scores than those who did not kill but were in heavy combat (MacNair, 2002).

Statistics were also done on this sample to see if the pattern of symptoms differed, comparing those veterans who said they did kill with those who said they did not. It showed that intrusive imagery—nightmares, flashbacks, and unwanted thoughts one cannot get rid of—was especially high for those who said they had killed. Temper, irritability, and violent outbursts were also particularly high. Commonly high, but not as strong, were hypervigilance, alienation, and survivor guilt. The issue of justified guilt was not covered in the database. Concentration and memory problems, however, seemed to be more characteristic of those who said they had not killed (MacNair, 2002).

Only recently has quantitative data been gathered. Throughout history, however, the world's literature has given expression to this phenomenon. This would be expected if it were a psychological understanding of something that is common to human beings, not dependent on their cultures. People need not have the concept in mind in order to have the experience.

An example comes from part of a poem written sometime around 1899 by a British soldier in the Anglo-Boer War. This is beginning a period, rising with the world wars and even more dramatically with the American war in Vietnam, in which veterans use poetry to describe their own emotions.

I Killed a Man at Graspan, by M. Grover

I killed a man at Graspan
I killed him fair in fight;
And the Empire's poets and the Empire's priests
Swear blind I acted right . . .
But they can't stop the eyes of the man I killed
From starin' into mine.

We do not yet have enough studies to know how much this applies to soldiers who see what they do, or whether the ability to be far off and push a button without seeing graphic results protects people from intrusive imagery. It has been suggested that there may still be some of the same effect. One history professor noted from her interviews that

technology still failed to render the dead completely faceless. Combatants used their imagination to "see" the impact of their weapons on other men, to construct elaborate, precise, and self-conscious fantasies about the effects of their destructive weapons, especially when the impact of their actions was beyond their immediate vision. . . . So while technology was used to facilitate mass human destruction, it did very little to reduce the awareness that dead human beings were the end product. (Bourke, 1999, pp. xviii–xix)

The concept of PITS can be applied beyond veterans of combat. People who carry out executions are another example. James Berry was a hangman in Great Britain from 1884 until 1892. Unlike most executioners, he kept an extensive diary that included his feelings. Justin Atholl wrote a book using this diary, published in 1956. The entire book shows a man portraying the symptoms of PTSD, which because it resulted from his own actions of killing could be called Perpetration-Induced Traumatic Stress. Atholl says:

Outwardly Berry was unchanged after seven years during which no month had passed without his taking his leading part in the ceremony to which the tolling bell supplied the descant. . . . After a hundred hangings, signs began to appear that Berry's nerves were being affected. He had been a teetotaler when he started. Now he was drinking a good deal. Where formerly he had always been genial he was inclined to become snappy with reporters. His nights were sometimes sleepless and when he slept he was agitated by dreams. When he started as an executioner his nightmares had been the products of his secret fears that things would go wrong, "of things that never happened and never could happen," as he put it. Now they were not products of imagination, but the re-playing by shadowy figures of real scenes which needed no embellishment from a troubled mind to make them nightmares. (Atholl, 1956, p. 158)

Similar accounts come from more recent participants in executions. Stories can also be found among police who have shot in the line of duty, the Nazi methodical killers, abortion providers, those engaged in blood sports or slaughterhouse activities, and regular homicide criminals (MacNair, 2002). The prevalence and severity fluctuate widely among groups, probably because of varying circumstances and the differences in social approval. The field of ascertaining how such differences affect individuals involved is just beginning; researchers have many aspects to cover. Psychology as a science is relatively young, only a little over a century old, and this is one of the fields in which researchers can become pioneers.

Acute Reactions at the Time of Killing

At the time of perpetration itself—the killing—there are certain features that make the later development of posttrauma symptoms more likely. They include:

Distancing/Avoidance

Avoidance of reminders of events is one symptom, so trying to avoid the reality of killing at the time it happens would make sense. One might think that it would help avert later problems, but it does not seem to have that effect.

Dissociation and Time Distortion

As in all traumas, there can be a sense of unreality. Things are happening as in a dream, or with mind separated from body. Time can often seem to slow down during the event. In film, this was portrayed during battle scenes in the movie *Saving Private Ryan* with sudden silence and slowness in the midst of battle.

An example comes from a highly stressed warden overseeing the execution of Connie Evans:

Everything seemed magnified—every sound, every whisper. Though it was only a few feet to the cell where Connie had spent the last seventy-two hours, I moved more slowly than usual. My feet were heavy, I felt as though I had to force my legs to move, and I could feel my heart pounding in my chest. How long the final minutes would be for both of us! I turned to speak to one of the physicians, but I was interrupted by the shrill ring of the red telephone on the wall behind me. The sound came without warning, and it instantly drowned out all other noise in the room . . . The telephone was still ringing, but somehow it sounded far away. (Cabana, 1996, p. 12)

Such dissociation seems to have a worsening effect on later development of PTSD symptoms. In a study of reports by American veterans of the war in Vietnam, researchers concluded that even though the tendency to dissociate during the event may have given the person some sense of detachment, distancing, and unreality, the dissociation did not give long-term protection against PTSD. Instead, it seemed to be a risk factor for it (Marmar et al., 1994, p. 906).

The Thrill of the Kill

There can be a sense of exhilaration that goes with the act of killing. This may be where the term "bloodthirsty" comes from. Researchers have ideas about how it may be biological, with opioids generated by the brain at times of trauma, but this has not yet been studied enough to say what the cause is. Nor do we yet know if those who have this reaction are more prone to PTSD than those who do not. It does seem likely that it at least does not protect them. That is why even a sense of euphoria, which is normally a desirable thing, does not keep the act of killing from being classified as a trauma.

This concept of *addiction to trauma* has been applied to victims as well, to people who continually seek out situations in which they are victimized. At this stage, it can only be accounted as speculation, or as a hypothesis in need of testing. Addiction to trauma has neither been well confirmed or disconfirmed; it is, however, based on long observation.

An example from an American veteran of Vietnam:

In the following interview, one veteran . . . was asked to explain his own understanding of the feeling process in re-experiencing combat memories, or "flashing back," and replied: "Yes, the rush or the feeling that you get from this is one of an addiction to adrenaline, addiction to cocaine, cocaine is a high that actually takes you up and this, the flashbacks, the terrible dreams, things like that also do the same . . . to you. I find it hard to function in an everyday capacity simply because of this rush. When I get into this high it is just like being in Vietnam, the thrill of killing, the thrill of destroying. And it's something I just cannot overcome, even with medication. From time to time my nightmares are like that of something of a terrorist that would actually feel this high. It's hard to duplicate this high with drugs, except the only drug I know is cocaine, that would reproduce this high for you, the same type of high of killing, of destroying. . . .

"I feel I should be dead. I feel like a lot of times I felt I want to destroy myself simply because there is no one else that I feel like I could destroy. Like moving out, to myself, it is very, very lonely and it actually consumes you." (Solursh, 1988)

WIDER CIRCLES OF VIOLENCE

Victims of Structural Violence

Structural violence includes poverty, racism, misallocated resources, and workers who labor under exploitative or dangerous conditions. These victims are not facing an acute crisis, as with direct violence. They face chronic conditions.

Some of the earlier studies of the effects of racism on African American children were done by Kenneth and Mamie Clark, and cited in the U.S. Supreme Court's 1954 *Brown v. Board of Education* decision on desegregation of schools. Children were shown Black dolls and White dolls and then asked which they liked and which was most like them. This projective technique showed the strains that messages of inferiority gave to Black children. This is the one of the first historical instances of psychological studies having a direct and stated impact on public policy (Clark & Clark, 1947).

Some of the specific psychological effects of living under chronic violence caused by institutions that have been studied include:

- a sense of depression, of being overwhelmed
- feelings of powerlessness, futility, hopelessness, fatalism
- a sense of fear and loss of safety
- a lack of trust and further social isolation when danger rather than safety is the organizing principle of relating to others
- transmission of these feelings from parents (who may lack the appropriate skills for caring and nurturing) to their children
- a psychological defense mechanism of denial, deliberately avoiding painful information
- a psychological defense mechanism of emotional numbing, allowing the emotions to ignore what the intellect cannot
- aggressive attitudes and behavior due to an acceptance of violence as a way to solve problems, as is seen chronically in the environment
- aggressive attitudes and behavior in a defensive maneuver to align with the powerful for protection (as with gangs)—by modeling themselves after the powerful, they feel safer

- substance abuse with drugs and alcohol
- obsessive thinking about material goods, associated with their deprivation

PTSD-type symptoms can also be expected. This is most commonly called *psychosocial trauma*.

A wide variation is likely, depending on the form of the violence. Some people in poverty live under a dictatorship or brutal foreign occupation with sporadic, unpredictable outbreaks of violence from the government. They may have differences in severity and pattern of problems than people who live in poverty in a democracy, where advancement beyond poverty is theoretically possible though not in practice, and the sporadic unpredictable violence is due to crime from other poor people. People who are suffering from health effects of pollution may never be aware of the structural violence and may not suffer psychologically at all, except for the psychological repercussions that normally accompany physical symptoms.

Additionally, there will be many people who live under remarkably adverse circumstances and nevertheless show resilience, living lives they find satisfying. Coping mechanisms include those that normally relieve stress: social support, religious activities, music, and humor.

Instruments of Structural Violence

Psychological ramifications of causing structural violence are another area that has received only a little attention. It has occasionally been noticed as a problem, as when Archbishop Desmond Tutu argued that Whites were also liberated when all-race elections occurred in South Africa (Tutu, 1999, p. 8). Quaker writer Thomas Kelly said, "The hard-lined face of a money-bitten financier is as deeply touching to the tender soul as are the burned-out eyes of miner's children, remote and unseen victims of his so-called success" (Kelly, 1941/1992, p. 81).

In psychology, Kenneth Clark suggested that racist ideas of superiority that relied on putting others down rather than on their own achievements hurt the self-esteem and creativity of White children. These children also suffered moral confusion over being told to play fair but not to play with children of another color. This could lead to problems of guilt feelings or of increased rigidity and hostility in stereotypes in order to deny the confusion (Clark, 1955, pp. 78–80).

Responsibility for structural violence by its nature is not something that can be pinned directly on individuals as easily as direct violence can. It is defined as violence by institutions rather than by individuals; nevertheless, individuals inhabit those institutions. The more extreme cases—slumlords, owners of unsafe factories, weapons sellers—can be distinguished and studied. Rather than calling them "perpetrators," the institutional nature of this form of violence makes it more logical to call them "instruments."

What are some of the psychological constructs that may be applied in these cases? To what extent might the concept of PITS apply? There has been so little study that what can be offered are some possibilities researchers might consider:

- a sense of depression, of emptiness
- feelings of guilt
- a sense of paranoia, a form of fear that considers possible reactions of victims
- an associated lack of trust of others, which further develops social isolation
- transmission of such feelings from parents to children; and by leaving children in the care of servants, giving them less of a sense of self-worth, or a sense of self-worth that relies on material possessions rather than human interaction
- the tension of cognitive dissonance—an image of one's self as a good person interferes with the reality, thus causing contorted reasoning to justify the reality, resolved with the intellectual defense mechanism of denial of facts
- a psychological defense mechanism of apathy and emotional numbing, allowing the emotions to ignore what the intellect cannot
- cynical attitudes and behavior due to acceptance of violence as a way to solve problems, as is seen chronically in the environment
- aggressive attitudes and behavior due to actually being powerful
- substance abuse—drugs and alcohol
- obsessive thinking about material goods, because wealth accumulation has taken on an addictive quality

The parallel points with victims, as listed in the previous section, is intentional. There are obvious variations between being powerless and powerful, but many of the problems mirror each other. In both cases, people are caught in the same unhealthy social system.

The power of the situation would be a major component, since structural violence essentially means violence of the situation. For example, in the Stanford Prison Experiment (discussed in chapter 1, under "Institutions"), there was a consultant who had been a prisoner himself. When playing the role of the parole officer, he found himself behaving in ways he had detested when he was the prisoner. The psychologists running the experiment got so immersed in their roles that they became obsessed with preventing a rumored prison break rather than collecting data. They experienced the sense of frustration that went with trying to run a prison, not with running an experiment. In the Milgram experiments, the authorities that kept people giving the shocks even when it was clearly distressing were also so immersed in the structure they had set up that they did not perceive their actions as violence. In real life and long-term institutions rather than short-term simulations, the short-run effects may become long-term aftermath. This point has not yet been studied well enough to draw any conclusions.

The varying levels of responsibility also lead to differences in reaction. Scientists who worked to invent the atom bomb, for example, can be expected to differ psychologically from those who decided to use it in Hiroshima, who differ from the citizenry that supported this decision, and so on. In the aftermath, the peacetime buildup of weapons led to different thoughts. Many of the scientists, such as Edward Teller, advocated strongly for the use of the atom bomb. Others were appalled at the new situation, opposed the buildup, and founded the *Bulletin of the Atomic Scientists*. In discussing the beginning of the bulletin, one scientist describes a clearly psychological reaction to participating in atomic bomb development:

Watching the flash of the first atomic bomb explosion at Alamogordo, the scientists had a vision of terrible clarity. They saw the cities of the world, including their own, going up in flames and falling into dust . . . In the summer of 1945, some of us walked the streets of Chicago vividly imagining the sky suddenly lit by a giant fireball, the steel skeletons of skyscrapers bending into grotesque shapes and their masonry raining into the streets below, until a great cloud of dust rose and settled over the crumbling city. (Rabinowitz, 1963, p. 156)

How often do those who have been involved in institutions of violence have vivid imagination of the real or potential consequences? Is there any connection of this to the PTSD symptom of vivid intrusive imagery? The answers await further research.

Another aspect of mental consequences is that those who engage in structural violence frequently do so for the purpose of becoming or remaining rich. What is the psychological effect of being rich? For most people, self-ratings of happiness are high and do not vary with income once basic needs are met (Meyers, 2000). The rich are neither higher nor lower in happiness ratings than anyone else who is not in deprivation-level poverty. Yet there could be a subcategory of the rich who are different because their work includes harmfulness. Do landlords who provide good housing at reasonable prices fare better psychologically than slumlords? Do CEOs who conscientiously treat employees well and follow environmental and safety practices throughout their companies fare better psychologically than CEOs apathetic to such concerns? This requires much more study. There is some study of the nonworking rich that suggests psychological problems arise when wealth is too highly valued (Wixen, 1973), but this would only be a start for a more thorough analysis.

Another possibility is that people participating with each other in institutions of structural violence could suffer tensions from cognitive dissonance. John Noonan (1979) suggested this in the case of slavery in the early years of the United States. He examined puzzling behavior by those who favored slavery. Political prudence would have suggested making allowances here and there, yet slavery advocates insisted on extremes. This was evident in the *Dred Scott* court case, which made Northerners watch as escaped slaves were taken off in chains, and did not allow slavery to be contained within Southern borders.

Noonan sees this poetically connected to the ancient Greek mythical beings called the Furies:

Why did the slave-holders act as if driven by the Furies to their own destruction? . . . Why did they take such risks, why did they persist beyond prudent calculation? The answer must be that in a moral question of this kind, turning on basic concepts of humanity, you cannot be content that your critics are feeble and ineffective, you cannot be content with their practical tolerance of your activities. You want, in a sense you need, actual acceptance, open approval. If you cannot convert your critics by argument, at least by law you can make them recognize that your course is the course of the country. (Noonan, 1979, p. 82)

Abraham Lincoln recognized this in a speech at Cooper Institute in 1860. When he was asked what would convince the slaveholders that his party had no designs on their property or the Constitution, he replied, "This, and this only: Cease to call slavery *wrong*, and join them in calling it *right*. And this must be done thoroughly—done in *acts* as well as *words*. Silence will not be tolerated—we must place ourselves avowedly with them."

Slavery is an easy case since practically everybody opposes it now. All view of the furies of self-destruction can be seen in the cool light of historical analysis. Current controversies, however, will raise more heated discussion. Noonan himself applies the principle to the abortion controversy, contending that those who favor abortion legalization have gone to extremes in the same way to support abortion practice. A vegetarian group distributed a pamphlet suggesting certain activities of the meat industry fit this model, since they believe that meat production is violent. Those in opposition to abortion and meat production are also known for having advocates who are extreme in their views and who engage in counterproductive activities. This makes it difficult to distinguish between behavior that may be due to a cognitive dissonance strategy of bolstering one's own case in spite of values to the contrary, and behavior that is due to an emotional commitment to one's cause and desires for consistency and purity of purpose.

There are at least three ways that the concept of *cognitive dissonance* can apply to people involved in structural violence:

1. *Effort justification*—As covered in chapter 1, a downward spiral can occur, as people are unwilling to admit that all their previous effort has gone to waste.

2. *A desperate drive for acceptance*—As stated above, people demand agreement rather than mere acquiescence.

3. *A desperate drive for clearly good by-products*—Providing extra justification for the violent institution. Finding additional good uses is usually admirable. It becomes a problem as a tension-reduction technique when people ignore evidence that the alternative is actually undesirable and does not have the features of goodness they had hoped. Nuclear energy, for example, needs to be considered on its own merits, not on a hope that it can be a good by-product of nuclear weapons.

Effects of Violence on Nonparticipants

For some who are aware of violence committed by others, the response will be one of the psychological defense mechanisms of *denial*. This can be illustrated by those Germans who knew, at least in a vague way, of the death camps being run by the Nazis. Opposing the camps would have required much energy and risk. Admitting what was occurring without doing anything would likewise be emotionally painful. When people are either unwilling or powerless to do anything, a common reaction is to deliberately avert the eyes and deny there is anything to react to.

In some cases where action is possible, whether or not an intervention occurs often depends on other factors. A famous case was an incident on March 13, 1964. A young woman, Kitty Genovese, was brutally attacked and stabbed to death outside an apartment building while several people watched from their windows. The assault started at 3:15 in the morning, and there were three separate times when the man attacked, but no one called the police until 3:50. By then, the woman was dead. Since police arrived in two minutes, an earlier phone call would probably have saved her life.

In this case, there were two problems. One is *social referencing*, when people use cues from the reaction of others to determine whether something should be reacted to as an emergency or not. The other is *diffusion of responsibility*—they all knew that other people were watching and thought that someone else would surely call the police.

Subsequent field and lab experiments have shown people are much more likely to offer help when it is clear they are the only ones available, so that responsibility is not diffused. Someone stranded by the side of the road with car problems will more likely have a passing traveler stop to help if they are on a lonely stretch of road rather than a busy highway. Experiments cannot ethically use violence to test the principle, but real-world news stories suggest the principle is the same.

This shows the power one individual can have. The social referencing effect occurs because people remain calm while looking at others to see if there is reason to classify a situation as something that requires action. If everyone else is doing the same, then what a person sees is that everyone is calm. One person deciding that it is time to act will bring about action from others. The diffusion of responsibility can also be dealt with quickly if one individual simply assigns tasks to specific individuals in the situation. Someone who is directly asked to call the police or an ambulance generally will.

The presence of violence in which one is not participating can be highly anxiety provoking. Watching others being assaulted or killed can trigger Posttraumatic Stress Disorder. While this is especially true when the others are loved ones, it can still happen when the victims are strangers. Other types of stress reactions, and acute reactions, are common. As with all traumatic situations, physical reactions such as headaches or substance abuse to counter the anxiety provoked by memories of the traumas can be expected. Even people who are quite actively helping in a situation, such as medical personnel who come to assist after a bombing, can get PTSD from what they have neither suffered nor participated in, but witnessed.

Therapists who have dealt with individuals who have been through violence have reported a kind of visceral stress response, called *secondary traumatization*. Their high levels of empathy and professional listening skills make them vulnerable. The chair of the Truth and Reconciliation Commission in South Africa reported that this secondary traumatization was a major problem among the commissioners and journalists who spent so much time listening to stories of brutality as part of their work. People reported sleep disturbances, short tempers, quarrels, and drinking. (Tutu, 1999, p. 286).

Those working in cleanup efforts after violence, from war to riots to domestic violence, should be sensitive to this possibility and take it into account when planning the most effective way to assist victims. Not only the victims need help—those who help the victims often require support themselves.

Finally, there is the question of those who are aware of structural violence such as poverty, racism, pollution, or widespread unsafe working conditions or appalling harmful medical practices. Several reactions are possible: fatalism about an inability to do anything; apathy or denial; cynicism about the human condition; optimism about the ability for change to occur; a desire to help by working with individuals affected; a desire to help by working on institutional causes of the problems; feeling overwhelmed; and a sense of urgency in solving the problems.

The sense of urgency can lead to a greater problem. If a form of violence is short-lived and can be resolved quickly, then a sense of urgency can be helpful. For example, a person who spent every day working to end the

Gulf War of 1991 while it was occurring would find that it was over before exhaustion set in. However, trying to end poverty or pollution or a long-lasting war such as the American war in Vietnam would take much more time and patience. A lifestyle of chronic activity to deal with chronic conditions is a necessity for which the insights of psychology can be applied. The psychological causes and effects of nonviolent action to counter violence, covered in the next two chapters, can help in this regard.

Potential Vast Violence: Nuclear Weapons

Several psychological features accompanying nuclear weapons policy have been identified. These were especially strong throughout the Cold War, and their residual effects are still being felt. While the fear of full-scale annihilation has receded with the collapse of the Soviet Union, it has not disappeared. Technological capabilities for it are still quite present.

The mechanisms of moral disengagement can be applied in various ways. For example, the use of euphemism is quite common with what would otherwise be terror-filled realities: "nuclear exchange," "nuclear yield," "escalation," "counterforce," or "window of opportunity."

A mechanism of minimizing or distorting the detrimental effects was also common. In line with this, Robert Jay Lifton identified, as psychological components, several illusions that drove nuclear policy throughout the Cold War years (Lifton & Falk, 1982):

- *The illusion of limit and control*—A limited nuclear exchange would occur and then both sides would show restraint and go no further. Lifton says the assumption defies all psychological experience.

- *The illusion of foreknowledge*—Events would occur in such a way as to allow preparation.

- *The illusion of preparation and the related illusion of protection*—People have experience with evacuation plans and shelters for more limited attacks, but assumptions of nuclear attack preparations were wildly unrealistic. A fantasy structure became fixed in many people's minds, radically divorced from reality. The psychological term for this is "delusion."

- *The illusion of stoic behavior under nuclear attack and the related illusion of recovery*—Based again on previous experience of entirely different kinds of attack. How people actually behave under nuclear attack can be seen by those who have undergone the experience, in Hiroshima and Nagasaki. Lifton's interviews there (as mentioned previously in "Effects of Direct Violence on Victims") show that people went into slow motion, extreme psychic numbing, a sense of being ghosts or in the realm of dreams. Recovery was only possible in those cities because there was still an outside world with an intact social structure able to help survivors. A full nuclear exchange would not have that feature.

- *An illusion of rationality*—Nuclear war is treated as a reasonable tool of policy.

For those more acquainted with reality and not subject to these illusions, some became activists and others became cynical. A sense of detachment was a protection against having to take action. Declaring the situation to be hopeless protected against the responsibility for action that goes with hope.

This sense of resignation and cynicism is well portrayed in the 1985 movie *War Games*. An ex-nuclear weapons systems designer has secluded himself in an island off the coast of Oregon, taking care that he was near a major target to be killed in the blast and spared the horror of survival. When two teenagers visiting him try to get him to take action to prevent a computer game-induced accidental launch, he declines on the grounds that it would only postpone the inevitable. He shows them a film on dinosaurs and talks of nature's way of extinguishing and starting over. The teenagers do eventually convince him to take action, but his initial attitude was not uncommon at the time.

The pervasive imagery of extinction—meaningless, technological extinction—may also have had social consequences. Psychological destruction occurred without the weapons even being used. While it would be difficult to test, with no control group possible, Lifton notes that a strong sense of foreshortened future may have contributed to the massive problems with divorce and overall avoidance of marriage that arose during the period. The upsurge in the abortion rate and other methods of not having children could be due to the same process.

In those government officials responsible for nuclear policy, Lifton offers two other noteworthy psychological components. One is an obsession with secrecy. The very place the atom bomb was developed, Los Alamos, was not only selected for its isolation, but had much to do with Robert Oppenheimer's knowledge of the area—he had camping trips there as a boy; the wilderness held secrets for him, and sentiment. The psychology of keeping a secret, and of seeing the revealing of a secret to be dangerous, arises in childhood and is exacerbated when the stakes actually are that high. Edward Shils (1956) calls his study of the period *Tormented by Secrecy*. The secret became the central issue, and drove much of the behavior.

When danger is involved, the components of the secret are forbidden knowledge, a sense of power, and a sense of shame. When these are strong enough, religious sentiment can start to play a role. The bomb managers can start to take on the trappings of a priesthood.

The other response of government officials is an anxious sense of executive impotence. If nuclear weapons are not to make of their possessors mass-murderers, the other option is to realize they cannot actually make credible threats with them. The sense of power that should come with such massive weapons was not realized in the real world, as wars continued and defiance remained common. American presidents felt a contradiction, as a power that should confer omnipotence actually conferred impotence. A quest for nuclear weapons "credibility" that could never be realized led to erratic political behavior throughout the Cold War. This may have been one of the contributors toward the American war in Vietnam, or the events that led up to the Watergate scandal.

CYCLES AND GOALS

Effects Turning into Causes

There are some ways by which the psychological effects of violence can turn around and become causes of further violence.

In situations where only individuals decide on violence, such as domestic abuse and street crime, some investigation has shown precise mechanisms for PTSD symptoms to be a risk. Silva and colleagues (2001) offer four categories of how PTSD symptoms can cause violent behavior. The first, and most mild, is sleep disturbance associated violence, in which there is physical thrashing around in bed—kicking, slapping, and so forth—and anyone sharing the same bed is at the receiving end of blows without warning and with no intention by the sleeper. The second category is associated with outbursts of anger, irritability, and hostility. The third is connected with flashback, and comes from flashback-induced misidentification of others, while the fourth is combat-addiction violence.

Flashback experiences, just like the dreams of PTSD, can seem quite real—especially since they are based on experiences the person has actually had in the past. On occasion, the flashback can be severe enough that it leads to a loss of ordinary understanding of reality. Authors offer as an illustration the case of Mr. A:

On one occasion, he had just won several games of pool and in frustration the losing party verbally attacked Mr. A. At that point, Mr. A noted that the man's face had transformed into the face of a Vietnamese foe who was wearing the traditional black clothes of the Viet Cong. Mr. A stated that for several minutes he was convinced that he was dealing with a dangerous Viet Cong soldier and therefore attacked the man perceived as the enemy with his hands. (Silva, Derecho, Leong, Weinstock, & Ferrari, 2001, p. 309)

Other forms of dissociation can also lead to confusion that contributes to violent events. The lower ability to distinguish real threats from circumstances that others would not regard as threatening can be disabling when the goal is avoiding unnecessary violence.

As for the combat-addiction violence, any kind of "repetition compulsion," or desire to get another adrenaline rush in the way that one has done in the past, or reenacting for any positive goal of excitement or post-action calmness, can lead directly to violent acts. To illustrate, Mr. D would frequent Chinatown and other areas of the city with significant Asian populations. There, he would engage in numerous physical fights with those reminding him of his former Vietnamese enemy. He sought these physical confrontations in order to "feel alive." . . . After those fights, he would welcome the sense of calmness. As is the case for many Vietnam veterans with PTSD, he often had feelings of emptiness and numbness that contributed to a lack of meaning in his life. His engaging in frequent physical fights brought about a sense of excitement that he described as "being alive again." His repeated violent addictive behaviors resulted in decreases in anxiety, tension, and other negative emotions. (Silva et al., 2001, pp. 310, 313)

These four categories deal only with the kind of chaotic violence not planned even by the individuals engaged in it. For more socially organized violence, some of the theories discussed in chapter 1 as causes of violence can be exacerbated when there are people who have PTSD. The following ideas are offered as possibilities for how this could work. More research needs to be done to see how much they apply:

Disconnections from People

From the American Psychiatric Association's (1994) definition of PTSD, symptom C(5) is a "feeling of detachment or estrangement from others," and symptom C(6) is a "restricted range of affect (e.g., unable to have loving feelings)." These symptoms can exacerbate, and sometimes initially cause, the practice of using dehumanizing language about the targets of violence and euphemisms about the actions against them. They support minimizing or ignoring the effects of the actions. Those two symptoms, along with symptom D(2), "irritability or outbursts of anger," render the occurrence of scapegoating more likely. Putting a mental distance between the doer and the deed, as with distancing, doubling, compartmentalizing, and intellectualizing, can be facilitated by the "numbing of general responsiveness" that helps define symptoms cluster C.

Destructive Authority

Those who already have PTSD may be more susceptible to destructive demands of authority. The estrangement from others, blocked emotions, and numbing take away one of the major resources available to cause noncompliance. Leaders suffering from PTSD symptoms can also influence why authority expects violent behavior and demands compliance. The same symptoms that make compliance more likely may also make the issuance of the orders more likely.

Oversimplified Thinking

The dissociation that can make individuals unable to distinguish real threats, when present in policymakers, can contribute to groupthink, war hysteria, and other forms of being unable to grasp the complexities of the situation. Detachment or estrangement from others would also reduce motivation to try to understand differing perspectives.

Homicide Rates after War

The idea that wars might increase crime and lawlessness has been suggested from scholars ranging from Erasmus to Sir Thomas More to Machiavelli. Winston Churchill and Clarence Darrow suggested that World War I specifically had this effect. Sociologist Emile Durkheim noted a sharp rise in the homicide rate after the Franco-Prussian War and suggested that war reinforces sentiments "alien to humanity and the individual."

Dane Archer (1984, pp. 63–97) conducted the most thorough study on this question. Archer found that, when the difference between prewar and postwar homicide rates was calculated, there was a very large effect for an upsurge in homicide rates. A sizable majority of nations that had been in war had increases, while this was not true of noncombatant nations from the same time periods.

Since some combatant nations did show unchanged rates or decreases, Archer looked further at what the differences between nations were. The main difference was in the size of the wars. Nations with larger combat losses showed increases much more frequently than nations with less extreme losses. While both victorious and defeated nations showed homicide increases, the victorious nations were more likely to do so. The increases occurred for both women and men and in all age groups. Economic conditions after the war made only a slight difference. Inasmuch as they had an effect, the nations with improved economies were more frequently among those with increased homicide rates.

Why these results? If social disorganization were the cause, then defeated nations should show more frequent increases than the victorious, as should those with worsened economies. Nevertheless, the opposite seems to occur.

Another suggested explanation is a greater number of violent veterans. This has been considered since at least as early as the American Revolutionary War, when Judge Aedanus Burke said in a charge to a grand jury that men who had become accustomed to plundering and killing during the war had since turned upon their neighbors. Many have suggested the idea that violence has become a habit or an appetite. A spectacular example is the soldiers who rode with Quantrill's guerrillas during the American Civil War: Jesse and Frank James, well-known outlaws. This might contribute to homicide rates, as shown in the previous section, but the Archer study shows that the rate also went up among women and all age groups. If it were veterans alone, this would not be the case.

Archer proposes the most likely explanation is a *legitimation of violence model*, where civilian members of a warring society are influenced by the "model" of officially approved killing and destruction. This could explain why there are higher homicide rates with higher combat losses, more for victorious nations, and with civilians who are women or of nonveteran age. The data disconfirms other suggestions as listed above. That does not make this idea the correct one, but it does strengthen its case. As Archer puts it:

What all wars have in common is the unmistakable moral lesson that homicide is an acceptable, even praiseworthy, means to certain ends. It seems likely that this lesson will not be lost on at least some of the citizens in a warring nation. Wars, therefore, contain in particularly potent form all the ingredients necessary to produce imitative violence: Great numbers of violent homicides under official auspices and legitimation, with conspicuous praise and rewards for killing and the killers . . . Even though social scientists have in the past amassed impressive experimental evidence that violence can be produced through imitation or modeling, they have in general neglected the possibility that government—with its vast authority and resources—might turn out to be the most potent model of all. (Archer, 1984, pp. 66, 94)

The case for this model may be strengthened by the additional information that crime rates often go down during nonviolent campaigns. This has not been subjected to as rigorous a statistical study as Archer gave, but Gene Sharp does cite several instances in which this drop occurred (Sharp, 1973, pp. 789–793). Though Sharp does not use the term, if we were to make this parallel to Archer's suggestion, we could call it the *delegitimation of violence model*. Sharp suggests the idea that less violence occurs because the nonviolent campaign undercuts the ideas supporting violence.

Hoped-for Achievements of Violence

Another effect of violence is the goal people hope to achieve with its use. Of course, if the goal is not perceived by most as legitimate, as with crime, then the violence is not legitimate either. A well-defined goal that is perceived as legitimate can be achieved, such as stopping a sniper from shooting more people by shooting the sniper. Throughout history, governments have been toppled or protected from toppling through violence. This is separate from the question of whether there were nonviolent alternative methods that also would have solved the problem.

Often, however, there are certain categories of times when the violence is counterproductive to the goal:

Not Having a Clear View

If groupthink or a shift to war hysteria mode or oversimplified thinking is occurring, being out of touch with reality allows reality to turn around and bite. If war planners think of the enemy as monsters who would not react to what is done to them in a manner similar to the way the planners would, then untoward events can and often do ensue. The idea that something as serious as war should be done with clear thinking is not a controversial point; it would be readily agreed to by war planners if put to them that bluntly. However, if more of such clear thinking were introduced, much war would be mitigated or avoided.

Increasing Hatred

Causing in other people a desire for revenge can become counterproductive to a specified goal. A good stopping place for a spiral of revenge—a feud—is often hard to find.

Getting out of Hand

Experience shows that wars are difficult to control. In situations of massive violence, the behavior of others is not necessarily predictable, even the behavior of the soldiers and civilians on one's own side. While this is also true of ordinary life, it becomes more acutely so during war, and the consequences are more grim.

Sparking Defiance, Strengthening Resolve

If the features of war hysteria are sparked on the other side, so they unite behind their governments and demonize the enemy, that enemy may get different results than expected. An example is Hitler's bombing of London during World War II. Hitler expected that London's population would become demoralized, but the opposite occurred and the bombing strengthened their resolve. Psychologically, this is a typical response, especially when people are facing a faceless enemy with a technique such as bombing. War planners who expect demoralization or defections and are not taking this common reaction into account may find their plans ineffective.

Backlash

Not only resistance from the other side of a conflict, but anger from third parties and occasionally from the policymaker's own people can occur. Acts of violence that are not perceived as justified can lead to violence or at least protest from various quarters.

Giving the Violence-Prone an Excuse

Sometimes the government being targeted for a violent reaction actually wishes to engage in war or heavy repression of dissent, but knows it lacks the needed justification in the eyes of its citizenry or supporters. When it is offered violence, however, the government has its excuse and is itself enabled to use violence. Such a state of affairs is so desirable that a government might provide agents provocateurs to nonviolent groups to provoke them to violence. It might also exaggerate a threat to get its justification. Such exaggeration is easier to accomplish when there are real incidences of violence that already scare the citizenry.

Lies

War planners can be exceedingly cautious about trying to avoid civilian casualties. This is not only very difficult to do in any war that is not confined to clearly defined battlefields, but it means the other side can easily exaggerate or tell outright lies about how an attack is being made. As long as there is an attack happening, this both inspires the lies and exaggerations and makes them more credible.

As for the war planners themselves, it is a long-standing proverb that "truth is the first casualty in war." The mission-focused nature of most war makes the telling of falsehood or the hiding of crucial truths very difficult to avoid. The home population may accept this, especially when in a warlike mood. Nevertheless, there is always the danger the truth will come out, and that people will react negatively when it does. A loss of credibility, and along with it a loss of ability to accomplish policy goals, can follow. Though occasionally successful, strategies based on the idea the truth can remain hidden have proven to be commonly unworkable throughout history.

Loss of the Moral High Ground

If a country has been attacked in an outrageous manner, it can gain much sympathy. Others may then cooperate in developing effective ways of countering the attackers. Once a violent counterstrike occurs, however, then the situation degenerates into a fight between two countries. Especially if there are civilian casualties, third-party onlookers may gain a sense that neither side merits their sympathy, or perhaps only the victims of the most recent carnage. It is like the schoolyard brawl that a teacher breaks up and each side complains the other person started it. The teacher generally will not care who started it because it is difficult to determine, and in any case has become an irrelevant issue. What matters is that both sides inflicted a fight on the good order of the playground. In the same way, both sides are victims when a counterattack occurs. In the absence of the violent response, there was only one victim. Those who responded to violence with violence may have lost an opportunity for greater sympathy, and all the practical help that can include.

Interfering with Other Approaches

At times there are several effective things that can be done to solve a problem. In fact, it is probably more common that a problem will not be solved in just one way and needs several things accomplished. If one of those approaches involves the use of violence, it can interfere with the other techniques that do not. Violence can sabotage other good efforts directly, as with humanitarian aid shipments, or it can make it harder to get cooperation when needed because of the loss of moral high ground as mentioned above.

Blowback

"Blowback" is a term originally used by the U.S. Central Intelligence Agency (CIA) to refer to times when they trained individuals who then turned around and used that training against the United States. There have been times throughout history when weapons were given to a group to help in some war and later were used in a war against the people who gave the weapons.

Setting Examples

By using violence as a problem solver, others with similar problems are encouraged to do the same. This could be other countries, other groups, groups within the nation of war planners, or, if the homicide rate goes up, individuals within the nation's population. All could complicate policy tremendously.

Becoming the Abhorred

Revolutions begun to establish justice and liberty may succeed in putting new people in power but not in changing the tyrannical conditions. George Orwell illustrated this principle in his classic book, *Animal Farm*. The same principle can apply to defense when others attack. The attackers are decried as sinister for killing innocent civilians; then the defenders do the same.

Martyrdom

Kierkegaard remarked that when tyrants die, their rule ends, but when martyrs die, their rule begins. When people have sympathy for someone who was killed, then the group that killed the person to solve a problem has often created a greater problem.

Perpetration-Induced Traumatic Stress

Leaving soldiers who have fought in a war with PITS, and having both soldiers and civilians with the regular PTSD coming from victimhood, can have long-lasting repercussions for a nation that were never taken into account at the time of planning war.

Vulnerability to Nonviolent Resistance

This may seem odd, since any group who begins a war or similar campaign using violence is fully aware that people on the other side are likely to fight back violently, but there is also the danger they will fight back nonviolently. If they do, as in the case of India seeking independence from Britain, then those who engaged in violence can end up being highly embarrassed by what they have done. When people fight back violently, the original attackers can feel justified in using more violence. When that feeling of justification is taken away, many will have wished they had not engaged in the violence in the first place.

CONCLUSION

Connections among the varying effects of violence are easy to discern. The thread of posttrauma symptoms has run throughout. Related problems such as substance abuse, depression, denial, numbing, and rage are running themes within the various groups impacted by the violence. While differing groups can have variations in patterns and features that other groups do not have, or do not have as much, there is a core of problems that are similar. There is also not a clear-cut distinction between the causes of violence and its effects.

Additionally, violence can be a cause of counterviolence activities. This would be like saying that disease causes medicine or accidents cause safety measures. Causes of nonviolence—other than the existence of violence, which makes it necessary—is covered in the next chapter.

FURTHER READING

Effects on Victims, Witnesses, and Rescuers

Herman, J. L. (1992). Complex PTSD: A syndrome in survivors of prolonged and repeated trauma. *Journal of Traumatic Stress, 5,* 377–391.

Leavitt, L. A., & Fox, N. A. (Eds.). (1993). *The psychological effects of war and violence on children.* Hillsdale, NJ: Lawrence Erlbaum Associates, Inc.

Marsella, A. J., Friedman, M. J., Gerrity, E. T., & Scurfield, R. M. (1996). *Ethnocul-*

tural aspects of Posttraumatic Stress Disorder: Issues, research, and clinical applications. Washington, DC: American Psychological Association.

van der Kolk, B. A., McFarlane, A. C., & Weisaeth, L. (Eds.). (1996). *Traumatic stress: The effects of overwhelming experience on mind, body, and society.* New York: Guilford Press.

Effects on Perpetrators

Grossman, D. (1995). *On killing: The psychological cost of learning to kill in war and society.* Boston: Little, Brown and Company.

MacNair, R. M. (2002). *Perpetration-Induced Traumatic Stress: The psychological consequences of killing.* Westport, CT: Praeger Publishers.

Effects of Nuclear Weapons

Lifton, R. J. (1968/1982). *Death in life: Survivors of Hiroshima.* New York: Basic Books.

Lifton, R. J., & Falk, R. (1982). *Indefensible weapons: The political and psychological case against nuclearism.* New York: Basic Books.

CHAPTER 3

Psychological Causes of Nonviolence

Nonviolence is a poor word for the phenomenon to which it is applied. As a negative term meaning the absence of violence, it pertains to all that is not violent, in other words, to most things. If one expects something to be violent but it is not, such as "nonviolent crime"—shoplifting as opposed to assault—then it is simply a category. A nonviolent method of solving a problem may have more merit than a violent one, but most solutions to the majority of problems are and always have been nonviolent. The English language does not offer a good word for nonviolence as a positive concept.

Gandhi called it *satyagraha* ("truth force"), and "moral jiu-jitsu" after a martial art involving putting people off balance. Military metaphors are not uncommon, with terms such as "brigades" and "blockades" being used. Even the term "campaign" was military in origin. The kind of bravery, self-sacrifice, and perseverance strategy necessary to violent campaigns is also necessary to nonviolent campaigns.

Solving the problems of violence, then, involves not only understanding its causes and removing them. It also involves understanding the causes of behavior that counters violence, and determining how this can be encouraged.

Accordingly, our first task is to look at some of the causes of violence discussed in chapter 1 and examine what psychology knows about countering or removing them. We then move on to what psychology identifies on the positive side, how to cause active nonviolent behavior. Finally, Maria Montessori called education the "armament of peace," and forms of education specifically designed for that purpose will be of special interest.

This chapter covers:

- Opposites of Violence—methods of removing the causes of violence
- Building Nonviolence—the positive causing of counterviolence activity
- Peace Education and Research—teaching and finding out more about removing violence and causing nonviolence

OPPOSITES OF VIOLENCE

Resisting Destructive Obedience

As mentioned in chapter 1, the psychology experiments of destructive obedience using electric shocks found that people were most likely to rebel when:

- the authority is not present, allowing for "cheating"
- the person giving the orders does not have the aura of authority
- authority is not united
- other people in the same circumstance are seen to be rebelling

If a nonviolence campaign needs to encourage noncooperation with authority, then that last point can be especially powerful. When Gandhi marched to the sea to make salt, many of the British were disdainful. They said they had been afraid he was actually going to *do* something and were relieved that he was only being symbolic. Yet Gandhi did have the sympathy of millions of people, so the example of only one was sufficient to get a group to come with him, and that group inspired huge numbers more to join the campaign. When conditions are right, it is sound psychology that one person can set the example that brings about behavior change in many others.

Leaving Violent Institutions

What happens in violent institutions (or at least those believed to be violent by some) when people leave them? People can leave because they retire, are fired, decide there is another job they prefer, or because they finally come to oppose the institution. Whatever the reason, the psychological dynamics of their participation are removed.

If the power of the situation is great, and people are thoroughly immersed in an institution with its expectations and the shared perceptions of those with whom they work, then what happens to them when they leave? In many cases, they remain advocates of the institution. Having spent a major portion of their lives within the institution, they are more likely to find it unacceptable to admit that they were doing something wrong. Nevertheless, there are sizable portions of people, depending on circumstances, whose freedom from the powerful situation leads them to reflect and turn to the opposition.

Robert Jay Lifton discusses examples of people who have been part of the nuclear weapons establishment. He identifies Admiral Hyman B. Rickover, Robert Oppenheimer, William Lawrence, and Secretary of War Henry Stimson as men involved in the nuclear establishment who came to oppose it, in what he calls "nuclear backsliding." Lifton comments:

I would stress the release from a whole constellation of man-weapon nuclearistic emotions with which those closely involved with the bombs become bound. . . . Provided with a measure of distance . . . one can extricate oneself from relying on the weapon for one's own vitality and larger connectedness or symbolic immortality. And one then can convey, often with eloquence and passion, truths about the weapons learned from the inside. (Lifton, 1968/1982)

Another example is the veterans of the American war in Vietnam who formed the organization Vietnam Veterans Against the War. While the same effect did not occur in previous wars, or among the Vietnamese veterans on the Vietnamese side of that war, there was a wider antiwar movement that provided additional psychological support to those veterans who coalesced with each other. More recently, the "refuseniks" among Israeli officers gave support to and took support from the Israeli peace movement.

Those responsible for carrying out executions are another example of people who, upon retirement or moving on to another job, often find they now oppose the death penalty. The same occurs in the case of people who provide abortions. Howard Lyman is an example of a man who owned a large ranch and decided for both health reasons and cruelty to animals to become a major vegetarian spokesperson. Occasionally, the most effective spokespeople against a dictatorship are those who have left its service.

It is common that there is a large social movement supporting such people as being the most effective of converts. The existence of such movements may well be an essential component in a majority of cases—at least, the cases in which converts become outspoken rather than merely disgruntled. People who remain in the institutions are more likely to perceive them as traitors who are worse than other opponents.

The role of Perpetration-Induced Traumatic Stress (PITS) in those who leave violent systems has yet to be explored. The antiwar poetry that expresses PITS leaves an impression that having such symptoms could easily contribute to the sense of opposition. In cases where individuals were expected to carry out direct violence, the aftermath of PITS symptoms may have a role in increasing opposition.

Countering Groupthink

Irving Janis, who first proposed the concept of groupthink, also proposed ten hypotheses of ways to avoid having decision makers get into dangerous groupthink situations. These are still in a state of development, with researchers trying to find which are effective and which might need to be refined.

1. Have policymakers informed about groupthink before a situations arises.
2. The leader of the group should begin by offering information without stating preferences.
3. At the outset, the leader should make it clear that group members are expected to air objections and doubts.
4. Someone should be assigned the role of "devil's advocate," offering convincing arguments against the most favored policy proposal. This should be a respected status in the group.
5. Outside experts should be brought in.
6. Members of the policy-planning group should discuss points with trusted associates. People who are not involved in the meetings or in making the decisions can have valuable reactions and ideas.
7. When a rival group is involved, a sizable block of time should be devoted to considering the rival's possible reactions. Warning signals and alternative scenarios from the rival's point of view should be focused upon.
8. Hold a "second chance" meeting. Once a consensus has emerged on the best policy alternative, hold a meeting whose entire purpose is to express reservations and work them through.
9. Have subgroups. When alternatives are still being considered, the policy-planning group can occasionally divide into two or more subgroups and meet separately. Several discussions will occur with perhaps different dynamics, and the groups can then come together to hammer out their differences.
10. Routinely have independent policy-planning and evaluation groups.

Personality Traits

The *egalitarian personality* can be regarded as the opposite of the authoritarian personality. People inclined to see human beings in egalitarian terms as a long-standing trait are more likely to behave in ways that do not back up authoritarian presuppositions. It is a useful concept in the study of child-rearing, whether it is the absence or presence of certain practices, which tends to bring about the differing traits.

The opposite of the Machiavellian personality is the *altruistic personality*. People with this personality care deeply about the moral course of action. If a person is consistently motivated to engage in altruistic acts, this can be associated with countering violence, or at least with human betterment.

After much study, the altruistic personality, as detailed in social psychology, offers two major features:

1. *Empathy*—The ability to experience the emotional state of another, and practice constantly doing so.
2. *High internalized standards*—Standards that range from moral principles to simple values, and are not externally imposed but involve an internal commitment.

However, though it can be related, this is not the same as practicing nonviolence, for at least two reasons:

- Nonviolence can actually be for selfish or self-defense reasons. Even if justice is involved, it may be for one's self rather than for another.
- Altruism can lead to violence; soldiers often use altruistic reasoning.

Appeal of Nonviolent Campaigns

William James's ideas of what makes war attractive (listed in the section entitled "Passions of War" in chapter 1) can also apply to nonviolent campaigns. Some are similar, but some are not:

1. Any kind of nonviolent campaign gives pride in one's self by belonging to a greater group and helping achieve its ends. It gives a sense of aliveness as part of the vast undertaking.
2. A nonviolent campaign can give meaning and purpose to a life that is otherwise boring.
3. Because the "target" is treated like a set of real human beings and community and agreement with them is sought, a more healthy sense of accomplishment and satisfaction is available.
4. Nonviolent campaigns also require cohesion and unity among participants.
5. The admirable virtues of discipline, courage, and self-sacrifice are every bit as necessary for a nonviolent campaign against a more violent foe as they are for a violent campaign.
6. The anxiety of uncertainty dissolves, not because the uncertainty does, but because the anxiety does. An ability to be unsure on certain points gives the opponent an opening to find an area of agreement, which is to be encouraged.

Richard Gregg further develops these ideas beyond William James, as shown in his remarks below:

In summary, we see that nonviolent resistance resembles war:

1. In having a psychological and moral aim and effect,
2. In principles of strategy,
3. In a discipline of a parallel emotion and instinct,

4. As a method of settling great disputes and conflicts,

5. In operating against the morale of the opponents,

6. In requiring courage, dynamic energy, capacity to endure fatigue and suffering, self-sacrifice, self-control, chivalry, action,

7. In being positive and powerful,

8. In affording opportunity of service for a large idea, and for glory. . . .

It is realistic in that it does not eliminate or attempt to eliminate possibilities of conflict and differences of interest, and includes all factors in the situation both material and imponderable, physical and psychological.

It does not avoid hardships, suffering wounds or even death. . . . Nevertheless, the possibilities of casualties and death are greatly reduced under it. . . .

It does not surrender the right of self-defense, although it radically alters the nature of the defense . . .

It is much superior to William James' suggestions for a "moral equivalent for war," in that it does not require State organization, direction or assistance, it is not used against the exterior forces and conditions of Nature but against human wrongs and evils. It is, therefore, much more dramatic and interesting and alluring. (Gregg, 1972)

Countering War Fever

Remarkable events occurred after the September 11, 2001 attacks in the United States. More people were killed that day than at the surprise attack on Pearl Harbor sixty years earlier that sparked American entry into World War II. Unlike Pearl Harbor, the great majority were civilians. The situation was practically a social laboratory experiment in an upsurge of popularity for war. The contrast with previous wars is instructive.

After Pearl Harbor, approximately 120,000 people of Japanese ancestry were put in internment camps for several years by the government without being charged, more than two-thirds of whom were American citizens. After the September 11 attacks, governments at various levels went to lengths to give the message that Muslim Americans and Muslim foreign guests were to be treated well. President Bush went to a mosque and there declared that anyone who behaved unkindly to them should be ashamed. There were some hate crimes, and the government did detain more than a thousand noncitizens on minor charges. This was nevertheless progress compared to sixty years earlier.

The threat to civil liberties was real, as is customary in war circumstances, but those who complained about it were not jailed, nor entirely ignored in the media. During World War I, a former U.S. presidential candidate, Eugene V. Debs, was put in prison for opposing the war. The equivalent in 2001 would have been to imprison Ralph Nader, an idea that was never even seriously mentioned. While war protests did bring about some impassioned opposition, as would be expected, there was nothing like the animosity that had been directed at them in previous years.

The Saturday after the attacks, the major television network ABC aired a two-hour show in town-hall format to explain things to children. The children (as the audience, with some adult experts) considered at length the question of why the hijackers did what they did, and offered some rather sophisticated answers, delivered in child-level language. The very question is not in line with war fever, which takes an oversimplified view of villains. There were many articles dealing with the questions of how to oppose this new threat most effectively, rather than assuming a war response. The first Hollywood telethon was a remarkably nonbelligerent affair, with tributes to heroes of the events, a plea for understanding Muslims, and barely any remarks that could even be interpreted as hatred of those who did this or a desire to hurt them.

It is true that the reactions of war hysteria (outlined in the section entitled "Passions of War" in chapter 1) were easy to find. It would be amazing if this were not so, given the circumstances. However, instances where such thinking clearly did not take hold were also easy to find for someone seeking them. The amount of war hysteria that did *not* happen may receive less attention, but it may behoove peace psychologists to study this.

Preparation by the civil rights movement, the peace movement, and movements to rectify past mistakes such as compensating and apologizing to Japanese Americans for their internment, all may have had an effect. There was even an effect for people familiar with previous work in psychology, as with the article headlined "Groupthink a Danger for White House War Planners" (Shapiro, 2001).

It would be easy for those who wish to move to a more peaceful society to be discouraged by the war rhetoric and bombing. The perception of backsliding would seem clear when legislators and executives move toward a more warlike stance and policies. Still, the contrast of this reaction with previous reactions bears further study. Perhaps we can learn more about what was done well. This will likely lead to greater enthusiasm for working toward peace than dwelling on the negative aspects of the situation.

BUILDING NONVIOLENCE

Moral Development

Studies by Lawrence Kohlberg have put forth the most widespread theory of individual moral development:

Kohlberg's Moral Development Stages

Level I: Pre-conventional Morality
Moral value resides in a person's own needs and wants.

Stage 1: Obedience and Punishment Orientation
Individual's moral judgment is motivated by a need to avoid punishment. If one is punished, it must have been a wrong thing to do, and if one is rewarded, it must have been right.

Stage 2: Instrumental-Relativist Orientation
Individual's moral judgment is motivated by a need to satisfy his or her own desires. Methods include sharing or hitting back when hit.

Level II: Conventional Morality
Moral values reside in performing good or right roles, in maintaining the conventional order, and in pleasing others.

Stage 3: "Good Boy/Nice Girl" Orientation
Individual's moral judgment is motivated by a need to avoid rejection, disaffection, or disapproval from others.

Stage 4: Law and Order Orientation
Individual's moral judgment is motivated by a need to not be criticized by a true authority figure.

Level III: Postconventional Morality
Moral values reside in principles, separate from those who enforce them, and apart from a person's identification with the enforcing group.

Stage 5: Legalistic Orientation
Individual's moral judgment is motivated by community respect for all, respecting social order, and living under legally determined laws.

Stage 6: Universal, Ethical Orientation
Individual's moral judgment is motivated by one's own conscience.

Points that Kohlberg considered important to understand about the theory are:

- Stage development is invariant. One must progress through the stages in order.
- People do not understand moral reasoning at a stage more than one stage beyond their own.
- Individuals are attracted cognitively to reasoning one level beyond their own present level when it resolves more difficulties. For example, two brothers both want the last piece of cake. The bigger, stronger brother will probably get it, so the little brother suggests that they share it. He is thinking at level two, rather than at level one. The solution for him is more attractive: getting some rather than none.
- Movement through stages happens when cognitive disequilibrium occurs.
- People look for solutions at the next level when their current outlook is not adequate to cope with a specific moral dilemma.
- It is quite possible for a human being to be physically but not morally mature.

The stages have the style of reasoning, not the content. Someone at Stage 2, for example, might favor a war because the enemy nation behaved badly and deserves to be punished. Yet at the time of the American war in Vietnam, Mohammed Ali resisted the draft in part because he said the Viet Cong had never done anything to him and it was therefore not right to hurt them. This is Stage 2 reasoning. Whether the reasoning reaches violence or nonviolence depends on much more than the stage itself.

Still, it was found that people at Stages 5 and 6 were more likely to disobey in the Milgram experiments (see the section entitled "The Power of the Situation" in chapter 1) than those in lower stages. There may be some correlation between moral reasoning level and violent behavior. On the other hand, there have been studies that have not found a significant relationship between nonviolence tendencies and the Kohlberg stages (Keniston, 1990; Kool & Keyes, 1990). More study is needed before a conclusion can be drawn.

Some have argued that Kohlberg was overly influenced by the philosophy of Immanuel Kant in labeling Stage 6 by universal principle. The description of the stage left out the component of actually caring about others, as well as having the skill of noticing when there are moral problems or need for care present in one's environment.

One of the major needs for expansion or modification of Kohlberg's theory from the perspective of peace psychology is its application to wartime situations and to public policy. The moral dilemmas posed in the research tended to be individual matters dealing with cheating and stealing, as opposed to larger institutional violence. Kohlberg himself had an interesting history on this. Fresh out of high school, right after World War II, he volunteered to help smuggle Jewish survivors of the Nazi Holocaust into what was then British-controlled Palestine. Many Western countries were still refusing to accept the refugees, and Britain had a sea blockade at Palestine to keep them out. Kohlberg (1948) described how he lied to port workers by telling them the freight was bananas. In this case, they found the stowaways and turned them back.

Kohlberg went on to graduate studies in psychology and a career in hypothetical dilemmas, with more real-life dilemmas added later. In the case of war, he studied one man who said he had been present at the My Lai massacre in Vietnam but had refused to shoot. Kohlberg (1984) seemed to suggest that failing to shoot was the most moral choice. There was another man on that occasion who had risked his life and a court martial to intervene to prevent murders, and succeeded. There are those who would argue that this form of moral behavior in wartime has more to recommend it than a mere refusal to shoot. The moral reasoning that went into intervening to save lives would be of special interest.

Ruth Linn has done some research in the moral reasoning of selective conscientious objectors, especially among Israelis (Linn, 1996). She found many of them justified their actions through Stage 4 reasoning. They os-

cillated between a sense of connectedness and one of detachment, another
dimension of moral development that Linn believes needs more attention.

There are actions within war and actions within nonviolent campaigns.
There are other methods of countering violence, such as lying in order to
smuggle people, as well as moral dimensions of public policy in general.
The basic points of empathy, attention to environment, social relationships, context, and desire to actually behave in line with moral reasoning
all deserve more exploration. The theory of moral development through
invariant stages may be modified, abandoned, or simply expanded upon.
Peace psychologists not only have a keen interest in applications, but can
also make good contributions in research because of the expanded
perspective.

Operant Conditioning/Role-Playing

The same idea of operant conditioning that can train people in violence
can also apply to nonviolence. In terms of that which is not violent, it
already does. Everyone from airplane pilots and attendants to astronauts
to emergency personnel train extensively on what to do in crisis situations.
They train so well that they do not even need to think, but automatically
do what is needed. With nonviolent campaigns, the "conditioning" can
be different, but in some cases, it is just as automatic. For example, there
may be a rule that says "in case of confrontation, sit down." In other
instances, though, the training requires not automatic actions but an ability to think quickly.

For this purpose, role-playing is ideal, and has been widely used. It is
simply the practice of possible confrontations beforehand in a training
session. Variations on what could go wrong can be thrown at participants.
Sitting, standing, or lying quietly, or answering softly but with firm resolve the demands of authority or mobs can be practiced in a safe setting.
It then is easier to do the same in reality when tense situations arise.

In addition, the emotion of fear that can be expected in confrontational
situations can be reduced with these mechanisms. Therapists deal with
stress reactions through conditioning and/or through cognitive restruc-
turing. Practice sessions ahead of confrontation can serve a similar
function.

Technology

The technology of nonviolence is entirely different from the technology
of violence. It can be close with nonlethal weapons, ones that restrain
people in riots or similar situations. There have been experiments with
the use of nets and foam and various technologies (that fit military methods) for emergencies. They are not destructive, but are also not construc-

tive to long-term resolution of conflicts in favor of social justice. They are useful only in emergencies; this is all that would be expected of them.

The major technological achievement that allowed for an explosion of nonviolent action in social movements was in communication. Media coverage of nonviolent rebellions allowed for a much wider audience of onlookers. Before, the word of what few eyewitnesses there might have been would have spread relatively slowly.

The benefits and pitfalls of this technology for promoting peace were noted in a post–World War II book called *Tensions That Cause Wars:*

> The development of modern means of swift and wide-range communication is potentially a great aid to world solidarity. Yet this development also increases the danger that distortions of truth will reach a great many people who are not in a position to discriminate true from false, or to perceive that they are being beguiled and misled. It must be a special responsibility of U.N. organizations to utilize these means of mass communication to encourage an adequate understanding of the people in other countries. This must always be a two-way traffic. It will aid the course of peace if nations are enabled to see themselves as others see them. (Cantril, 1950)

There are also advocates of the idea that peace can be better achieved through decentralized and ecologically sustainable technologies such as solar and wind power and "appropriate technologies" designed to meet the needs of the specific localities in which they are used. Any effect of such technologies on alleviating poverty automatically reduces the violence caused by material deprivation.

Even among the affluent, however, decentralized technologies can be regarded as a matter of security. Those who would like to impose massive disruption—an enemy nation, an internal coup d'état, or terrorists— would be thwarted if there were no central target to hit. For instance, houses with photovoltaic cells on their roofs, producing electricity directly from sunlight, suffer no complete power outage when a central power-producing plant is hit.

Much of the research done on such technologies has been on technical aspects, how to best market them or allow them to fit into differing cultures. More study needs to be done on psychological aspects of reducing poverty, pollution, and dependence on vulnerable centralized arrangements, along with how this might relate to building peace.

Resilience

The field of health psychology has looked extensively at what enables people to cope with stress. Since infliction of violence would be a major stressor, as would knowledge about it happening to others, coping with this would be a necessary component of nonviolence. More to the point, an ability to cope well with stress is of obvious benefit to those engaged in nonviolent confrontation.

Kobasa (1979) has proposed the concept of the *resilient personality*. Another common term for this is "hardiness," a set of personality characteristics serving as resistance resources for stress. There are three components:

1. *Challenge*—The belief that change is normal, and that it provides incentives rather than threats to growth.
2. *Commitment*—The belief that what one is doing is important and valuable, and the willingness to exercise influence within one's situation.
3. *Control*—The belief that destiny is the result of one's own efforts.

The challenge orientation involves openness and flexibility, which are essential features of problem solving and the generation of more and better alternatives. Commitment involves a developed sense of purpose that clearly works well in nonviolent activism. Psychologists refer to an attitude toward control that maintains it comes from inside a person as an *internal locus of control*. In other words, the location of the control is inside. The opposite is an external locus of control, whereby people believe others control their destiny, an attitude clearly at odds with effective nonviolent activism.

The proactive attitudes involved in hardiness are also related to the concept of *self-efficacy*. When one is confident that one's actions will have an effect, one is more likely to take those actions. The effect need not be total or speedy—after all, with resiliency, setbacks are positively seen as a challenge.

A related construct is one by Antonin Antonovsky (1979) called *sense of coherence*. This also has three components:

1. *Comprehensibility*—The belief that things are understandable.
2. *Manageability*—The belief that things can be handled. It is not necessary that one is in control, but only that *things* be in control. For example, the doctor may be in actual control of the sick child, but the mother who gives this control to the doctor has lowered stress.
3. *Meaning*—The belief that there is a point to things that may be going wrong.

Some of this involves subtle differences in points of view. *Challenge* could be a form of giving *meaning* to events, for example. The differences on control and manageability are slight (though not to those who argue them).

Does the sense of coherence relate to the nonviolent personality? Clearly, those engaged in productive nonviolence could benefit from it. Antonovsky himself believed there was no connection between the sense of coherence and morality, saying that complete jerks were quite capable of having a high sense of coherence (Antonovsky, 1993). However, initial studies correlating scores on his Sense of Coherence Scale with the Machiavellian Scale did show strong negative correlations between the two (MacNair, 1998). That is, as one goes up, the other goes down, and vice-versa.

Both constructs are well known in the scholarly literature on stress, and both are still matters of evolving debate. Joanne M. Joseph (1993) suggests that resilience is a precondition for productive nonviolence, and discusses how the traits are related to peace activists who engage in proactive actions while ordinary citizens who may agree with them do not act.

Beliefs and Emotions

Beliefs underlying nonviolent action include that it would be effective. The just world view would mainly be replaced by an understanding that there are injustices that are not the faults of the victims and do need to be addressed. Realpolitik would be replaced by a belief that moral means should be used for moral ends, and power for its own sake is not the ultimate and only thing groups are looking for. Machismo would either be replaced by an egalitarian ideal or at least by an ideal that manliness need not involve violence. A belief that violence is inevitable or part of human nature would be absent. It may or may not include a belief that nonviolence is the human instinct, with hatred or violence needing to be taught. Pacifists believe violence is never a last resort. Nonpacifist nonviolent activists may believe it is, but they are usually much more leery about it.

As with violence, there are emotions that help with nonviolent campaigns; some of them are the same and some are the opposite. Many have already been discussed, but the following bear further comment:

Courage

Courage is crucial to nonviolent action. This does not distinguish nonviolence from most planned violence, but those who disdain a nonviolent approach often think this feature is absent. It cannot be absent if the nonviolence is to be effective. This is illustrated by a joke:

In the days of the United States' Old West, many people were making merry in a saloon. A drunken cowboy came charging in, waving a gun, announcing loudly, "All right, all you mangy varmints, git out. Give me some elbow room." With great haste, everyone departed quickly. Except for one man, a Quaker in a broad-brimmed hat, sitting in the corner, quietly sipping orange juice.

The cowboy went over to him, glaring, and said, "I don't believe you heard me, partner. I said for all the mangy varmints to clear out."

The man looked up pleasantly and answered, "I heard thee, friend. And I must say, there certainly were a lot of them, weren't there?"

The Quaker did not merely refrain from offering violence. He also refused to reward the cowboy for the violence he threatened. Everyone else offered neither violence nor nonviolence, but cowardice. Nonviolence advocates can be just as disdainful of the options of cowardice or apathy as are those who believe that violence is necessary for establishing justice.

Forgiveness

On a personal level, research in therapy is showing that forgiveness is a major component of healing for inner peace. It relieves depression, anxiety, and resentment, and serves the forgiver very well, even if it does nothing for or is not known about by the forgiven. When clearly separated from a situation in which continued abuse is allowed, forgiveness appears to be therapeutic. On a societal level, once a nonviolent campaign is firmly committed to ending continued abuse, then forgiveness has a crucial role. The head of the Truth and Reconciliation Commission in South Africa entitled his book *No Future without Forgiveness* (Tutu, 1999). If the abuse and therefore the campaign are still ongoing, then forgiveness may not be given with the kind of finality that can be achieved when it is in the past. Yet the tempering of anger and resentment, anxiety and depression, is crucial to the success of a nonviolent campaign.

Dennis, Sheila, and Matthew Linn (1997) propose that when we have hurts inflicted upon us, these are like small deaths. They applied to a process of forgiving the stages that Elisabeth Kübler-Ross proposed for people who are in the process of dying. This was not a perfect fit, since "bargaining" was relatively unrealistic under Kübler-Ross but healthy and realistic behavior under the Linn scheme. More importantly, the psychological concept of "stages" does not apply because they are often out of sequence, and not all have to occur each time. They will therefore be called "components" here.

The first component is *denial*, studiously ignoring the hurt. This can have the advantage of keeping events from being overwhelming, so the hurt can be mentally set aside until it is easier to handle. However, it has the disadvantage of making it impossible to resolve the problem, and manifests itself in health problems or unhealthy behavior.

The second component is *anger*. This has the advantage of locating where the hurt is, and how deep it is. It is a sign of sensitivity to injustice. As Thomas Aquinas put it, virtue consists in being angry with the right person for the right reasons and for the right amount of time. Anger indicates the hurt has surfaced and is ready to be healed. It energizes us to correct what needs correction and helps us to protect ourselves and others from being victimized by injustice if possible. As with denial, disadvantages also include health problems or unhealthy behavior.

The third component is *bargaining*. In the case of healing from a hurt, this is the creative working through of the problem. It helps define the boundaries, and gives ideas on how to resolve the difficulty. Some of those ideas may not be so helpful on first thought, but can lead to things that are beneficial. Some fantasies about how to resolve the problem are unrealistic, but can be further reflected upon to find more practical solutions.

The fourth component is *depression*, a feeling that the problem is one's own fault. It has the advantage that it helps people to admit real guilt and think about where they themselves need to make amends. There may be opportunities for change in one's self. This keeps one from being a victim of waiting for others to change. It is a way of seeing shared humanity, and avoiding dividing people so much into clear-cut oppressor/victim categories, both of which are helpful for nonviolent resolutions. As with denial and anger, however, being stuck in depression can include health problems and unhealthy behavior. In addition, if the guilt felt is untrue and the fault is not reasonably placed on one's self, then that inaccuracy can cause further problems.

The final component is *acceptance*, when one is at peace with those who did the hurting, whether the relationship continues or not. There can even be gratitude for what is learned from the experience. People can feel energized, and may have more courage to face future risks.

The Linns apply this to nonviolence specifically with a quote from Barbara Deming, that nonviolence gives us two hands upon the oppressor: "one hand taking from him what is not his due, the other slowly calming him as we do this." Ironically, even though their book advocates a process of forgiveness, they entitle it *Don't Forgive Too Soon*. Just as both violence and cowardice are to be avoided with nonviolence, so are both continued resentment and allowing one's self to be treated like a doormat. None of these is beneficial either for the person who has been hurt, or for those who did the hurting. The Linns suggest that firmness in establishing rights is an integral part of forgiveness when done in the service of nonviolence.

Tolerance for Ambiguity

Tolerance for ambiguity is the ability to live with situations that are not clear. Different interpretations of what is happening are possible, and the outcome is uncertain. It is the ability to accept complexity, not insisting on simplistic solutions. A low tolerance for ambiguity is one of the features of the authoritarian personality.

Since nonviolent campaigns are full of situations that are not clear-cut, a high tolerance for such circumstances causes a greater ability to handle them. The existence of differing interpretations is one of the rich resources for the strength of nonviolent campaign. It allows for creativity in reaching solutions that offer the opponent a way of saving face and yet still be satisfactory for the justice goals of the campaign. The desire for simplistic solutions often translates into a motivation for violent solutions. This is shown by the features of the "mythic mode" or war hysteria (see section entitled "Passions of War" in chapter 1), and the problems with "integrative complexity" in those decision makers moving toward war (discussed in the section on war in chapter 7). The ability to handle the greater complexities of nonsimplistic, nonviolent solutions helps promote them.

Commitment

The desire to see change, or protect against undesirable change, means little if people are not willing and able to take necessary action. Being *willing* is an *active orientation*, as opposed to a passive orientation. In other words, one is not a mere sympathizer, but someone inclined to act. Being *able* is an *internal locus of control*. "Locus of control" means the location where a person believes the control over events comes from. An external locus of control means that events are imposed by the outside, and nothing much can be done about this. An internal locus of control is a belief in an ability to impact events. It is related to the concept of having a sense of self-efficacy. In an article on "Components of Pacifism," Elliott (1980) proposed that these two features, an active orientation and an internal locus of control, are essential—along with a commitment to nonviolence—in defining the kind of pacifism espoused by Gandhi. It could also apply to nonviolence activists who were not entirely pacifist.

Stress Reduction

The discussion so far has been of societywide peace, what could be called "outer peace." Many people include "inner peace," or mental tranquility; in psychological terms, this means stress reduction. Stress reduction includes relaxation exercises for direct reduction, including meditation, guided imagery, muscle relaxation, massage, and so on. These are aided by aerobic exercises, healthy diet, ability to express, social support, a sense of coherence or resiliency (as covered above), and having tasks organized in low-stress ways.

High amounts of stress are a common consequence of violence, both direct and structural, to the victim, the perpetrator, and the onlookers. Such stress then increases the toll of violence by having a high cost in physical health, from heart disease and cancer to osteoporosis and diabetes (Sapolsky, 1994). Stress reduction techniques help to heal the consequences of violence.

Since stress can come from things that are not violent, such as a desire to finish certain difficult tasks, or a lack of sufficient control in being able to finish those tasks, the stress reduction techniques are also necessary to basic peace in social organizations and workplaces. A less stressful workplace is more compassionately organized for the workers.

Stress reduction aids the mental skills that go with courage, forgiveness, and tolerance of ambiguity. Mental states of stress are suggested to be associated with unclear thinking in a variety of ways. Oversimplified thinking, in the form of war hysteria, stereotypes, or an inability to understand another side's point of view, is often associated with high stress. There are psychologists who propose that stress is a major contributing factor to these mental undercurrents of violence. Calmness allows for better decision making, decisions that are more likely to take complex circumstances and varying views into account. Presumably, then, stress reduction techniques can aid in the mental skills necessary to building peace under a wide variety of circumstances. At least, this is a hypothesis worth further research.

Nonviolent campaigns themselves can certainly be quite stressful. Stress reduction techniques can make campaigners better able to continue their work.

Spirituality

Mohandas Gandhi regarded spirituality as a crucial component of nonviolence. Martin Luther King, Jr., was a minister who liberally sprinkled Bible verses and religious imagery into his speeches. These were often sermons, and practically always indistinguishable from sermons. From the Philippines to Poland to Latin America, the Catholic Church has been prominent in nonviolent struggles against dictatorships. From ancient times, spirituality has been connected to nonviolence. For example, King Ashoka of a province of India in the 200s B.C. converted to Buddhism and thereby changed from a war-prone king to a peaceful one. The Hebrew prophets railed at the injustices of their day, and asserted that justice was something other than what the king declared it to be. While there have been campaigns that did not make use of spirituality, many have used the religion common to their time and area in the nonviolent pursuit of justice.

One of the features of religion used this way is a tendency toward ecumenism. In other words, those united in a campaign tend to become more tolerant of religious differences. Gandhi was a Hindu, but Muslims were crucial to a campaign for Indian independence, and the opponents he was dealing with were Christian. With Christians, Jews, and Sikhs supporting his campaign, Gandhi took a universalist attitude toward religion, so all could be welcome. Martin Luther King, Jr., was in the southern African American Christian tradition, with Christians of various other views also involved, and Jews well represented. The campaign would only be successful if Catholics and Protestants, Christian and Jews, were happy to work together, having a sense of fellowship not sabotaged by doctrinal strife.

In some cases, the conflict that requires peaceful solution is one in which ethnic groups have so identified with religion that establishing peace must include a greater acceptance of differences in religions. Catholics and Protestants in Northern Ireland are a prime example.

Religious institutions also supply instrumental help to nonviolent campaigns. They often provide practice needed for nonviolence, courage, forgiveness, tolerance of ambiguity, and other emotions, along with the rationale for their importance. They provide a ready-made system of social support, which provides not only needed emotional sustenance but also essential practical provisions. They provide disciplines, rituals, memories, symbols, and facilities that allow for relaxation and stress reduction. In practical terms, their locations may be the only relatively safe place to hold meetings.

Many argue that the prayer and divine guidance, the connection of the worshipper to the divine, are indispensable. The role of psychology would be to study the impact of this belief on the behavior of all involved.

PEACE EDUCATION AND RESEARCH

History of Peace Education

In 1628, a Czech bishop and teacher, Jan Amos Comenius, started publishing a popular series of books on education reform. Some were translated into various European languages, Arabic and Persian. He was invited to help establish reform of schools in several European countries. He asserted that education should be universal, the same for all regardless of class or gender. Comenius thought that if people were educated on different religions, languages, and ways of life, and had an internationally oriented education, this would help develop peace.

Peace education efforts saw a surge of growth at the beginning of the twentieth century, with Europeans and Americans forming peace societies and warning against the saber rattling that led to World War I. In 1912, the School Peace League had chapters in nearly every American state. Between the world wars, many teachers thought schools had encouraged war by indoctrinating children in nationalism. They taught international studies so students would be more understanding of different cultures (Scanlon, 1959).

During these years, Maria Montessori developed an education method that has grown in popularity and is still commonly used. Dr. Montessori was the first woman in Italy to get a medical degree, in 1894. In a psychiatric clinic and later as director of an asylum for mentally retarded children, she came to believe that such children could be more educated than others thought. When she was successful, she decided to also apply the method to children of normal intelligence. In 1907, she opened the first

Montessori school in the slum district of Rome. Within a year, people were coming from around the world to see the program. In subsequent years, she wrote several books on its principles.

The method includes having several projects available from which to learn. Students select projects by being attracted to them. Part of the idea is that children learn better when following their interests. Of relevance to peace education, Montessori also reasoned that children who did not follow authoritarian teachers automatically might also not do so for authoritarian government leaders urging them to war. She thought education should free the spirit and promote love. The success of the method under conditions of extreme poverty in Italy bode well for its future successes elsewhere.

In 1934, Montessori fled Italy because of the takeover of Fascist rule. Her stay in Spain was short-lived, as a civil war broke out there. She went to the Netherlands, but from 1939 to 1947 she lived in India and Sri Lanka before returning to the Netherlands and dying in 1952. During all this time, she continued writing and developing the Montessori method of education.

The first college-level peace studies program began in 1948, at Manchester College, Indiana. The interdisciplinary field of peace studies has been growing ever since.

Throughout the 1950s and 1960s, fear of the new nuclear threat was uppermost on educators' minds. During that time, much of peace education for children was focused on international understanding.

In 1970, Brazilian educator Paulo Friere proposed an educational method of *conscientization* in a book called *Pedagogy of the Oppressed*. This is a process of understanding sources of oppression, in which various forms of violence are studied and nonviolent alternatives are developed. Friere was trying to use a form of education to help the poor escape from structural violence.

In 1974, the Quaker Project on Community Conflict published a book with a curriculum called *The Friendly Classroom for a Small World Handbook*. This helped pioneer the approach of teaching children conflict-resolution skills. The book has gone through at least twenty-five editions and has been translated into seven different languages. The goals for the classroom were to promote community and open communication, to help children gain insights into human feelings, including their own, and to explore ways to respond to problems and prevent and solve conflicts. Other curricula using similar approaches have also been published since then, and research on their effectiveness is ongoing.

The United Nations has taken a particular interest in the idea of a transition from a culture of violence to a culture of peace. Peace education is one of the major areas to be addressed for this. Many hold the idea that well-done peace education is a major cause of nonviolence, and naturally, psychology in particular would be amenable to this point of view.

Approaches to Peace Education

There has been a diversity of approaches to peace education. Different countries naturally focus on whatever aspect of peace education is uppermost on their minds with regard to their own conflicts. For Japan in the 1950s, the teachers' campaign for peace education was manifested as "A-Bomb Education," in reference to the recent bombings of Hiroshima and Nagasaki. In Ireland, peace education is called "Education for Mutual Understanding," since the main problem there is centuries of animosity between Catholics and Protestants. In Korea, peace education has been called "Reunification Education." In Latin America, it is sometimes referred to as "Development Education," where strategies to address the structural violence of poverty are the most prominent concerns.

There is also a diversity of approaches outside of national problems. Many advocating peace education have focused on specific concerns. These approaches are not mutually exclusive; they complement each other well.

International Education

Intended to counter: war

Intended to foster: a sense of being a world citizen

This focuses on understanding international systems, appreciation of other cultures, preventing hostilities, and reducing international tension. To counter the demonizing of the "enemy," education to humanize those perceived as enemies is included.

Conflict Resolution Education

Intended to counter: interpersonal conflicts

Intended to foster: skills in peaceful problem solving

Conflict resolution programs focus on mediation and communication skills, promoting empathy, and increasing abilities in problem solving. Programs in schools range from preschool to high school with age-appropriate curricula. Research has shown this not only decreases aggressiveness and increases cooperation, but also seems to be associated with better academic performance and positive attitudes toward school.

Nonviolence Education

Intended to counter: all forms of violence and demonizing of opponents

Intended to foster: nonviolence activism

Nonviolence education, with a more Gandhian approach, focuses on understanding the power of nonviolence, not demonizing opponents but using courage, forgiveness, and loving approaches to solve injustices.

Human Rights Education

Intended to counter: ethnic hatred

Intended to foster: multicultural understanding

A focus on human rights and the rights of minority groups includes knowledge of how such rights are abused in various places with or without explicit wars. Nongovernmental organizations often help protect by documenting and interceding. Multicultural understanding aims at reducing stereotypes and hostilities between groups, hoping to thus eliminate adversarial mind-sets and encourage more positive group interactions.

Violence Prevention Education

Intended to counter: street crime, domestic violence

Intended to foster: personal responsibility

Violence prevention programs are particularly aimed at those who have committed or are at risk of committing nonauthorized violence against others. The programs are often associated with the court system, and tend to focus on anger management, learning about causes and costs of violence, self-control, personal responsibility, and support groups.

Development Education

Intended to counter: structural violence

Intended to foster: peace building

Development programs promote democratic thinking and conservation skills, critical thinking and building for the future. The purpose is to build peaceful communities by having an active democratic citizenry interested in an equitable sharing of the world's resources and ecological sustainability.

Environmental Education

Intended to foster: ecological sustainability

Environmental education offers a holistic approach to how humans and nature interact. Sustainable development and appropriate technology are emphasized. Lifestyles, businesses, and governmental policies are all involved in the basic work of making peace with the planet.

Character Education

Intended to foster: individual responsibility and helpfulness

This form of education is more likely to be favored by conservatives, though liberals and others also find it helpful. It would not necessarily be peace education if the values of courage and self-sacrifice included participation in war. Nevertheless, encouraging the virtues of honesty and integrity, courage and patience, temperance, and concern for the well-being of others will have peace-promoting effects.

Moral Education

Intended to foster: higher levels of moral development and use of democracy in education

Kohlberg further developed his theory of moral development into the idea of moral education with the concept of the "just community," especially applying to schools. He argued that democratic decision making is crucial in forming a just community, not merely because it is just, but because it also aids in moral development. Democratic decision making involves real-life problems and real-life resolving. Equalizing power relations encourages students to think for themselves, not depend on others to do their thinking for them. Errors are more likely to be corrected with open expression and examination of opinions. It encourages people to follow the rules since they voted on them. With a communitarian ethic, not a tyranny of the majority, the process is not one of voting, but of deliberation, understanding others, and balancing concerns.

Religious Education

Intended to foster: religious knowledge and practice, commitment, and community concern

Some forms of religious education are intended to foster peace. Most contemporary religions can motivate adherents for works of charity, social justice, inner peace, and societal peace. Any of the approaches covered so far could also be fit into religious education. Some people are more comfortable with a religious context. Religions also offer education for practices such as prayer, ceremony, and social support for others. Many people find these helpful during nonviolent campaigns and other efforts for human betterment.

Education on Specific Issues

Intended to counter: specific forms of violence or threats to peace

Intended to foster: a knowledgeable citizenry, motivated to take action

Specific forms of ongoing obstacles to positive peaceful conditions can be addressed directly. Education efforts about details concerning particular issues can be aimed at students, other specific groups, and members of the public in general. One common method includes wide dissemination of communications such as books, films, pamphlets, newsletters, magazine articles, Web pages, letters to the editor, and Internet forums. Another common method is a sponsored speech by a knowledgeable person, or a program of speeches organized into conferences or teach-ins. Question-and-answer sessions help encourage interaction and greater amounts of reflection. Other possibilities include informational picket lines, displays at conferences or on the street, street theater, and ordinary conversations with friends and coworkers. This is an area where creativity in "getting the word out" is especially helpful.

Culture of Peace

Intended to foster: peaceful imagination, creativity, and insight

The use of art forms for peace education is as old as ancient parables and fables, stories with a moral point. The parable of the Good Samaritan, for example, made the point that love of neighbor includes ethnic groups that are regarded with disdain. Aesop's fable of the sun and the north wind arguing over who could make a man take off his cloak made the point, when the sun won, that gentle persuasion works better than blustery force. Ancient poetic images include the Hebrew prophets' idea of a day when people would beat swords into plowshares, an inspiration that has been turned into a famous sculpture outside of the United Nations. Songs have also served this function, from the ancient Psalm 46 to the modern folk song. Drawn pictures and photographs have shown the devastation of war or the realities of nonviolent campaigns. These art forms can help coping with emotions, but they can also be educational.

Peace Studies

Intended to foster: an interdisciplinary field of study, teaching, and research

There are now hundreds of peace studies programs at colleges and universities worldwide, including departments, certificate programs, and designated courses. There are also scholarly conferences in various countries. Practically every academic discipline has made some contribution to understanding and promoting peace.

Definitions for Peace Research

Peace research, while practiced for millennia, as a disciplined form of inquiry began in the 1960s with the founding of the International Peace Research Association. Norwegian Johan Galtung was particularly prominent in peace research and is often cited for two conceptual distinctions.

The first is the difference between *negative peace* and *positive peace* (Galtung, 1969). Negative peace means the absence of war and other forms of direct violence. It is achieved when a war or crime that might have happened is prevented. Positive peace is a condition where nonviolence, social justice, and ecological sustainability remove the causes of violence. It is achieved when social institutions of peace are in place that make the idea of using war or other violence unlikely to occur.

The other distinction is between *direct violence* and *structural violence.* Direct violence involves intentionally harmful actions carried out by individuals. They may choose to do them alone, under someone else's authority, or they may be the authority commanding that the actions be taken. Structural violence is instead carried out by social organizations. It does not target individuals, but leaves them in poverty or otherwise puts them in harm's way, such as unsafe working conditions, dangerous products, or disease from pollution. Table 3.1 details the differences.

An anthology of peace psychology readings, *Peace, Conflict, and Violence:*

Table 3.1
Differences of Direct and Structural Violence

Direct Violence	Structural Violence
Kills People Directly	Kills People Indirectly
Kills Quickly	Kills Slowly
Dramatic	Commonplace
Personal	Impersonal
Acute Insult to Well-Being	Chronic Insult to Well-Being
Episodes May Be Prevented	Inertia May Be Mitigated

Source: Christie, D. J., Wagner, R. V., & Winter, D. D. (2001). *Peace, conflict and violence: Peace psychology for the 21st century.* Upper Saddle River, NJ: Prentice-Hall.

Peace Psychology for the 21st Century (Christie, Wagner, & Winter, 2001), uses this distinction to organize its readings, with the first section on direct violence and the second on structural. The remaining two sections are on the form of making peace that goes with these, as shown in table 3.2.

Another distinction in kinds of violence is between *physical violence* and *psychological violence* (Elliott, 1980). Physical violence—behaviors intended or threatening to inflict bodily injury or death—is the most straightforward and visible. Psychological violence is behavior or threat of behavior intended to humiliate, degrade, intimidate, or otherwise demean the dignity of others. The distinction is relevant because there could be people who will use nonviolent tactics such as strikes and boycotts for practical reasons, yet feel delight if events conspire to humiliate an opponent. There are other people who do not engage in physical violence and yet are still very abusive to others psychologically, as is common with family abuse. Such people do not perceive the violence because it is not physical.

Definitions are important because the first thing to do in research is to operationalize a concept. This means to find a definition for something abstract by designating an operation to define it. For example, if a researcher wants to measure the extent to which people's overall philosophy tends toward the violent or the nonviolent, a scale could be developed in which participants circle numbers for how much they agree or disagree with certain statements. The numbers are then added up to give a total

Table 3.2
Differences of Peacemaking and Peacebuilding

Peacemaking	Peacebuilding
Reduces Direct Violence	Reduces Structural Violence
Emphasis on Nonviolent Means	Emphasis on Socially Just Ends
Reactive	Proactive
Limited in Time and Space	Ubiquitous
Goal: Prevention of Violent Episodes	Goal: Promotion of Social Justice
Interest in the Status Quo	Threat to the Status Quo

Source: Christie, D. J., Wagner, R. V., & Winter, D. D. (2001). *Peace, conflict and violence: Peace psychology for the 21st century.* Upper Saddle River, NJ: Prentice-Hall.

score, which can be correlated with scores from other scales, studied for how subtopics within the scale seem to coalesce together, or used to compare different defined groups to one another. A number of such scales for measuring nonviolence attitudes are currently being developed (Elliott, 1980; Kool & Sen, 1984).

Other methods of research include lab experiments, in-depth interviews, and even biological tests. Results of many such studies done in the past are reported throughout this book, as are suggestions for further research.

Biological Questions for Peace Psychology Research

The field of biopsychology is still fairly young, but quite of bit of progress has been made in such areas as what parts of the brain have which functions, what chemicals in the bloodstream do, and a wide variety of biochemical and biophysiological responses. Research is still in the preliminary stages on most areas that would bear directly on peace psychology. Following is a list of some of the major questions:

Addiction to Trauma

As detailed in "Effects of Direct Violence on Perpetrators" in chapter 2, a question has been raised as to whether there is a biological component to the sense of exhilaration that has been observed with the act of killing. Some studies have suggested that there may be a release of opioids in the brain (van der Kolk, Greenberg, Boyd, & Krystal, 1985; Southwick, Yehuda, & Morgan, 1995). This is a stress response that normally helps people and animals by avoiding pain in a crisis situation. The pain caused by the crisis could interfere with taking needed actions to avoid further harm. The biological pain avoidance is "exactly the sort of stress-response needed to keep that zebra functioning when it is injured yet still must get away from the lion" (Sapolsky, 1994, p. 177). In the world of artificial drugs, opioids are related to morphine, heroin, and cocaine, known for their addictive qualities. Does a biological component of the reaction help explain the observation that in some people the behavior seems to be addictive? If so, what interventions might effectively counter this problem?

Posttraumatic Stress Disorder

The physical reaction to reminders of the trauma—increased heart rate and blood pressure and galvanic skin response—can be measured. Hormones show something of a particular profile. There is a suggestion that brain structures may differ, such as those suffering Posttraumatic Stress Disorder (PTSD) having a smaller hippocampus. Longitudinal studies are still being done to find out if people with a smaller hippocampus are more predisposed to PTSD or if having the condition tends to shrink the hippocampus. The difference from PTSD that comes from being a victim as opposed to the apparently more severe form that comes from being a perpetrator in the trauma is yet to be considered. Biological studies can help us understand the causation of PTSD and its treatment; some pharmaceutical treatments have already been tried. The biological aspects of PTSD are being intensively studied (Friedman, Charney, & Deutch, 1995). In an article on a Web site focusing on PTSD (http://www.trauma-pages.com), van der Kolk phrases it as "The Body Keeps the Score."

General Stress

The biology of the general stress response is one of the better-understood points of biopsychology (Sapolsky, 1994). Traumatic stress has some biological differences and some differences in how it is experienced. General stress is much more common. Stress responses can also be medically measured, as can the effects of stress on bodily functions such as the immune system. This can lead to understanding differences in violence and nonviolence. For example, one study showed that stressful tasks like trying to meet a deadline strengthened the immune system, while exposure to TV violence weakened the immune system (Bosch et al., 2001). This was measured by immunoglobulin A in the saliva. Conversely, watching films of loving interaction with Mother Teresa (McClelland & Krishnit, 1988) or humor (McClelland & Cheriff, 1997) caused rises in the immunoglobulin A, indicating a better immune system and better resistance at least to colds. It seems, therefore, that the biological impact of violent or nonviolent behavior—on those who do it and on those who watch it—has implications for physical health.

Biological Contributors to Violence

This is tricky, since some people with the idea that criminality or violence is hereditary have supported racism or continued denigration of certain classes. Still, there are questions concerning such things as testosterone and seratonin levels as being connected to violence. Consumption of alcohol and other intoxicants can also be a biological route to violent behavior.

The Brain's Decision Making

Medical scans of the brain have become quite sophisticated, and researchers have been able to see what areas seem to be most active while people do certain tasks. Some decisions seem to rely more on the memory area, and others on the emotion area. Some studies may have application to decision making that has to do with war or other forms of violence, as well as decisions to engage in nonviolent campaigns.

Spirituality

Some studies have suggested biological correlates to spiritual practices (Austin, 1998; Newberg, d'Aquili, & Rause, 2001). Brain scans of meditation by Buddhist monks or deep prayer of Catholic nuns has shown a quieting of a kind of self-orientation area. When such people report a sense of feeling at one with the universe, a mystic loss of the sense of the boundaries of their own selves, the brain scans show what is happening biologically. The area of the brain we have all developed to orient us to the boundaries of our bodies, handy in everyday life, quiets down. People lose the sense of boundaries of self in the same way they lose their vision when closing their eyes. The direction of causation is not yet known; it may be that the quieting of the orientation area of the brain causes the sensation. Or, instead, it may be that the sense of loss of boundaries of self causes the area to shut down as not needed, just as closing the eyes does not cause prayer, but a decision to pray often leads to the closing of the eyes. The connection of spirituality to nonviolence has been strongly believed by many of its practitioners. Biological associations with spirituality can be of interest in finding what causes or results from nonviolence.

CONCLUSION

With nonviolence, there is no blame to apportion to others, and euphemisms are unnecessary. Rather than disengaging, people are engaging. Rather than using dehumanizing language, people are using humanizing language, which is more realistic. Practices such as distancing, doubling, effort justification, or a just world view are irrelevant. While the willingness to suffer for a cause one believes in may be puzzling to some, it does not differentiate the doer of nonviolence from the soldier.

The addition of peace education adds a major component that was absent in the chapter on violence. There is education for violence with strict discipline in such places as military school or police training. However, these are generally not intended to cause incidents of violence that would not otherwise occur, but rather to make violence more effective in achieving specified goals. Education for violence by fostering attitudes and techniques, as is done in places varying from Hollywood movies to prisons, does have the effect of increasing violence. Nevertheless, those who do it generally have other motivations in mind than an actual intention to cause violence. Peace education is intended to have an effect on actually causing peace to develop. These people are educating deliberately with the hope that this aim will be achieved. Preliminary research suggests that, at least on a small scale, some forms of such education are successful.

FURTHER READING

For more on the opposites of violence, see the reading list of chapter 1, which gives resources on the violence that is being directly countered.

Moral Development, Reasoning, and Behavior

Kohlberg, L. (1984). *The psychology of moral development: The nature and validity of moral stages.* San Francisco: Harper & Row.

Linn, R. (1996). *Conscience at war—The Israeli soldier as a moral critic.* Albany: State University of New York Press.

Staub, E., Bar-Tal, D., Karylowski, J., & Reykowski, J. (1984). *Development and maintenance of prosocial behavior: International perspectives on positive behavior.* New York: Plenum Press.

Nonviolent Personality

Joseph, J. (1993). Resiliency and its relationship to productivity and nonviolence. In V. K. Kool (Ed.), *Nonviolence: Social and psychological issues.* Lanham, MD: University Press of America.

Kool, V. K, & Keyes, C. L. M. (1990). Explorations in the nonviolent personality. In V. K. Kool (Ed.), *Perspectives on nonviolence.* New York: Springer-Verlag, pp. 17–38.

Mayton, D. M., Diessner, R., & Granby, C. D. (1996). Nonviolence and human values: Empirical support for theoretical relations. *Peace and Conflict: Journal of Peace Psychology, 2,* 245–253.

Oliner, S. P. (1988). *The altruistic personality: Rescuers of Jews in Nazi Europe.* New York: Free Press; London: Collier Macmillan.

Stress and Stress Reduction

Sapolsky, R. M. (1994). *Why zebras don't get ulcers: A guide to stress, stress-related diseases, and coping.* New York: W. H. Freeman and Company.

Peace Education

Aber, L., Brown, J., & Henrich, C. (1999). *Teaching conflict resolution: An effective school-based approach to violence prevention.* New York: National Center for Children in Poverty.

Bodine, R., & Crawford, D. (1999). *The handbook of conflict resolution: A guide to building quality programs in schools.* San Francisco: Jossey-Bass.

Boulding, E. (2000). *Cultures of peace: The hidden side of history.* Syracuse, NY: Syracuse University Press.

Friere, P. (1970). *Pedagogy of the oppressed.* New York: Seabury.

Green, N. S. (2001). *The giraffe classroom.* La Crescenta, CA: Center for Nonviolent Communication.

Harris, I. (1988). *Peace education.* Jefferson, NC: McFarland & Co.

Marshall, J., & Wheeler, L. (1996). *Street soldier: One man's struggle to save a generation—one life at a time.* New York: Delacorte Press.

Patti, J., & Lantieri, L. (1994). *Waging peace in our schools.* Boston: Beacon Press.

Power, C. F. (1989). *Lawrence Kohlberg's approach to moral education.* New York: Columbia University Press.

Prothrow-Stith, D. (1991). *Deadly consequences.* New York: HarperCollins.

Prutzman, P., Stern, L., Burger, M. L., & Bodenhamer, G. (1988). *The friendly classroom for a small planet: A handbook on creative approaches to living and problem solving for children.* Philadelphia, PA: New Society Publishers.

Reardon, B. (1988). *Comprehensive peace education: Educating for global responsibility.* New York: Teachers College Press.

Salomon, G., & Nevo, B. (Eds.). (2002). *Peace education: The concept, principles, and practices around the world.* Mahwah, NJ: Lawrence Erlbaum Associates.

Web site for high school level program, "Help Increase the Peace": http://www.afsc.org/hipp.htm.

Web site for program of workshops primarily for prisoners, "Alternatives to Violence Project": http://avpusa.com.

Peace Research

Peace and Conflict: Journal of Peace Psychology, a quarterly scholarly research journal available from: Lawrence Erlbaum Associates, 10 Industrial Avenue, Mahwah, NJ 07430–2262. Sponsored by Division 48 of the American Psychological Association.

Web site for the International Peace Research Association: www.ipra.org.

CHAPTER 4

Psychological Effects of Nonviolence

The recipients of nonviolent action are generally not victims of it; they are usually the violent attackers. That is what makes them subject to non-violent countermeasures. The response of onlookers is also important to the success of nonviolent campaigns. Both receivers and observers are therefore targets, groups the nonviolent campaign is aimed at. Conse-quences to them are different than they are to groups at whom violence is aimed.

Similarly, it would seem odd to many to call participants in nonviolent campaigns "perpetrators" (though some of their direct targets may feel so). Still, we are roughly paralleling chapter 2 by considering the effect on targets first and then on those active in causing events. The effects on the active are divided into two parts, positive and negative. The latter is a caution about a major negative psychological effect for those who do not pace themselves—burnout. Finally, paralleling the chapter 2 dis-cussion of how well goals are achieved with violence, nonviolence is considered.

The sections of this chapter, then, are:

- Impact on Targets—how attackers and onlookers react
- Positive Impact on Participants—features of the effects on those actively involved
- Burnout—negative risk to participants
- Goals—a comparison of nonviolence to violence in achieving its aims

IMPACT ON TARGETS

Attackers

A classic rendition of the impact of assertive nonviolent resistance comes from Richard Gregg, who offered the following in a book he wrote as a gift to Mohandas Gandhi on Gandhi's sixty-first birthday. After suggesting that a violent attack of A on B in which B responded in kind would make A feel justified and allow for continued attack, counterattack, and long-lasting feuds, he offers a different scenario, where A attacks a different sort of person, C:

The attitude of C is fearless, calm, steady, unusually good-humored and kindly . . . He does not respond to A's violence with counter-violence. Instead, he accepts the blows with smiling cheerfulness, but also with good-tempered reasoning, stating his belief as to the truth of the matter in dispute . . . asking for an examination of both sides . . . and stating his readiness to abide by the truth . . .

The first feeling of A will be surprise . . . A's first thought may be that C is afraid of him . . . But C's look and posture show not fear but courage . . . A vaguely realizes that C has taken and maintained the moral initiative . . . perhaps A was not going to lose anything after all; that all his fierce exertion was unnecessary, wasteful and a little foolish . . . If there are onlookers, A perhaps begins to feel a little undignified in their eyes . . . He, of course, doesn't want to acknowledge it but his feelings betray themselves in his hesitance or decreasing firmness . . . The onlookers perceive it, and he himself senses a loss of public support. . . . That hurts his pride, his anger flares up and he strikes or wounds C again . . .

Yet C continues in an attitude of respect toward A, and appeals to A's better nature and finer instincts. Strangely, he seems even to trust A. . . . A's fear of humiliation goes, and thereby his anger fades. He sees that his original fear . . . has no grounds. (Gregg, 1972, pp. 5–26)

Gregg suggests that the new idea in the situation tends to stimulate the attacker's imagination, which can have a powerful influence over conscious will power. He proposes that strong conviction of any sort is contagious and stimulating. He believes imitation is a powerful psychological force, and conscious or unconscious imitation by the attacker in this kind of situation leads to more peaceful outcomes. He argues that the energy of the nonviolent resister may be great, but compared to the violent foe it is applied more intelligently and efficiently. The angry or violent person tends to be shortsighted, often using short leverages based on insufficient analysis. The nonviolent person uses longer, more psychological leverages that may move slower but are more permanent. Overall, the nonviolent resister has less need for physical, tactical information than the military by being in a nonspatial realm of attitudes and feelings. Psychological information is what is important.

There is more recent work on social psychological mechanisms used to account for the success of nonviolent action or *satyagraha*:

Attribution Theory

People commonly try to understand themselves and others by designating intentions and motivations to them. That is, they make *attributions* to account for their own behavior and other people's as well. An insight of *attribution theory* is that when people see other behavior as normal in a situation, they tend to attribute it to the situation, but when they see other behavior as abnormal, as unexpected, they tend to attribute it to internal disposition. In other words, the expected response to violence would be violence in return. However, when violence is offered and the response is nonviolence, this deviates from expectation, and the behavior is attributed to a nonviolent disposition (Mayton, 2001).

Self-Serving Bias

The *self-serving bias* is the psychological term for the observation that people tend to take credit for their successes but not for their failures. Successes are due to internal factors like their own good character or talents, while failures are due to external factors of the situation. If a nonviolent campaign provokes a violent response, yet those who are responding with violence wish to continue to view themselves favorably, then they will attribute their violence to external factors. The law or practice that is being protested fits the bill for being such an external factor. If it is changed, then the external factor no longer exists, the violence disappears, and those engaged in the violence can continue to think of themselves as people who are not violent by character. They attribute their behavior to the situation instead. Since the point of the nonviolent campaign was to change that specific situation, this works out well for all concerned (Mayton, 2001).

Out-Group Homogeneity Effect

The in-group is the group a person belongs to and identifies with. The out-group is a group a person considers to be other people. People can easily see the differences between individuals in their own in-group; for instance, one person is shy, another obnoxious, one is punctual but not trustworthy, and so on. There is a tendency for these understandings of individual differences to drop when a person looks at an out-group. The less known the out-group is, the greater the *out-group homogeneity effect*. People in an *out-group* are distant, so differences get blurred. The more distant the group, the greater the blurring. This is where the idea comes from, in referring to another racial group, "they all look alike."

The resulting deindividuation can easily become dehumanization. One of the things a nonviolent campaign seeks to do, whether aware of this mechanism or not, is to reduce the out-group homogeneity effect by reducing the sense of its group as an out-group in the minds of its opponents. Those in power tend to see opposition forces as being a mass of people rather than a set of individuals. They are fully aware that the people they deal with in their own group are individuals, but a group of people protesting them tends to be stereotyped as being homogeneous. If those people use violence, the distance is maintained and the out-group retains its status all the more. Efforts at humanizing interaction break down those stereotypes; the out-group homogeneity effect lessens as the distance between groups erodes.

This works both ways. People who want to start nonviolent campaigns against those in power may also tend to see these people as more similar to each other than they are. Demonizing the opposition and viewing them as homogeneous are strong psychological tendencies in a conflict. Paying attention to ways of having human interaction with people from this *out-group* will result in a fading of the bias to see them as similar, when the reality of their individual differences becomes clear.

Social Referencing and Role Expectations

When a situation is unusual, people cannot rely on habit to tell them how to react. A common way to deal with novel circumstances is to monitor the actions of surrounding people, to figure out how to define the situation and what to do (social referencing) or to respond to social interactions in the ways normally expected (role expectations). If, for example, a protester approaches a police officer with a cheerful expression and a hand held out for shaking, the police officer often responds in kind. Not all officers will, but it takes the officer more effort to respond with hostility than to do what is normally expected and respond in a friendly way. If the officer came onto the scene with a hostile attitude but is met with a friendly response, then the situation becomes redefined for the officer. There will be times when the officer's response will continue to be hostile, but persistent contact in which it is clear that the activists expect a different way of interacting can and often does wear this down over time. The same is true of counterdemonstrators or officials with the protested institution. They often come into the situation in a belligerent mode and end up willing to be in a dialog mode. This is less difficult than maintaining a belligerent approach that is not reciprocated. Nonviolent activists are deliberately and consistently changing the reference and the expectations of social situations.

The converse can also apply: when demonstrators lack a nonviolence orientation and arrive with a belligerent attitude, police can and often do calm things down by treating people in a friendly manner. Though some demonstrators maintain a stereotyped view of police, the police can use the same dynamic of expectations in the interactions to change attitudes, either immediately or with some time.

Cognitive Consistency

The theory of *cognitive dissonance,* one of the more highly studied concepts in social psychology, has been used to account for otherwise puzzling behavior. Many rationalizations and mental gymnastics have been used to make contradictory ideas seem consistent, and this is a problem when violent behavior is the focus of justification. However, if people have a drive to avoid letting their values, ideas, facts, and behavior have contradictions, this can be an enormous aid in nonviolent campaigns. Such campaigns deliberately appeal to values, offer ideas, fastidiously document facts, and have a goal of changing behavior. A drive to *cognitive consistency* can be used to their advantage.

This is done in at least three ways (Pelton, 1974):

1. A person is given facts that contradict previous attitudes. He or she deals with the contradiction by changing the previous attitude to match the new information. This is called persuasion. It is the ideal form of nonviolent action, since it is the easiest, quickest, and most effective. Therefore, this is the first thing to try. If it works, the campaign succeeds. Of course, it often is not sufficient to work, but still serves as a foundation for later confrontations and acts as something an opponent can back down to in a face-saving way.

2. If people are induced to behave in a way contrary to their attitudes, their drive for cognitive consistency can make them change their attitudes to fit their behavior. This makes the social change more permanent. Such behavior changes are often necessitated by campaigns of noncooperation. For example, in the Montgomery bus boycott, business leaders eventually found it in their best business interests to allow for the racial integration being demanded. A cynic could say this was due to greed rather than a change of heart. Greed may have been what changed the behavior, as it overrode the racial prejudice; however, once the behavior changed, so did the racial prejudice. When people noticed they were behaving in a new way, they accounted for it by adopting an attitude that was consistent with the behavior.

3. Nonviolent campaigners can expose individuals to already existing inconsistencies between their values, attitudes, and behavior. People generally like to think of themselves as humane and just. There will be parts of their philosophies or religions that contradict inhumane or unjust behavior. Sometimes, bringing the contradictions to their attention causes a belligerent response as a way of denial, but occasionally the contradiction is seen and addressed by changing the behavior to fit the better of the previous values. Nonviolent campaigners generally call this "appealing to conscience."

It can take time for these mechanisms to apply. They sometimes work quickly, especially in interaction among individuals. At other times, particularly in large group settings or long-standing institutions, and when nonviolent opposition begins slowly and builds, the first reaction of those in power is likely to be one of using the tools long available to them to maintain their power.

In a chapter called "Challenge Brings Repression," Gene Sharp (1973, pp. 521–571) documents historically how once a nonviolent campaign has coalesced, polarized the status quo, and brought an unavoidable challenge to those in power, the initial response is frequently one of attempts to repress the movement. This can involve control of communication and information, psychological threats, confiscation and economic sanctions, bans and prohibitions, arrests and imprisonment, exceptional restrictions, and direct physical violence. Thus, direct violence to support previous structural violence can be the first reaction of those who believe they benefited from the original arrangement.

Because this is a large-scale situation, persistence by the nonviolence group is then necessary on a large scale. The idea of those in power is that their repression will have the effect of eliminating their problem. When they see this is not so, then the dynamics as mentioned above can occur through the course of time. Commonly, it will take a very long time in large situations; struggles can take years or decades.

Observers

A major part of where nonviolence gets its strength is in the reaction of onlookers. Those people who are violent are more disconcerted when onlookers disapprove, so part of their violent technique includes trying to hide what they are doing. This is why techniques such as massive letter-writing campaigns on behalf of political prisoners are so effective. Mere exposure of violent or polluting activity to public scrutiny is occasionally sufficient to stop it.

Nonviolent activists suffering under the weight of a violent reaction know the importance of having the onlookers on their side. They take great pains to publicize what the violent wish to keep hidden because they know that onlookers who are enraged are one of their major sources of support in any campaign.

Experiments have been done to further study the psychology of the observer (Mann & Gaertner, 1991; Mann, 1993). One experiment asked whether observers rate disproportionate force as more inappropriate. It also looked at whether they are more lenient toward force used by their own country. A group of U.S. psychology undergraduates were given different scenarios. One variable was the invading country: in one-third, it was the United States, one-third England, and one-third the Soviet

Union. The country invaded was Nigeria. The second variable was the invader's tactic. Half of the scenarios had them shooting and killing four hundred defenders. The other half arrested four hundred defenders. The third variable was the defenders' tactic. Half had them mildly violent, weakly and sporadically shooting at invaders. The other half had them engaged in nonviolent resistance—demonstrations and street blockades.

Results showed, according to prediction, that the more disproportionate force was rated as more inappropriate. Highly violent force was most inappropriate when used against nonviolent defenders, less so but still inappropriate when used against the mildly violent, and the same for the invader's milder tactic used against the nonviolent defenders. Rated as the least inappropriate was for moderate force used against moderate violence. As for the country, the actions of the Soviet Union were always rated as more inappropriate than that of the United States or England. This was also expected, and adds another complication into the understanding of the observer.

An obvious limitation of the study includes that it is not known if people would act on these perceptions. As with studies in general, it tells us some things but not others. How well does a relatively artificial condition generalize to the real world? It does at least add to the list of research that helps us eventually come to a greater understanding.

A second study looked at observers' responses to the My Lai massacre, the slaughter of several hundred civilians carried out by American troops in Vietnam. This study was a content analysis of congressional speeches in response. The purpose was to see what was uppermost in the minds of those who thought the massacre was justified (there were only two), those who thought it was not justified (there were thirty-six), and those who thought it was ambiguous. Both of those who thought it justified appealed to military necessity and nothing else. Those who cited principles that it was not justified were by far most strong on the theme of noncombatant immunity, that non-soldiers should never be targets. In this real-world situation, some of the features of the theory of the psychology of the observer were confirmed: people can oppose disproportionate use of violence by troops from their own country, and the noncombatant nature of the victims was what bothered them most. In this case, they were not observing a nonviolent campaign, but the same principle can apply.

An earlier set of experiments was done on the question of how people respond to someone else's suffering, back when the deceptive appearance of giving painful electric shocks was still allowed (Pelton, 1974). People who watched what they thought was another experiment lowered their ratings of liking for the actor who apparently received shocks and expressed distress. She was rated even less likable when participants had seen one session and knew they were about to see another. The suggestion to account for this is the *just world view*: the person who suffered must have deserved the suffering, and therefore is less likable. This is compounded if one is about to be subjected to seeing it again. However, when people were able to cast a vote that the person being shocked had finished and would be compensated with money, almost all did so—and the dip in likability ratings disappeared. This still fit the just world view, which does not require justice all along, but in the end. When people were able to take action to cause a happy ending, sympathy for the person increased.

Ironically, the same just world view often supporting violence can be turned around to serve nonviolent campaigns. People want to think the world is just, and therefore safe. If they can help in some small way to arrange a happy ending for those suffering, they will often do it, and their sympathy for the sufferers goes up. If onlookers feel completely helpless to do anything, a blame-the-victim strategy may be used to ease the discomfort. However, if they have the power to do something, however small, the desire for a happy ending to the story makes them likely to take action.

POSITIVE IMPACT ON PARTICIPANTS

Direct Effects

The subsection on "Appeal of Nonviolent Campaigns" in chapter 3 already discusses some of the positive impacts of nonviolent campaigns. In the causal loop common to psychology, positive effects can be a cause of behavior because people seek those effects.

Gene Sharp is a very prominent scholar of nonviolence. He lays emphasis on its practical aspects and advocates using it not merely for moral reasons, but because it works. For impact on participants, he suggests (Sharp, 1973, pp. 777–799):

Ending Submissiveness

Within a nonviolent group, and the larger grievance group, there must be a change from passive acceptance, helplessness, or any sense of inferiority or fear. Without this, there is no nonviolent action. With nonviolent action, these diminish. A self-image involving self-deprecation is potent for inhibiting independent actions. When these independent actions happen and spread, those who are active find a decrease in the self-deprecation. This tends to spread out to other members of the grievance group.

Learning a Technique That Reveals One's Power

With a variety of techniques available, people who gain skill also gain confidence. Seeing the effects in front of one's eyes is a powerful learning experience. Once the goal is attained, this learning remains and can be applied in other situations.

Increasing Fearlessness

Not only is casting off fear one of the prerequisites for nonviolent action, it is also an effect of that action. People learn through discipline and training and then through experience that they can remain firm in the face of threats. They can refuse to be terrorized.

Increased Self-Esteem

When the view of an aggrieved group's inferiority changes, behavior changes along with it, which then strengthens the view. People have enhanced self-perception when they see what they can do.

Bringing Satisfaction, Enthusiasm, and Hope

People feel lively and energized, and remember participation in nonviolent campaigns with some exhilaration.

Effects on Crime and Violence

The use of nonviolent struggle by so many ordinary people clarifies that humans are not by nature violently aggressive. It undercuts the ideas and practices entailed in street crime and everyday violence, and these therefore sometimes subside. Sharp cites instances when crime rates dropped during times of nonviolent campaigns.

Increased Group Unity

It is common during strikes, boycotts, series of demonstrations, and other campaigns that the solidarity of the group is noticeably magnified.

Increased Internal Cooperation

The reverse side of defiance is mutual aid. Members of the group must provide support for each other to make up for what they are deprived of due to the campaign.

Contagion

As word of even moderately successful nonviolent techniques spread, so will the use of the technique by others.

Sharp suggests that, while it is important to understand the effect of nonviolence on its recipients, it may be even more important to understand its effect on participants. The effects on the opponent are immediate, but the effects on participants are long lasting. Strengthening of these groups can alter relationships in more permanent ways.

Martin Luther King, Jr. offers his observations on this, reflecting on the aftermath of the Montgomery bus boycott:

Although the intense solidarity of the protest year has inevitably attenuated, there is still a feeling of closeness among the various classes and ages and religious denominations that was never present before. The increased self-respect of even the least sophisticated Negroes in Montgomery is evident in the way they dress and walk, in new standards of cleanliness and of general deportment . . . There has been a decline in heavy drinking. Statistics on crime and divorce indicate that both are on the wane. (King, 1958, p. 187)

Humor

Tom Mullen explains part of the dynamics of how humor relates to nonviolent action:

Those able to see the humor of a situation are usually more understanding of the human condition than those who can't. Seeing the funny or ironic side of events is a way of seeing the truth they contain. An inability to laugh at human foibles is blasphemy. It treats human beings as if they were godlike, and they aren't. I foul up. You foul up. All God's children foul up, and laughing about our foibles is a form of confession. . . .

Relief results both from formal confession . . . and informal confession—poking fun at our pretensions. Those able to laugh at themselves find relief, and they release others around them to do the same . . . an inability to laugh about our concerns too often results in idolatry of the cause . . .

If Karl Marx's revolution had had a healthy dose of Groucho Marx's comedy, lives would have been saved—and the resulting regime would probably have been more humane. . . .

Cheerful crusaders are cheerful lovers of humanity—sinners and saints alike. They relate to the human race as if they were part of it. (Mullen, 1989, pp. 49–52)

Humor's place in active nonviolence comes from several features:

- It can be used as a prophetic instrument in nonviolent campaigns, cutting the pretensions of the powerful.
- It can be used to keep activists from burnout (see section on "Burnout" below).
- By deflating their own pretensions, it can keep activists from descending into arrogance that leads cause-oriented people to violent thoughts.
- Forms of humor that opponents are able to share can lead to communication breakthroughs, or at least to greater friendliness.
- It can make it easier to understand differing points of view, differing sides of an issue.

- Nonviolent campaigns by their very nature involve clear-eyed views of human foibles. Without the kind of haughtiness and disdain for the enemy generally required for violence, humor comes naturally as a side effect.

Humor can also, however, have the opposite effect. Hurtful humor can be violent in itself. Jokes that are racist or sexist, which make fun of victims or make fun of the "enemy" can be vicious. Instead of bursting pretensions, they reinforce stereotypes, and can easily become a form of semantic dehumanization of victims. They can sting, even without physical violence.

Mullen (1989) identifies two simple "acceptability" tests for a distinction between satiric humor that fits nonviolence and vicious humor, which does not:

1. *Is it true?*
   If there is truth to the joke, it is a satire, even if it is poetic truth rather than scientifically factual. If it feeds a stereotype rather than reality, it fails this test.
2. *Is it told in fun?*
   The intention of the joke teller matters. Is it laughing *with* or laughing *at?* Is it intended to be hurtful, or is it something the target could reasonably respond to without humiliation?

Optimism

Every part of life can be expected to provide failures. Failure makes everyone feel momentarily helpless. For pessimists, the hurt lasts; for optimists, there is more resilience and the hurt goes away. Optimism has also been connected to good physical health, achievement, and lack of depression.

The studies of Martin Seligman (1991) in this trait are well known. He says optimism or pessimism results from learned habits that can be relearned. These habits come from the *explanatory style* people use to explain successes and failures in their lives. Do they explain events in a way that gives them hope, or takes it away?

Three Features of Explanatory Style

1. *Permanence*
   Pessimists tend to attribute bad events to permanent causes—"I'm all washed up," "The boss is a jerk." Optimists attribute them to temporary causes—"I'm tired today," "The boss is in a bad mood." Conversely, pessimists attribute good events to temporary causes—"I'm lucky today." Optimists attribute them to permanent causes—"My normal good luck is holding."
2. *Pervasiveness—Universal vs. Specific*
   Pessimists take the problems from bad events and let them invade other parts of their lives. For them, the cause of the bad events is universal—"All teachers

are unfair." Optimists keep the bad events localized, so a job loss does not invade their exercise workout schedule. They attribute bad events to specific causes—"The teacher for this class is unfair." As above, the converse is true for good events. Optimists think good events have universal causes, and so will enhance all they do. Pessimists attribute good events to specific causes, making it impossible to generalize.

3. *Personalization: Internal vs. External*
   Optimists attribute good events to internal factors, such as their own skill or charming personality. They attribute bad events to external circumstances and people. Pessimists blame themselves when things go wrong, and attribute good events to outside circumstances that cannot be counted upon to be repeated.

The personalization feature is the trickiest. People should take responsibility for themselves, and not be extrapunitive about blaming others if they are not truly to blame. However, it can be helpful for people to think they can change if they know they are internally changeable, that internal character traits they find undesirable are not permanent.

Studies in the technique of getting people to change their explanatory style have proven successful in treating depression, along with other benefits. An optimistic explanatory style seems associated with greater achievement, since people are more motivated to do things necessary to achieve. That alone makes it worth recommending to those who wish to engage in counterviolence activity.

Normal beliefs underlying campaigns of nonviolence fit into this form of explanatory style:

1. *Permanence:* Nonviolent activists, to do what they do, must believe that violent opponents are capable of changing their minds, and that bad events are temporary and changeable. As for good events, activists are appealing to shared values and a basic desire for goodness, which are permanent.

2. *Pervasiveness:* Nonviolent activists believe their violent opponents are violent only in specific areas, the areas under contention. They do not generalize specific bad actions as being done by entirely bad characters. When violent opponents do relent, however, and repair damage or stop inflicting it, it is attributed to common humanity.

3. *Personalization:* Nonviolent activists are happy to allow their violent opponents to attribute the violent actions to external circumstances and join them in making that attribution. The alternative is to insist that opponents admit to being inherently bad people.

The opposite also follows. People given to violence have a tendency to be pessimists. Justifying violence against others goes well with assuming that problems are permanent features of those against whom the violence is aimed. Only in the personalization feature do violent perpetrators withdraw from the pessimist paradigm, since they also tend to attribute the problems to external circumstances or people. Internalized self-loathing may also be a contributory factor, but only in some cases.

An optimistic explanatory style is therefore both a cause that helps make nonviolent action possible and a side effect that naturally follows for those who practice it regularly. This has associated benefits for physical health, achievement, and avoidance of depression.

Of course, there are many times when activists become very discouraged, and events may cause them to start a pessimistic explanatory style. It may be that those who maintain this will tend to drop out, and those who go back to the optimistic style will tend to remain. This would be another helpful area of research.

The Creativity of the Foreclosed Option

In an episode of *Star Trek: The Next Generation*, the Klingon Worf was in an accident leaving him paralyzed. According to Klingon tradition, this meant he should commit ritual suicide, and he was intent on doing so. The doctor was appalled. She tried to research Klingon physiology to find treatment, but since the Klingons always committed suicide on such occasions, they had no advice to give. Various creative things were tried for allowing him to live and function with dignity, even if not with full use of his legs, and finally a procedure that cured him was found. A solution could be found because one option—suicide—was foreclosed in the doctor's mind.

When a specific option is unavailable, others must be sought. When the option is made unavailable because it is undesirable, other avenues may be preferable. Medical breakthroughs, along with treatment choices and other caring alternatives for those with disabilities, require that the option of suicide be off the table.

Once a violent solution is on the table, it precludes the development of alternatives. Violence as a problem-solving technique has the apparent advantage of being quick and efficient. One need only ignore the long-term aftermath and other negative impacts on society. Nonviolent alternatives must of necessity take more care, attention, resources, and time. They have obvious advantages in the long run, but the short-term consequence is more work.

This leads to the ironic outcome that foreclosing an option means *more* options available, rather than fewer. Vegetarians, for example, who foreclose the option of eating meat, actually have more variety in their diets than those eating standard fare (Beardsworth & Keil, 1992). There is no reason in theory why those who eat meat cannot also eat the variety of vegetarian options. Often they do, but excluding meat seems to open up creativity in the diet. Those who oppose abortion have a much more extensive and complex set of services offered through crisis pregnancy centers, maternity homes, mentoring, and government social services than the relative simplicity of the abortion clinic. Similarly, those who oppose nuclear energy propose a wide variety of alternative energy options.

In the psychology of creativity, this is called *divergent thinking*. Many possible solutions are generated when people do not limit themselves to the obvious or conventional.

In the case of war, those who by definition foreclose it as an option entirely—pacifists—have offered a wide array of ways to deal with problems of violence and injustice, some of which are discussed in the next two chapters. People inclined to resort to weapons are less likely to be creative in finding alternative ways of resolving problems. Those who oppose war must of necessity come up with such alternatives. Therefore, creativity is another of the side effects of assertive nonviolence.

BURNOUT

What happens when people in helping professions, nonviolence campaigns, or similar intense undertakings of compassion focus on problems but lack positive feedback? What happens when they lack a sense of improvement in what they are working on, have a high level of emotional stress, receive little support from or get further stress from coworkers, and feel overwhelmed? The answer is that they are in major danger of the *Burnout Syndrome*. This is defined as having three components; each of which tends to develop from what came before.

Components of Burnout

1. *Emotional exhaustion*—This is at the heart of the syndrome. It means feeling overwhelmed by the emotional demands imposed by other people.

2. *Depersonalization*—This is development of a detached, callous, even dehumanized response.

3. *Feeling of reduced personal accomplishment*—The feeling results from the uncaring actions with depersonalization.

Those who are most at risk of burnout deal with many people over an extended period of time, are on constant call, and expected to deal with problems in a caring manner. These people get very involved and get overwhelmed; too much is asked of them, and too little is given to them.

Many people facing a problem with burnout think it is their own fault; sometimes they think of it as someone else's fault. While there are some personality variables making it a little more likely, it is far too widespread for that to mean much. It is not a question of *who* is at fault, but *what* is at fault. The core problem is a *situation*. Much of the research on burnout comes from Christina Maslach, whose interest in burnout as a situational

problem was sparked after her experience in being the one who termi-
nated the Stanford Prison Experiment (see chapter 1).

Part of the reason people do not understand burnout as being caused
by the situation is that the situation has not changed from what it was
before the problem developed. Normally, a change can be seen as causing something, but burnout has the distinctive feature of being due to a
situation that has not changed for too long. Another reason people do
not see burnout as being due to circumstances is that they see other
people in the same circumstances who seem unaffected. Yet they themselves seem unaffected to those other people! Standards of being professional or cheerful or of having it be inappropriate to share negative
feelings can keep people from realizing their feelings are normal and
also held by others.

There are a few demographic variables of interest in how susceptible
people are to burnout. Gender makes no difference in prevalence. In the
United States at least, White and Asian people seem to be most susceptible
and Black people appear to be less susceptible. The clearest difference is
due to age: young people are far more likely than older people to have
burnout. Part of this may be due to greater experience and longer coping
by older people. Part of it may simply be that the younger people who
suffered enough burnout left the field and those remaining are those who
had developed the coping mechanisms before this happened.

Interestingly, married people are much less likely than single people to
develop burnout, as are those with children. Children and family do *not*
provide an extra emotional drain, but instead tend to be helpful social
support.

Below is a more detailed list of known ways to cope with or avoid
burnout. It is crucial that people who intend to enter professions that deal
with direct assistance to individuals or who intend to work in social
change organizations are familiar with these. This will not only help with
stability of such professions or campaigns, but will also be a model of
compassion in the workplace, expected of other workplaces in a peaceful
society.

Coping with and Avoiding Burnout

1. *Work smarter, not harder.* As when going uphill, it is better to shift into an appropriate gear rather than putting on more gas.

   a. *Set specific, realistic steps.*
      When done, one can see that progress has been made. The final goal of justice
      may be after one's lifetime. The final goal of a specific campaign may be
      years away. Have accomplishments defined in concrete terms, and have
      daily, weekly, or monthly goals that can reasonably be done in that time
      frame.

   b. *Do the same thing differently.*
      Avoid ruts. Find what can be varied, and experiment with what is effective.
      If one makes choices rather than simply following directions, one has a
      greater feeling of autonomy. The change may also be an improvement in
      effectiveness, and can be abandoned if not.

   c. *Take breaks and rest periods.*
      This gives both relaxation and a chance to get some psychological distance
      in order to get some perspective, to see things more coolly.

   d. *Take a "downshift."*
      This is not a break, but doing other aspects of the work. Get paperwork or
      reading done, organize files, do some cleaning. These downshifts can be
      scheduled, or taken when a person starts to feel overwhelmed.

   e. *There is no need to take it personally.*
      See other people's problems objectively. Much anger is directed at whoever
      is present, and not at the true target.

   f. *Do not take it home.*
      Ideally, leave problems at the workplace and have a different space where
      the work does not intrude.

2. *Caring for One's Self.* The best way to help others is to be in good shape.

   a. *Accentuate the positive.*
      The point of helping professions and nonviolent campaigns is to focus on
      what is wrong. Finding the good makes the bad less overwhelming. Pay
      attention to accomplishments, minor as well as major—including sharing a
      joke, having an interesting conversation, and so on.

   b. *Small talk is important.*
      It may be irrelevant to the problem itself, but it helps people manage.

   c. *Ask for positive feedback.*
      Sometimes people do not think of giving compliments or are not sure it is
      appropriate. Asking for feedback about what is helpful along with what
      could use improving can bring encouragement.

   d. *Know yourself.*
      Be in tune to inner feelings. Constructive self-analysis may include keeping
      a log for a while.

   e. *Use relaxation techniques.*
      As with physical exercise, these come in many forms, and the best to use is
      the one that fits the individual well.

   f. *Have a life of your own.*
      As for social and organizational approaches, workplaces can be designed to
      see that resources are available, and work is divided to allow for breaks and
      downloading. Organizations should see that personal time is protected, not
      allowing or insisting that work spill into personal time. Vacations are im-
      portant. Social support at the workplace is extremely important—the com-
      panionship of colleagues gives help, comfort, insight, and ability to make
      comparisons.

Support groups might be helpful, especially for people who work in isolation, as happens with housewives who often volunteer, and with peace workers who may be the only employee in the office. This only helps, however, if the sessions are supportive and not overly laden with griping or confrontations. Some people are disinclined to participate, and groups are not helpful if they are imposed.

Humor is especially important. It helps one see the bright side and lift spirits.

There was once an American woman who went to a Latin American country with a concern that people were being treated violently by the government. She was to spend six weeks, and felt a keen sense of emergency. She was disconcerted to find that many of the local people, after a hard day's work on the campaign so vital to them all, had organized a dance. She could not understand how they could do something so frivolous when the stakes were so high. She was gently told that, while she could handle a nonstop emergency feeling for six weeks, the local people were in this campaign for several years. They scheduled in a "ministry of joy." This not only has merit in itself—people in favor of peace usually also favor joy—but it was a wise way of helping to ensure the longevity of the campaign.

GOALS

Hoped-for Achievements of Nonviolence

In considering how well nonviolence has the effect of achieving specific goals, we apply the same list of problems that can hamper the effectiveness of violence, found in chapter 2, to nonviolent campaigns. In some cases, this gives us clear risks that need to be addressed. Nonviolence planners may do well to be aware of these problems just as military planners would. In other cases, the use of nonviolence simply avoids the problem that violence must beware.

Not Having a Clear View

The mechanisms that support violence can and often do creep into those who are trying to practice nonviolence. This includes demonizing opponents, or having an enemy image of them. It is a constant danger when people are investing so much of their energy into a campaign. The very fact that they are not contemplating violence against anyone can make the use of an enemy image all the harder to perceive.

Groupthink can be just as much a danger for nonviolent campaign planners as it can be for military campaign planners. The list of the symptoms of groupthink under "The Power of the Situation" in chapter 1 shows that every one of the features, except for the enemy image, can apply in nonviolent campaigns.

Nonviolence is most effective, then, if it has self-correcting mechanisms to prevent or alleviate forms of unclear thinking. This is also true of techniques of violence. However, the use of more clear and realistic thinking, unencumbered by unrealistic psychological mechanisms, will in the case of violence most likely lead to less violence. In the case of nonviolence, it will most likely lead to more nonviolence. Goals are better achieved in both cases.

Increasing Hatred

One of the major strengths of nonviolence methods is that, over the course of time, they decrease hatred by refusing to participate in it and bringing about a similar response from their opponents. Nonviolence practitioners have only opponents, not enemies, and the category of "opponent" is regarded as temporary.

Getting Out of Hand

Nonviolent campaigns are quite capable of getting out of hand. They do not always run according to plan like a smooth-running business. Businesses do not always run according to plan either, as is especially well known by those who run them.

The primary way of getting out of hand is that, by sparking a spirit of resistance and breaking down apathy or submission, violent outbursts occur. In the Indian independence campaign and the American civil rights movement, for example, riots arose due in part to this reason.

Any nonviolent campaign is likely to have opinionated people—those are the kind most attracted to the activity—and opinionated people can lead to factions within a movement. There are also the ordinary personality conflicts and struggles over bureaucratic territory. If people elect to use nonviolence, this does not alone turn them into saints; human failings are still evident.

In those situations where the only alternatives are violence or submission, then participants may find these risks worth taking. Participants in violent campaigns are not likely to be less opinionated, and factions and personality conflicts and fights over territory still occur. Because of the approval of violence, these can be more deadly and therefore more likely to get seriously out of hand, especially in violent revolutions or coups by soldiers. Using the alternative of submission to violent conditions means things have already gotten out of hand, by definition.

Sparking Defiance, Strengthening Resolve, Backlash

Responses of intense anger and repression are often sparked by nonviolent campaigns. This is not due to their nonviolence, but due to their assertiveness. They are demanding changes, or defending against undesired changes, and those wanting the status quo or the undesired changes will naturally react more negatively to this than they would to acquiescence. They want submission, and therefore can react violently to any kind of resistance, whether violent or nonviolent. With well-done nonviolent campaigns, however, this response may last for years but still be relatively temporary. Part of the technique of nonviolence is to weaken the resolve of opponents to continue with laws or practices that are harmful.

Giving the Violence-Prone an Excuse

The nonviolent campaign does often spark a reaction of violent repression. It therefore brings about acts of direct violence that would not have occurred in its absence. However, the initial and continued nonviolence in the face of a violent response undercuts the perceived justifiability of the violence. This is common for onlookers, and can eventually come about even for the attackers themselves. The nonviolent campaign is not an excuse for violence a government had hoped to do.

Lies

Nonviolent campaigns are certainly vulnerable to being lied about, and this danger is so common that planners take it into account. Opponents who are violent are frequently also deceptive. They use whatever technique they think will work and tend to demonize their opposition, so they may also spread untrue rumors that they actually do believe themselves.

The extent to which a nonviolent campaign is able to keep its nonviolence intact makes the lies and rumors less credible, especially as time goes on. Those who use violence, no matter how well they believe they are fitting just war criteria, are less likely to have this option. Because of this, those facing a nonviolent campaign often send in agents to provoke violence in the group. If they succeed, it helps their case tremendously.

Loss of the Moral High Ground

One of the major strengths of nonviolence is its ability to keep the moral high ground. Inasmuch as practitioners fail to do so, they have also failed to follow nonviolence principles.

Interfering with Other Approaches

Humanitarian aid can be offered to refugees at the same time as a bombing. Bombing interferes with the humanitarian aid, but not vice-versa. Violent approaches can interfere with nonviolent approaches. However, assertive nonviolent approaches only interfere with violent ones by making the violent ones seem less appealing as problem-solving options, by providing sound alternatives.

Blowback

When people who are trained in nonviolence turn around and use the techniques against those who trained them it results in less dire consequences than when violence training or weapons are used against the group that provided them. A good example of this actually happening is hard to come by, except perhaps in school or family situations where teachers or parents find out their students or children learned only too well.

Setting Examples

Setting the example of what nonviolence can do generally has good consequences. Unlike wars, during which the homicide rate goes up, the rate of violent crime often goes down during nonviolent campaigns (Sharp, 1973, pp. 789–793).

Becoming the Abhorred

Nonviolence when successful does not change its practitioners so they become what was abhorred, but instead does the opposite: it changes the abhorred people so they become less objectionable. The effect on practitioners of the technique is more positive, as discussed above.

Martyrdom

Nonviolence practitioners *are* the martyrs. If they cause martyrdom in other groups, then by definition they are not nonviolent.

Posttraumatic Stress

By virtue of not perpetrating violence, nonviolence practitioners cannot be subject to Perpetration Induced Traumatic Stress (PITS). Some of them, however, may be motivated by previous experiences that led them to have PITS, such as Vietnam Veterans Against the War.

There is still the danger of Posttraumatic Stress Disorder (PTSD), however, as people become involved in campaigns in which violence is aimed at them and their friends. Any violence they suffer can have the kinds of effects trauma has. Spending long terms in prison can have the same kind of traumatic impact prison has on most prisoners.

If people deliberately choose to go into situations in which they risk suffering violence or imprisonment, does this make posttrauma symptoms worse than normal? Does the choice and deliberate planning serve to alleviate posttrauma symptoms? Or are such problems the same for this group as for other victims of trauma? Research has not yet answered these questions. Providing aid in terms of therapy and having a community of support, however, may be as necessary for nonviolent campaigns as it is for soldiers in war.

Vulnerability to Nonviolent Resistance

There is a story from the Indian campaign for independence from Britain on nonviolent protesters being subjected to nonviolent resistance. Protesters were carrying out a planned march when they came to a bridge. The British soldiers, tired of the negative fallout when they used violent responses, used the technique of their opponents: as a group, they sat at the entrance to the bridge and blocked it. They were totally nonviolent, but did stop the march. Finally, when lunchtime came, the marchers opened their lunches and shared the food with the soldiers. This broke the impasse. The soldiers left the bridge and let the marchers cross. Thus, a battle occurred that was nonviolent on both sides, and the more assertively nonviolent side won.

CONCLUSION

As said before, there are many links and connections among these subjects. There is value in laying them out clearly in a pattern. The reality, as always, is not nearly so neat.

Humor, optimism, and creativity, for example, were listed as effects of nonviolence, but they also serve as causes. Their absence can either serve as causes of violence or be another of its effects. Nor are they necessarily absent from the violent, since unrealistic optimism about the outcome of a war can contribute to the war happening. Humor can be malicious. It can also relieve the stress associated with battles just as well as other forms of stress.

Burnout can be a result of helping behavior for those who are not careful, but it can also be a result for harming behavior for similar reasons. It can contribute to harmful behavior by causing deadened feelings and irritation. For example, a social worker who snaps at a client can make the structural violence suffered by that client all the more burdensome. A therapist not up to par during counseling sessions can have the same effect on victims of direct violence.

The impact that nonviolence has on recipients could also serve as a cause of nonviolence. People who see this effect are more likely to engage in nonviolent action than those who despair of such results.

FURTHER READING

Impact on Targets and Participants

Gregg, R. B. (1972). *The psychology and strategy of Gandhi's nonviolent resistance.* New York: Garland Publishing, Inc.

Pelton, L. H. (1974). *The psychology of nonviolence.* New York: Pergamon.
Sharp, G. (1973). *The politics of nonviolent action: The dynamics of nonviolent action.*
     (Vol. 3). Boston, MA: Extending Horizons Books.

Optimism

Seligman, M. (1991). *Learned optimism.* New York: A. A. Knopf.

Burnout

Maslach, C. (1982). *Burnout: The cost of caring.* Englewood Cliffs, NJ: Prentice-Hall.
Maslach, C. & Leiter, M. P. (1997). *The truth about burnout.* San Francisco, CA:
     Jossey-Bass.

CHAPTER 5

Conflict Resolution

To some, conflict resolution is the prime alternative to violence. Governments use diplomacy, not only to resolve specific conflicts but also to avoid war. The existence of the war is sometimes regarded as a result of failed diplomacy. Groups that have been in violent conflict—for example, different countries at war, different sides in a civil war, and different gangs in informal gang warfare—may well need conflict resolution techniques and someone skilled at mediation to extricate themselves from a situation they know has gotten out of hand. More commonly, ordinary people in everyday situations have conflicts that arise as a simple matter of normal experience. Long-standing conflicts can also degenerate into circumstances that, if not outright violent, are certainly not peaceful either.

This chapter covers:

- Principles—an overview of the basics
- Special Applications—a look at some particulars for specific groups and situations
- Chronic Conflict—long-standing group hatreds
- Public Policy—various applications to government

PRINCIPLES

The Peaceful Approach to Conflicts

As early as 1924, social psychologist Mary Parker Follett did an analysis of conflict in a book called *Creative Experience*. She suggested three ways conflicts are settled: domination, compromise, and integration.

Follett argued that the first two were unsatisfactory because they merely rearrange material; what is already there is adjusted, but nothing is created. Integration means analyzing the desires or intentions of the parties and working out a new solution to satisfy all. This concept of *integrative solutions* is still a major foundation of current conflict resolution models.

There are many such models. The common parts of conflict resolution models include that conflict resolution is a cooperative endeavor. The foundation is an understanding of the parties' interests, the solutions sought are integrative ones, and both the process and the outcome are nonviolent.

The point of cooperation does distinguish conflict resolution from the kind of nonviolent campaigns that must be waged when one party is powerful and has no intention of caring about the needs of others. When cooperation is impossible, then other means of nonviolent struggle are called for. This is covered in chapter 6.

The *interest-based approach* allows for a search for a win-win solution. It differs from a *rights-based approach,* which makes decisions according to legal rules that are set up as a win-lose situation. By taking *interests* rather than *positions* into account, the possibility that a solution will be satisfactory to all parties becomes more likely. The classic example is a brother and sister who both take the position they want the one remaining orange. It turns out that the brother is interested in eating the inside, while the sister wants the rind to make marmalade. Once this is clear, the solution is obvious; the interests of both can be satisfied. Because they went beyond positions to actual interests, they were able to find an integrative solution.

The solutions that meet the interests and needs of all parties, or at least do so as well as can be figured out, distinguish conflict resolution from a competition or zero-sum game where one side wins and the other loses. They also distinguish conflict resolution as a form of conflict settlement. Other forms of settlement might include compromises or impositions. Lingering dissatisfactions in some cases means the conflict is not truly settled, but only remains quiet for a time until its issues rise again.

It is important to know what type of conflict is involved. There are three major types:

1. *Zero-sum*—a win-lose conflict
2. *Mixed motive*—both can win, both can lose, or one wins and the other loses
3. *Pure cooperative*—both win or lose

The difference matters because strategies and tactics differ. People who believe they are in a zero-sum conflict when they are not can behave in ways contrary to their own interests. Zero-sum conflicts are much more rare than many people realize.

It is also a good idea to determine whether a conflict must be faced or avoided. Conflicts that will soon evaporate on their own, or are inherently irresolvable, may well be avoided. Other conflicts may lead to festering problems if avoided, and need to be faced with discernment.

Communication skills during conflict are among the most crucial. Resolution is more likely when people listen attentively, understand the others' perspective, and continually check that they are doing so successfully. People need to communicate clearly, in a way that makes it apparent that they do understand the others' perspectives.

People trying to resolve conflicts should be alert for natural tendencies to bias, such as misperceptions, stereotyped thinking, oversimplified black-and-white thinking, and narrowing the range of perceived options. Of particular concern is the *fundamental attribution error,* the tendency to attribute the aggressive actions of the other to the other's personality while attributing one's own to external circumstances such as the other's hostile actions.

People also need to know themselves well, and how they as individuals typically respond in situations of this kind. Knowing and being accepting of how other people are on certain dimensions can also be helpful. Do they tend to avoid conflict or be excessively involved? Do they have a hard or soft approach, rigid or loose, intellectual or emotional, escalating or minimizing, revealing or concealing? Being aware and accepting of such differences in approach can help things go more smoothly.

The most important principle is that everyone should be mindful to remain a moral person and consider people on the other side as a member of the same moral community. All sides have people entitled to care and justice.

Application to an Issue Controversy

Following is an example of a current controversy to which the principles are applied by way of illustration. The conflict over the teaching of evolution or creationism in the schools is chosen because of three features it has for applying the above principles:

1. People have well-defined positions, but the underlying interests are not always clearly stated. People on the other side may be able to understand the opposing view better if they were aware of the interests.

2. Only two of various conflicting positions are defined, which oversimplifies the nature of the conflict. Not only can nuances be missed, but also other viewpoints are entirely ignored. False dichotomies help make the conflict more dramatic, but less resolvable.

3. While many people would see this as a philosophical conflict having nothing

to do with peace issues, both sides have asserted that their position is in line with the interests of peace and the other side opposes them.

Conflict: What should be taught in schools about scientific knowledge of origins?

Side 1: Darwinian-style evolutionists believe humans came about through random chance and natural processes such as natural selection.

Side 2: Young-earth creationists believe the Bible is factually true and that the creation account in Genesis is scientifically accurate.

What type of conflict is it? It is a mixed-motive conflict. What is taught in schools could be only evolution, only creationism, both, or neither. Additional alternatives include a curriculum focusing on how science knows what it knows and using this debate as an example.

Another problem is that there are also people who take neither side of the debate, but an alternative position. One such group believes in "intelligent design," a process that accepts the evidence of lengthy time and gradual development, but not the random chance and materialism required of the Darwinian view. It also does not accept the fundamentalist view of biblical facticity. Another group, especially of Eastern religions, holds that human existence is an illusion. Ancient peoples believed in the actions of various gods. In current Western thinking, both sides of the conflict as defined above are minority views. The view of intelligent design (essentially, divinely-guided evolution, or evolving creation) is about as prominent as that of the young-earth creationists. The strict materialist evolutionists are a much smaller group.

This complicates the question of what should be taught in the schools. In media, courts, and legislation, this has been regarded primarily as a fight between the two sides defined above. While the theory of ancient gods is primarily of interest only as a historical point, and the view of existence as an illusion cannot by definition be scientific, the hypothesis of intelligent design is more prominent and yet tends to be disinvited from the two-sided debate.

What are the positions, and what are the interests?

Position, Side 1: Only evolution should be taught because it alone is scientific. Creationism is religion and has no place in the science curriculum.

Position, Side 2: Creation science should be taught in addition to evolution, which is not as scientific as many suppose. Science requires consideration of all theories, and religion should not be discriminated against.

Interests, Side 1:

1. Religious dogma has been tremendously harmful. We have an interest in ensuring that it does no more harm.

2. From the squelching of Galileo to the Crusades and Inquisition and on to current experience, rigid religiosity has been cruel and impeded knowledge.

3. Religious fanatics are currently causing political havoc on public policy issues. They support excessive military and nuclear weapons and ignore the needs of the poor. Those with an interest in peace issues have an interest in seeing that they do not get too much power.

4. Teaching science in a science class is basic. Religion should remain in church, synagogue, and temple.

Interests, Side 2: (Note: Parallel interests are numbered the same way.)

1. The radical materialist view of random-chance evolutionists means human individuals are not made in God's image and therefore not worth much. The stakes are very high in firmly establishing that each human life has value. It is not something that can be thrown away as a mere product of random chance.

2. The Nazi and Soviet genocides resulted from this kind of mentality. Darwin was really trying to find a way to justify the bloody exploits of the British nineteenth-century upper class by saying that natural selection had made them more fit and therefore more entitled.

3. An attack on the Bible is an attack on what give us our self-esteem as human beings. Social Darwinism, with its racism, classism, and anti-charity attitudes, is a major threat to humane policy today. Its connection to the biological evolution theory is not coincidental.

4. Teaching science does not mean teaching atheist propaganda. Science is supposed to consider alternative explanations for facts. Evolutionists are trying to squelch an alternative explanation because they know a consistent rigorous scientific debate would show the weakness in their reasoning. Repressing other views is the only way they can maintain their anti-religion agenda.

Are there converging interests? (Again, points are parallel.)

1. Can creationists agree that many people have been hurt by a rigid religious approach and understand that pain? Can evolutionists agree that the worth of individuals is a very important point? Neither of these interests is a problem for many people on the other side to accept.

2. Can both agree that any killing done in the name of their respective views is a distortion of those views?

3. Can both agree that public policy should be humane? How much can they agree on what humane means?

4. Is there an approach to teaching science that allows different views to be taken into account? Can the subject of origins be used as not just a presentation of conclusions, but also as a good case study in how science works?

How much are the interests as stated above based on stereotypes that can be resolved by more accurate views? There are evolutionists who are religious, after all, and those who are atheist are often passionate about humane and ethical views. There are fundamentalists who do maintain an open mind and are quite capable of reasonable dialog. There are also those who believe in intelligent design who are stereotyped if either side lumps them into the same category as the other side.

How well this analysis helps will depend on individuals involved in specific instances. It can at least perhaps be helpful in allowing people to delve more deeply and understand where the actual interests are. This can keep them from making arguments that are simply puzzling to others.

In other kinds of conflicts, the points in contention might be more purely factual (who was responsible for planting the bomb) or more purely philosophical (should the tasks be divided equally). Conflicts range from the personal to institution-wide to multinational. This one was offered to illustrate a complicated, nonfictitious case.

SPECIAL APPLICATIONS

Debates

In the public forum, when people debate issues, there is a strong tendency for them to use the arguments that make most sense to them and fuel their own passions. They do not necessarily seriously address the main concern of the other side, or of the audience.

For example, those who oppose a bombing campaign may discuss how much harm it is doing to civilians, how much they do not want this done with their money or in their names, and how the roots of the conflict were never properly addressed. Proponents of the bombing campaign may then counter that it is necessary and challenge opponents to come up with alternatives. To proponents, the idea that the bombing is necessary and will prevent violence in the future is the important point. Civilian targets are regrettable and the roots of the conflict are in the past. As long as their bottom-line argument is being ignored, they see nothing but naiveté on the part of those arguing against them. If opponents start out their debate making a case that the bombing is actually counterproductive, then they have gone to the heart of the matter. If they can in fact reasonably make such a case, then spending time on arguments that mean little to the unconvinced is not a productive use of time.

Other examples can be found on both sides of the debates on the death penalty and abortion. Proponents of the death penalty generally believe it deters murder and addresses the emotional needs of the victim's families. Opponents believe executions are murder and teach potential murderers that killing is a way to solve problems. Side issues may be of relevance to people whose positions are weakly held, but if either side of the debate does not understand or acknowledge the main concern—the most important argument the other side has—it is losing the opportunity to make its own case most effectively. Opponents of abortion believe it is killing babies, and any arguments that mothers somehow benefit from their babies being killed puzzles them. Proponents of abortion availability believe it is essential to women's freedom and ability to control their own lives. When they hear opponents not addressing this issue, they think that they are callous toward women. As long as proponents do not address the issue of violence to an unborn baby, and opponents do not address the issue of the needs of women, then neither side is listening to the bottom line of the other. A shouting match ensues.

This is not merely a strategic recommendation to manipulate a debate in one's favor. Addressing the bottom-line argument of the other side in a debate also shows that one is *listening* to the other side. Failing to do so is a way of saying that one's own views and attitudes are important, and those of other people are insignificant. That is what the opponents hear, and also what an audience witnessing the debate hears.

The side issues still deserve attention because there are some on which one can find *common ground*. With the death penalty, for example, everyone is in favor of finding ways to prevent criminal homicide. Establishing where the common ground is and where the disagreements are can help clarify the debate so it becomes a disagreement over specific views rather than a black-and-white confrontation of opponents. The perception of "enemy camps" and other military metaphors for a dispute can be avoided. Common ground is like the interest-based approach to conflict resolution, except the conflict is not resolved. The finding of common interests can mean projects or legislation both sides can favor, thereby making more progress both sides are happy with. The debate itself rages on, but at least some good is accomplished from the point of view of both sides.

On some side issues, one can even concede a point to the other side of the debate, thus avoiding the pitfall of dogmatism. For example, an American who was debating on the side in favor of the 2001 U.S. bombing of Afghanistan was given by the host of the debate the point that polls showed only 10 percent of the public opposed the war. The proponent of the war then pointed out that 10 percent of the American public constituted more than twenty million people, a lot of opposition. That point actually helped the other side of the debate. The technique was used by someone advocating the use of violence, but a willingness to understand various points of view can be done by anyone. An opponent of the bombing who concedes that this was a good technique for the proponent to use is utilizing the same technique.

Establishing that one is actually hearing what the opponent in debate is saying also has the beneficial effect of being able to ask the same in return. Most debaters are primarily interested in their own views, and will likely remain so as long as both sides follow that same pattern. Listening, perhaps paraphrasing back to the opponent in a positive way what has been said, clearly attempting to understand the other person's point of view, and then expecting reciprocation, generally leads to more productive debates. Once this dynamic is set up, opponents often reciprocate, or look bad to the audience if they do not. Both the debaters and the audience may then have more of a sense that they have gained more light than heat.

Children

There are developmental aspects to conflict and the skills to cope with it and resolve it. A review of the research (Schantz, 1987) finds four issues to be prevalent. During toddler and preschool years, most conflicts involve the possession and use of objects. The second largest category is distress over another child's action or lack of action. Other issues are social intrusiveness—unprovoked attack or intrusion into the child's activity, and violating conventional or moral rules.

As children get older, fewer conflicts are about the physical environment and more are about the social environment. Ideas, beliefs, and establishing what the facts were become more important.

Selman (cited in Schantz, 1987) suggested developmental levels for conflict resolution skills:

1. a physical, momentary "here-and-now" orientation—resolving conflicts by stopping interaction or using physical force
2. having an appreciation of the subjective, psychological consequences of conflict, for only one person in the conflict
3. gaining bilateral understanding, though not yet seeing it as a mutual disagreement requiring a mutually satisfying agreement
4. coming to understand that specific conflicts reside in the relationship itself, and solutions do need to be mutually satisfying
5. integrating a balance of dependence and independence, and recognizing symbolic and unstated ways of handling conflicts

In short, over time the development of how to deal with conflict changes in three dimensions:

• The temporal orientation moves from here-and-now to future interactions.
• The conflict focus moves from physical behaviors to people in a relationship.
• The understanding of relationships moves from unilateral to mutual.

Promoting resolution skills in children is more likely if parents have good skills themselves and model the appropriate behavior for their children to learn. This is so not only when children are watching parents interact with others, but also how unilateral or mutual the parents are when relating with the children.

Teaching conflict resolution skills in school can be done as early as kindergarten and is also done in middle school and high school. This is one of the approaches to peace education, and books for further reading on this subject are listed at the end of chapter 3.

Differing Cultures

Differences in cultural beliefs and assumptions would be an obvious area where sensitivity is crucial. Some simple things need to be known about how people understand things differently. For example, there is different meaning to looking someone straight in the eye. In much of the West, this is interpreted as honesty; in much of the Orient, it is a mark of disrespect.

Some of the different images used for conflict and conflict resolution say various things about how people see things. In Lederach's (1995) work in Latin America, he found the word *desmadre* used to describe conflicts. It connotes chaos, but literally means "without a mother." This says quite a bit about the role women play in the community in maintaining stability. Another word used for conflict is *enredo*, which essentially means to be caught up in a fishing net, to be entangled. The interrelationships are important, there are knots and connections, holes must be carefully sewn, and loose ends taken care of.

In the United States, Canada, and much of Europe, the image of conflict resolution involves going to a table. This suggests rationality, bureaucracy, and formal roles. In East Africa, by contrast, there is a proverb: "What old people see seated at the base of the tree, young people cannot see from the branches." This emphasizes the role of the elders in conflict resolution, and assumes this is done outdoors, using local resources and community tradition. Putting a table in and expecting them to go indoors may well be disruptive, and would look as silly to them as going outdoors and negotiating under a tree would look to the average Western diplomat in a business suit.

In addition to knowledge of some of these differences, there are a couple of points about the approach to be remembered in dealing with various cultures:

Giving Information to People vs. Getting Information from People

Many trainers who run sessions for conflict resolution understand themselves to be experts in the area, and expect their audience to see them this way. Their purpose is to give knowledge to the people being trained and guide their practice. Another approach instead uses the culture as a resource, where participants are expected to name their own realities and tools. The training session involves digging into participants' already existing knowledge, assumptions, and images, and coming up with a model of conflict resolution that might not be the same as another culture's. This method of training includes a process of discovering how people already think.

In discussing this based on his own experience in various cultures, John Paul Lederach (1995) argues that both are necessary. The trainer-as-expert approach alone misses a rich set of resources and can be too bossy. The approach of only eliciting from the audience means knowledge and experience that has been gained is not shared, and that was part of what the participants came to the training for. A good balance can be the most effective. In current practice, that means expanding more on the approach of eliciting from the audience.

Analytical vs. Holistic

Some people, when given a problem, have a natural inclination to make a list, or to look at component parts and try to figure out how they fit together. This is what the scientific mind tends to do, and it is therefore common to those with training in psychology. Other people tend to use analogies, metaphors, proverbs, and stories to work through a difficulty. The problem is kept whole, rather than looked at by its parts. The poetic mind is accustomed to this, and it is a common pattern in many cultures and in areas of psychology such as the Jungian approach.

Breaking down into parts is analysis, by definition, and putting parts together into a whole is synthesis and holistic. Since both approaches have advantages and disadvantages, many find merit in using both to gain the most insight. When dealing with different cultures, it is a point about which to be aware. People accustomed to thinking in one mode may find the other unhelpful.

There are undoubtedly many more points to discover in dealing with conflict resolution, peace education, and other forms of peacemaking across cultures. As the field expands, more of these will become better known.

CHRONIC CONFLICT

Causes of Group Conflict

The causes of group conflict receive much attention in social psychology. Group conflict is long-standing conflict between two groups based usually on ethnicity, nationality, or religion. A prerequisite for all group conflict is that people thoroughly identify themselves with one social group, and identify other people as being outside their social group. This is called *social identification,* or group identification.

One place this applies is the practice of trying to ease tensions between groups within a country by appealing to their common citizenship. People who are engaged in social identification with a smaller group that is opposed to another smaller group are encouraged instead to socially identify with the larger group to which both smaller groups belong.

Once social identification has occurred, it can lead to perceptual distortions. Causes for prejudice that have been identified include:

Scapegoating

Finding someone to blame for problems is very appealing because it offers a possibility that the problems can be solved with a quick fix. One of the appeals of violence is its seeming speed.

Zero-Sum Thinking

Sherif's (1966) "realistic conflict theory" suggests a thinking process whereby people believe there is only so much to go around. If the other group gets it, one's own group does not.

Relative Deprivation

Comparisons of one's own group to other groups can lead to an emotional response if it is perceived that the other group has relatively more of something desirable. If this is seen as unfair, conflicts are exacerbated.

The Fundamental Attribution Error

People know about the complexities of their own situations and therefore attribute their own negative or odd behavior to those situations. However, people are unfamiliar with the complexities that others encounter, and so attribute their behavior to their personalities or dispositions. The nuances of our own situations are clear, those of other people less obvious.

Attributive Projection

Since our own ideas about the world strike us as obvious, we tend to assume other people therefore also hold them. If we have evidence they do not, instead of considering how their culture or circumstances might differ, we believe they are incorrect. We also tend to believe they either know this and behave deceptively or are ignorant.

The Just World View

A desire to believe that if people are suffering it is because they deserve it can lead to callousness about other people's anguish.

Stereotypes

Lab experiments have shown that when people have more power, they are likely to stereotype others more than when they do not (Goodwin, Operario, & Fiske, 1998). Powerful people have motivation to oversimplify those over whom they have power and seek information consistent with previous categorizations. Stereotypes—especially negative ones—justify existing differences in power in their minds.

If conflicts are based not on ethnicity or nationality but on positions regarding issues, then the motivation for stereotyping is similar. For example, there was the pro-choice activist who in an accusing manner asked the pro-life activist if she were Catholic. The pro-life activist declared she was not and demanded to know if the pro-choice activist was atheist. Catholics and atheists are found on both sides of this debate. Long-standing groups include Republicans for Choice and Feminists for Life, Catholics for a Free Choice and the Pro-life Alliance of Gays and Lesbians. The desire to stereotype members of a movement who are in opposition to one's own is strong. If the opposition is reasonable or can understand nuances, after all, then one's own case weakens. The dichotomy of right/wrong or good/bad cannot then be stringently maintained. Since ethnic conflict frequently also involves ideas and not merely accidents of skin color or language, the same principle can also apply there.

Working with Diversity

It is common to call the solution to the problem of intolerance "tolerance." This is understandable, since it is clearly the opposite, yet it leads to unfortunate meanings. "Tolerating" the fact that other people have different ideas, cultures, or skin color is not the solution because it implies there is something wrong. Conversely, there is no virtue in tolerating violent harm. Tolerance is helpful for circumstances in which there is something wrong, but not extremely wrong. For instance, parents might tolerate their children's taste in clothing or music, believing the clothing to be ugly and the music to be mere noise. The children can tolerate their parents' taste in clothing and music on the same belief. Tolerance therefore increases harmony, but only when the implication there is something wrong does not cause disharmony itself.

The question here, then, is how to work with diversity, lower prejudice and unfair discrimination against differing groups, and prevent intergroup violence. There are basically two categories of approach on how to decrease prejudice between groups: *interdependency* and *contact*.

Interdependency

Sherif (1966) was one of the early scholars in this area. He proposed that one of the best ways to resolve group conflicts was the technique of providing "superordinate goals." This is a form of interdependency in which both groups must cooperate in order to achieve what they both need. In a classic experiment with two rival groups of boys at camp, he found this to work. Leaders often use this technique, sometimes consciously, to induce rival factions to coalesce for a greater goal. It is also one of the prime effects of war itself. People set aside arguments when there is a victory to be won, and bemoan the loss of unity when peace returns. Goals can instead be nonviolent, of course, and frequently are.

When discussing the tendency of those in power to stereotype others, researchers suggest one of the ways to avoid this is through mutual dependence. If the extent to which one actually depends on others can be made uppermost in the mind, then it becomes much more important to make accurate judgments and avoid the cognitive distortions of stereotypes. Paying attention to counter-stereotypical information becomes more likely (Goodwin, Operario, & Fiske, 1998).

In schools, this interdependency can be intentionally instilled with the *jigsaw technique*. First used in 1971, much experience has shown that this technique can be successful in reducing fear and mistrust. By requiring students to rely on each other to get a good grade, cooperation becomes mandatory. When forced to work together, students gain the ability to see other people as they really are, rather than as they are stereotyped. The ten steps of the jigsaw technique are:

1. The teacher divides students into jigsaw groups of five or six people. The groups come from assorted other groups of different gender, ethnicity, and ability.

2. The teacher appoints one student from each group as the leader. At the beginning, this is the most mature student in the group.

3. The teacher divides the day's lesson into about five or six segments.

4. Each student is to learn one segment. It is important that students have direct access only to their own segment.

5. Students become familiar with their own segments.

6. Temporary "expert groups" are formed when one student from each jigsaw group joins other students who are assigned to the same segment. Students can then discuss this same segment with others and rehearse their own presentations.

7. Students go back into their jigsaw groups.

8. Each student presents his or her segment to the jigsaw group. Others are encouraged to ask questions for clarification.

9. The teacher monitors the groups in case there are problems. An example would be if one person is dominating or being disruptive. Intervention is mild, preferably with whispered instruction to the leader until he or she figures out how to deal with such situations.

10. At the end of the class, there is a quiz. Grades do rely on administering this process properly.

Contact

In a 1954 book called *The Nature of Prejudice,* Gordon Allport put forward the classic construct called the *contact hypothesis.* The idea was that prejudice is based on the ignorance of others, and less ignorance would mean less prejudice. Contact with members of the out-group should therefore reduce the problem.

Some have suggested that it cannot be that simple. Whites in the traditional American South, for example, had ample opportunity for contact with Blacks and nevertheless had colossal amounts of prejudice. In fact, they had more prejudice than in areas where Blacks were such a small portion of the population that the mere difference in skin color of a few was barely noticed. However, the contact in the South was not under terms of equality; it was a form of contact designed to increase the privileged status for Whites.

Accordingly, Allport and subsequent researchers set the following conditions as necessary to see that contact was actually productive in reducing prejudice:

- It is supported by authority figures.
- It is voluntary for participants.
- Within the situation, participants are of equal status.
- There is cooperative interdependence among participants across groups.
- Individualized contact has the potential for friendships across groups.
- The interaction includes behavior disconfirming stereotypes that groups hold of each other.
- Members of the other group are seen as typical of that group, not a mere exception, so stereotypes are disconfirmed.

This is one of the most researched hypotheses in the area of intergroup conflict. Results are mixed—some experiments show a good success rate, and others are disappointing. The hypothesis has accordingly grown in complexity, with researchers looking for new avenues to increase its effectiveness.

Forbes (1997) argues that the problem with the contact hypothesis is that it analyzes at the level of individuals, where it experimentally does work. However, it does not analyze at the level of groups, where it does not work well. He proposes instead that if sympathetic contact with an out-group by some individuals does cause reduced tension for those individuals, it can be made up for by increased tension of other members in the in-group. These others may have increased resentment, and regard those in their own group who have befriended others as traitors to their group. Improvement in the attitudes of some insiders may make others more hostile. Forbes proposes that this is why something that works at an individual level may not have the same effect at the group level.

On the other hand, in a meta-analysis of approximately five hundred studies, Pettigrew and Tropp (2000) find strong support for the contact hypothesis. They ascertain that what is needed for greater understanding between groups is contact, in all but the most hostile and threatening conditions. When the above conditions are met, then the effect is even larger. Their analysis also found that the effect is primarily not from changed thinking, but from changed emotions. In other words, stereotypes may not change, but greater liking occurs. This explanation could also help account for mixed results. It is also true that a statistical finding of "greater understanding" of others does not mean that the understanding became great enough to avoid destructive conflicts.

In addition, the form of group tensions that needs to be reduced must be considered. The classroom jigsaw technique could also be looked at in terms of the contact hypothesis, for example. However, people who live in segregated enclaves and are close to civil war, with memories of loved ones having been murdered by the other side, may have passions requiring different approaches.

Dealing with the Past

Barbara Tint Alon (2002) suggests that those practitioners of conflict resolution who believe that interests can be better satisfied by looking forward—where the group would like to go rather than where it came from—may be missing an important piece of how conflicts can best be resolved. She starts with a distinction between history and memory, as shown in table 5.1.

History is objective. It is what it is. What happened, happened. Memory, on the other hand, is colored by feelings and contexts and subsequent events. History is what happened out in the world, while memory is a psychological phenomenon inside a person. History is static since once something has happened, the fact that it happened remains forever. Memory is fluid and can change the feelings, context, and priorities of what is most important, and the coloring of subsequent events. In other words, history is a fact, while memory is a feeling. History is generally what happened to the group as a whole and is therefore political. Memory is very personal.

A crucial distinction is that history, by definition, is in the past. Memory is in the present. It is memory that most needs to be dealt with. People can and do argue over what actually happened. These are arguments over objective, external, static facts. Political debates are full of such disputes.

Table 5.1
History and Memory

History	Memory
objective	subjective
external	internal
static	fluid
fact	meaning
political	personal
past	present
debatable	not debatable

Memory is not debatable in that way. People have the memories they have—subjective, internal, personal feelings. If they say they have them, they do; there would be no point in arguing the matter.

Though table 5.1 shows a list of opposites, the two concepts are certainly not opposites of each other. The distinctions are not clear-cut, and the two are not so neatly separated; it is a changeable framework.

Barbara Tint Alon found the distinctions useful in her research of extensive interviews with Israelis and Palestinians. She believes her findings can be applied across a large variety of long-standing destructive conflicts. Her conclusions are:

- People often challenge cultural or political history, but generally accept other people's personal and family histories.
- Historical stories promote nationalism. Personal stories promote conciliation.
- Those in positions of power are the ones most likely to suggest that the past is not important.
- People's memories often focus on their own victimization. They are less likely to see the victimization of others.
- Though people may say it is best to look forward, they quickly go back to past memories and injustices.
- Those who are entrenched in the past are less open to conflict resolution processes and are the most likely to keep the conflict going.
- The different perceptions of the past correlate directly to the different perceptions of the conflict and how it can be resolved.

- How much people actually suffered or lost is not necessarily correlated to their tendency to focus on the past.

Tint Alon suggests several important implications of these findings for how to deal with resolution of long-simmering conflicts. Parties may be unaware of it, but memory plays a substantial role in the conflict. Having parties argue about historical facts is not likely to be productive, but bringing it to the personal level may be. People more readily accept the personal histories of others, and those family and personal stories are also more likely to bring a sense of conciliation. Asking people to look only to the future may be unrealistic. People who are stuck in memories of victimization may be helped by eliciting different, more positive memories related to the conflict. This strong tendency to revert to memories is then transformed to something more helpful.

One extensive case in which these principles were applied was in the Truth and Reconciliation Commission of South Africa. Though the conflict had been settled through democratic elections in which all races participated with a peaceful transfer of power to the new government, it was recognized that some way must be found to deal with the past. Having Nuremburg-style trials of those who had participated in torture and murder was rejected as a method that would leave people mired in the past. Yet, ignoring the role of memory would not do either, because the past would continually return to haunt the present if it were not dealt with. The chair of the commission, Archbishop Desmond Tutu, illustrated this with the case of a young Afrikaner whose grandmother had recounted stories about the horrible conditions in the concentration camps set up by the British during the Anglo-Boer War. The young Afrikaner told Tutu that remembering those stories made him ready to fight the war all over again—and this was about a hundred years after the war was over (Tutu, 1999, pp. 28–29).

The commission accordingly was set up to hear people's stories about their experiences under apartheid. This was a very difficult process, but it was a way of working through memories that needed to be dealt with.

More study of this will help. The South African experience was dealing with memories as a way to finish resolving a conflict that had been settled. It is a successful case that may be applied in other postconflict situations. How well these insights can help in resolving conflicts that are still ongoing will take more experience.

PUBLIC POLICY

Diplomacy

One of the first uses of the approach of integrative solutions to conflict in international affairs occurred with a series of problem-solving workshops in 1965. They were labeled "Controlled Communication Workshops" (Burton, 1969) and were sponsored by the London-based Centre for Analysis of Conflict. They included a panel of third-party facilitators to keep the dialogue free of zero-sum thinking and traditional power and compromise-oriented negotiations. The facilitators' job was to see that acceptable outcomes would evolve through the meetings. Representatives came from Indonesia, Malaysia, and Singapore, countries that at the time were involved in a violent conflict. Meetings lasted for more than a week. How much they helped cannot be said for certain, but the fighting between the three parties did stop soon thereafter.

Results from further efforts were mixed, but the research on how to do this expanded. One of the facilitators at that first workshop, Roger Fisher, did coauthor a book with William Ury in 1981 called *Getting to Yes*, which was an immediate best-seller and longtime handbook for practitioners.

These informal processes are currently often used in what is called *second-track diplomacy*. Informal meetings are run parallel to formal negotiations. Non-official representatives of governments can state concerns and offer creative options that would be unlikely to come up or seem appropriate in the formal negotiations.

Nongovernmental organizations can also contribute to resolution of international conflicts by essentially running a second track themselves. There are times when nations may be more willing to engage in dialog when the third-party facilitators are more neutral, with an organization that truly has no stake in the outcome other than that it be peacefully resolved to the satisfaction of all parties.

Another feature of diplomacy is a technique used in the frequent case when both sides in a dispute do not trust each other. Since the lack of trust is a serious problem, and conflicts are difficult to resolve under such circumstances, negotiators can propose *confidence-building measures*. These are small steps that do not cost each side much, but are then intended to be reciprocated. They are both willing to take each step because they do not perceive that they would be in deep trouble if the other side does not reciprocate; however, each side will not take further action until the other side does reciprocate. In this way, the two sides can inch toward a settlement. A settlement is not the same as a resolution, and its major drawback is that the conflict is likely to be reopened because a satisfactory resolution is not reached. In some situations, however, a settlement is a good step on the way to resolution, and confidence-building measures are a good step on the way to settlement. Many disputes, especially international ones of long standing, take much time and care to resolve.

Postwar Reconciliation

Cleaning up after the damage of war is needed for humanitarian reasons, but there is also a prevention aspect. If war-torn societies experience little or inadequate reconstruction, the psychological wounds can remain deep and the lingering social hatreds invite more conflict. Reconstruction needs to include physical rebuilding so the meeting of basic material needs is eased. Psychologically, there is also work to be done with regard to reconciliation, which is a form of *learning* from the experience.

After South Africa held its first fully democratic elections, with all races participating, the new government set up a Truth and Reconciliation Commission. It was both process and outcome, serving as relationship-building, truth-seeking, acknowledgment of others' pain and humanity, and allowing for forgiveness and dialog. Perpetrators of murder and torture were offered amnesty, but only when they applied for it and made full disclosure of the events that occurred. They had to attend difficult sessions with the victims. Even without prison sentences, they did not get off scot-free. Victims got much needed information about what had happened to their loved ones, and a chance to have their stories heard. An account work of the commission is written by its chair, Archbishop Desmond Tutu, in his 1999 book entitled *No Future without Forgiveness*.

Restorative Justice

Restorative justice is a category of victim and offender encounter programs that can be regarded as a post-crime reconciliation program. Its core values are restitution, reconciliation, and reintegration for all concerned.

Victims, offenders, and members of the community take the active role in healing relationships broken by crime, so they replace the state as the primary participant in the search for justice. The state still has a role in facilitating the process. Retribution is replaced by restoration, which benefits the victims and makes the offenders less likely to re-offend.

In general, juvenile programs, where the idea is most workable, are the beginning point for restorative justice programs, which can then be expanded to adults when they are well established. There are many such programs in localities around the world, and the United Nations is doing some work in establishing guidelines.

One program that serves as an illustration is the Re-Integrative Strategy Classes (RISC) for juvenile offenders. A licensed psychologist leads the classes over the course of twelve weeks. They cover peer pressure, respect for authority, and diversity. Participants, who are there voluntarily, are assigned a mentor to see that they attend classes, fulfill aspects of their contracts, and otherwise become productive citizens in the community. In the final week, the victim and associates return and meet with the offender. The hope is for forgiveness and healing at this point, with the offender reintegrated in the community and no longer a threat to safety.

In other cases, restitution to the victim or community service may be called for. Mediation and conflict resolution may be necessary. In all cases, the means are tailored to the goal of psychological healing for everyone concerned.

The United Nations and the U.S. Department of Justice are among those who have taken an interest in this approach. Below are points of an overview of restorative justice process and potential taken from a Department of Justice publication (Nicholl, 1999, p. 91):

- Crime creates an opportunity for diagnosis of problems and changing social structures that promote criminal behavior.
- Problem identification requires involvement of everyone who has harmed others, has been harmed, or might have a role to play in addressing the harm.
- Problem resolution requires citizen involvement. The causes and consequences of harmful actions are often beyond the capacity of government alone.
- The process allows for learning about what factors contribute to crime.
- Learning applies to making changes in practices, policies, and priorities. This offers crime prevention, social justice, and more public safety.

In other words, this is a problem-solving approach rather than a violent approach to solving a problem of violence. Highly punitive measures have generally been used based on ideas of long standing, but not on experience of what actually works.

Mention should also be made of a concept that is often paired with restorative justice: *community policing*. In this case, police take a more problem-solving approach, which involves conflict resolution and prevention skills. It is a proactive rather than a punitive method that is becoming more widespread as empirical evaluation shows its effectiveness.

Marshall Plans

On June 5, 1947, then U.S. Secretary of State George C. Marshall gave a speech at the commencement of Harvard University suggesting, as stated in the front-page headline of the following day's *Washington Post*, that "Marshall Sees Europe in Need of Vast New U.S. Aid; Urges Self-Help in Reconstruction." The Marshall Plan stalled about ten months in the U.S. Congress, but events in Europe startled lawmakers as the Soviets made military inroads into Eastern Europe. Much of the idea of the plan was to keep Europe strong against such incursions. Japan also received a large amount of rebuilding assistance after the war.

The result has been that both Germany and Japan have been converted from war-ravaged nations of fascist ideology into peaceful and prosperous nations not perceived as a military threat to anyone. How could nations with so many citizens filled with a raging war mentality become nations where those who think that way are now on the fringe?

The conventional wisdom is that the harsh and punitive measures put on Germany after World War I were a major contributor to World War II, whereas the Marshall Plan was a major contributor to the absence of another such war. From nonviolence theory, this makes sense. The Marshall Plan was a major campaign of nonviolence.

It is a very peculiar form of nonviolence, since it relies on previous violence having occurred. Yet it uses the principles of considering the needs of those on the "other side," seeing them as real people, caring, and helping. People are not treated as the enemy; they are assertively and with great cost treated as friends. They then become friends. That is how active nonviolence is supposed to work.

This is also a peculiar form of nonviolence because it is commonly recognized as being a form of defense. Hard-nosed military planners understand quickly that this massive infusion of aid to a defeated enemy is important to future security.

Economic Conversion

There is a basic emotion that keeps military bases open and weapons being built long after the military itself sees no use for this: people's anxiety about losing jobs. When all other forms of reasoning have suggested that certain preparations for violence serve no security purpose, the behavior is maintained for an economic reason. People who disdain those on welfare continue to demand government subsidy for their own work without expectation that the work is of actual value to the taxpayer. The average taxpayer is so understanding of this anxiety that the argument to continue the subsidy for the sake of jobs seems sound to many.

The irony in this is that the military is second only to the space program in producing the fewest jobs for the money. Both military weapons and the space program use huge amounts of money on the material rather than the labor. The space program uses a much smaller portion of money and therefore has a smaller impact on the economy. For the military, the same amount of money spent on anything else—government services or left in taxpayers' pockets—produces more jobs than that money spent on the military. Nevertheless, the change from one way of spending to another is frightening to those with jobs relying on the status quo.

A nonviolent alternative is direct economic conversion. Rather than letting people loose on the market, a weapons-building factory or base could be converted to a similar use that allows people to keep their jobs. A proposal for conversion is likely to meet less resistance than the economic dislocation people otherwise fear.

CONCLUSION

In some group conflicts, the two groups have roughly equal power. If their leadership is interested in resolving the long-term conflicts, then the above techniques can be useful. From teachers who want to relieve tensions among a diverse student body to government officials who want minorities to have more opportunities, training of skills that involve resolution rather than confrontation would seem appropriate. When any unfairness that exists is relatively minor and can be understood and alleviated, or when compromise would not leave grave injustices in place, then mediation or negotiation are the best routes to peace.

When negotiations break down, however, this does not mean violent conflict or war are the only alternatives left. When a compromise is unacceptable because it does not address basic issues that will be left festering as resented injustices, there are still other options. In some cases, there will be creativity in involving third parties or using the legal system. In others, especially when all these options are unavailable and power is not evenly distributed between groups, more will be required. This is discussed in chapter 6.

FURTHER READING

For more on teaching conflict resolution, especially to children, see "Peace Education" in the reading list of chapter 3.

Principles

Deutch, M., & Coleman, P. T. (Eds.). (2000). *The handbook of conflict resolution: Theory and practice.* San Francisco: Jossey-Bass.

Differing Cultures

Lederach, J. P. (1995). *Preparing for peace: Conflict transformation across cultures.* Syracuse, NY: Syracuse University Press.

Ethnic Conflict and Prejudice

Alexander, M. G., & Levin, S. (Eds.). (1998). Understanding and resolving national and international group conflict (entire issue theme). *Journal of Social Issues, 54,* 629–846.

Chirot, D., & Seligman, M. E. P. (2001). *Ethnopolitical warfare: Causes, consequences, and possible solutions.* Washington, DC: American Psychological Association.

The Jigsaw Technique

Aronson, E. (2000). *Nobody left to hate: Teaching compassion after Columbine.* New York: W. H. Freeman.

Aronson, E., & Patnoe, S. (1997). *The jigsaw classroom: Building cooperation in the classroom* (2nd ed.). New York: Addison Wesley Longman.

Official Web site for the jigsaw technique: http://www.jigsaw.org.

Diplomacy

Rouhana, N. N., & Kelman, H. C. (1994). Promoting joint thinking in international conflicts: An Israeli-Palestinian continuing worship. *Journal of Social Issues, 50*, 157–178.

Postwar Reconciliation

Abu-Nimer, M. (2001). *Reconciliation, justice and coexistence: Theory and practice.* Lanham, MD: Lexington Books.
Tutu, D. M. (1999). *No future without forgiveness.* New York: Doubleday.

Restorative Justice

Nicholl, C. G. (1999). *Community policing, community justice, and restorative justice: Exploring the links for the delivery of a balanced approach to public safety.* Washington, DC: U.S. Department of Justice, Office of Community Oriented Policing Services.
Nicholl, C. G. (2000). *Toolbox for implementing restorative justice and advancing community policing.* Washington, DC: U.S. Department of Justice, Office of Community Oriented Policing Services.
Web site on restorative justice: www.restorativejustice.org.

CHAPTER 6

Nonviolent Struggle and Social Movements

Conflict resolution works well when people on all sides of a conflict have goodwill. It works best when the amount of power each side has is equivalent. However, there are many cases when one side has more power than the other, with no intention of being fair, or there is a disputed idea of what is fair. From a bully demanding other people's lunch money to a government trying to establish dictatorial laws, there are times when ordinary conflict resolution techniques are not appropriate and more extreme measures of nonviolence are called for.

Conditions that actually constitute structural violence appear to be peaceful to those in more powerful positions. To them, a nonviolent campaign of opposition is "breaking the peace." This is how they see it and how they try to present it to onlookers. They believe the opponents are causing the conflict, and that it could be resolved if the opponents would accept the status quo. Social strain results when there is pressure to change relationships within a structure to new ones; this is resisted, of course, by those who want no change. If the campaign is successful in removing the structural violence, however—such as segregation laws, dictatorships, unsafe working conditions, and killings in medical settings—it has achieved progress in building peace.

This chapter covers:

- The Psychology of Power—a foundational understanding of how the nonviolent can gain power
- Actions—the forms nonviolent campaigns can take

- Movement Dynamics—various aspects of social movements and strategic considerations
- Individual Situations—using nonviolent defense in everyday life, outside a movement context

THE PSYCHOLOGY OF POWER

Kinds of Power

Kenneth Boulding proposes three kinds of power in human situations. Political *power* is essentially the ability to cause certain things to happen, to cause people to behave in a certain way. The three kinds interact with each other:

1. *Threat power*—Things happen to avoid undesired consequences; people behave a certain way out of fear.
2. *Economic power*—Material things happen because people have mutually decided on them; people behave in a way they believe is in their self-interest.
3. *Integrative power*—Things happen because people see this as legitimate; people behave because they are persuaded it is right.

Threat power is the idea behind military force and to some extent judicial courts. It does often work in specific situations—"Put a coin in this meter or you will receive a fine." Military threats, however, have a tendency to be less clear-cut, more vague, and this often causes them to lose their potency. More to the point, this type of power can lose all effectiveness if it is not combined with the third type. If it is seen as not having legitimacy, then defiance becomes more likely. If the threat was a bluff, the threatener backs down; if it was not a bluff, the violence inflicted then has other consequences. If those consequences include a further lowering of public perception of the threatener's legitimacy, then it is actually the threatener who is in trouble.

Economic power can come from the successful use of *threat power,* as with conquest of land. More frequently, though, it comes from a voluntary exchange in which the seller can refuse to sell and the buyer can refuse to buy. Again, the cooperation necessary is more likely if participants perceive the power relationships as legitimate.

Integrative power includes persuasion, loyalty, sense of community, and other aspects indicating the powerful are regarded as a legitimate authority rather than a usurper. It is a gift to the powerful by those over whom they have power, and it can be withdrawn.

In other words, while we tend to think of power in terms of material weapons and material wealth, the most important component is psychological. For threat power, it is the component of fear that makes it work.

The same material circumstances without that psychological component makes the power diminish.

Economic power depends on the psychology of voluntary exchange. If the psychology changes, so will the economic arrangements. In most cases, it is perceptions of legitimacy that bring about the changes in material arrangements. Perceptions are the province of psychology. It is also ongoing learning processes that bring about changes; learning is prime as a psychological field.

Whatever happens in the material world also has a psychological impact, which then interacts to have more effect on it again. The world is complex and nonviolent campaigns can be difficult and lengthy. Psychological perceptions are not necessarily easy to dislodge. Learning takes time. Nevertheless, understanding how fundamental the psychological component is to power is crucial to understanding how nonviolent action can be and often is more powerful than violence.

Gandhi called active nonviolence the "power of truth." His name for it, satyagraha, is translated as the force or power of truth. Clearly, this fits in with the concept of integrative power, or power derived from perceptions of legitimacy. If power is perceived as coming from a lie or a half-truth, then it loses legitimacy. Only when power has truth on its side does this danger disappear. While lies can be powerful for a time, the very fact they are used shows how powerful the truth is. If the powerful could maintain their grip on power in spite of unpleasant truths being known, they would not need to bother with lies.

This also applies to the emotions of love and fear. Threat power is based on fear; as such, it often works even when truth is known. People cooperate with a power they perceive as illegitimate because they are afraid to do otherwise. If this fear disappears, however, the power of threat that was based on the fear disappears with it. If the fear is submerged in hatred, violence follows; if it is submerged in love, nonviolence follows.

This leads to a tricky course. The nonviolence movement must remove fear from the population in order to work. It is not uncommon that a result may be the outbreak of riots. This occurred in India with Gandhi's campaign and with the civil rights movement in the United States. The overcoming of fear was needed before anything more could be done. Large portions of people acting in love did help remove the fear in many, but not everyone responded to the removal of the power of threat with love. Some responded by turning back the power of threat on their tormentors.

The powerful tend to regard this as a delightful turn of events. It gives them back legitimacy that the nonviolent movement had taken from them. They may now respond with violence to reestablish order. In many cases, this dynamic is so clearly helpful to the illegitimately powerful that they have arranged agents provocateurs. These are people pretending to be part of the movement, but whose real job is to provoke violence that appears to come from the movement.

Boulding also thinks a case can be made for adding *organizational power* to this mix as being one of the major achievements in nonviolence in the twentieth century. The technologies of greater communication have allowed defiant people to achieve higher levels of sophistication in organizing to persuade others. Once the perception is widespread and the powerful are not seen as legitimately powerful, changes occur.

Losing Power

Hannah Arendt defines power as the ability to act in concert. Consider the distinction between "power with" and "power over." The first involves no violence at all, but engages the voluntary cooperation of a group. The second is the ability to get people to do something they do not want to do, and therefore frequently involves violence. To Arendt, the first is actual power and the second is not. Violence is a sign of the absence of power. The ability of violence to induce certain behavior in others is temporary; when the violence is removed, the behaviors stop. True power brings more permanent behavior because of free consent. Violence is resorted to when power is weakened.

Therefore, when events conspire to cause large numbers to withdraw their consent, regimes can topple remarkably quickly. This is often attributed to an "armed uprising," but the dynamic that caused the change has already occurred; the violence becomes superfluous.

In a contest of violence against violence the superiority of the government has always been absolute; but this superiority lasts only as long as the power structure of the government is intact—that is, as long as commands are obeyed and the army or police forces are prepared to use their weapons. When this is no longer the case, the situation changes abruptly. Not only is the rebellion not put down, but the arms themselves change hands—sometimes, as in the Hungarian revolution, within a few hours . . . Only after this has happened, when the disintegration of the government in power has permitted the rebels to arm themselves, can one speak of an "armed uprising," which often does not take place at all or occurs when it is no longer necessary. Where commands are no longer obeyed, the means of violence are of no use; and the question of this obedience is not decided by the command-obedience relation but by opinion, and of course, by the number of those who share it. (Arendt, 1972, p. 148)

Again, it is the psychology of the situation rather than the weaponry that makes the revolution successful. Power is a *relationship* among people, not a *property* owned by the powerful. Even the power to own property is based on the psychology of how people define their relationships.

In more recent times, there have been several examples where the power transfer was indeed done nonviolently, or with small amounts of violence clearly unrelated to the success of the movement. From the Philippines to several countries in Eastern Europe, the concept that opposition to a dictatorship requires violence is eroding into an understanding of the potency of "people power."

This follows previous lengthy but successful nonviolent campaigns to induce the British to leave India, and along with other colonizers to leave African countries. The dynamics that brought about an end to apartheid in South Africa and segregation laws in the United States were clearly the nonviolent ones.

The dynamic was noted as far back as the fall of the French monarchy. This was of course accompanied by violence, but Tocqueville observed that the monarch fell "before rather than beneath the blows of the victors, who were as astonished at their triumph as were the vanquished at their defeat" (Arendt, 1968, p. 260). This also shows another point: if violence is superfluous in achieving the goal of overthrowing dictators and tyrants, and it is nevertheless used under old beliefs that it is necessary, the dynamics involved in violence can then have a strong effect on what new government emerges out of the old.

Power needs numbers, while violence needs implements. If people are united and powerful and dedicated to a single action, there is no violence at all. If they are disorganized, feuding or apathetic, then a tyrant can terrorize them into submission with a small number of heavily armed soldiers.

In the real world, situations are usually a combination of the two. Events conspiring to allow a huge upsurge in public noncooperation are not common. Dictators usually do not attempt to rule by pure force but do have support from many within the population, especially the upper crust.

Sources of Power

Gene Sharp is the most well known of nonviolence theorists, having put out a 1973 three-volume set on *The Politics of Nonviolent Action*. He suggested that there are two views of power. Unlike the three (or four) Boulding offered, Sharp was not proposing that these are two kinds of power, rather, these are the *views* people have:

View 1: The Monolithic Theory. People depend on decisions of government or other hierarchical systems. Power is self-perpetuating, durable, and not easily or quickly changed. It arises from those at the pinnacles of society.

View 2: The Pluralistic-Dependency Theory. The government depends on the decisions and cooperation of the people. Power is fragile and requires constant replenishment of its sources from a multitude of people and institutions. It arises from those many parts of society.

For the most part, advocates of violence hold the first theory and nonviolent action relies on the second. The question then becomes which of the theories better fits reality. Under the monolithic theory, avoiding direct and structural violence would involve either voluntary self-restraint by rulers, or a change in ownership of the durable monolithic entity through elections, revolutions, and so on. Sharp argues that only when those who are ruled believe the monolithic theory does it actually work in the real world.

Why do people obey? Sharp suggests these psychological factors:

1. *Habit*—long-established practice. There must a belief structure to the habit. If that changes, or if a ruler is new, then other things must be done to keep people obedient.

2. *Fear of sanctions*—threats of punishment. This is especially important when other reasons for obedience become weakened. It is among the most expensive to administer, however, which puts a strain on resources.

3. *Moral obligation*—a sense that it is proper and necessary to obey. This comes partly from customs and socialization, but also from deliberate instruction. It leads to internal and voluntary compliance, and is therefore the least expensive and most effective for those in power. If those in power are in fact democratic and humane, then this factor is all the more likely to be effective. There are four origins of such a sense of obligation: a belief it is for the common good of society; a belief the ruler is superhuman, divine, supernatural, etc.; a belief the command is legitimate because the issuer is entitled; or the commands conform to accepted norms, like not lying or stealing.

4. *Self-interest*—offering incentives. To keep the support of at least some, rewards offered can include prestige, higher status position, direct financial gain, or indirect financial gain.

5. *Psychological identification with the ruler*—The triumphs and defeats of the rulers are seen as the triumphs and defeats of the entire group.

6. *Zones of indifference*—Some things are just not important enough to question. Even in the absence of habit, reward, or punishment, some things that do not arouse enthusiastic adherence nevertheless do not arouse determined opposition either.

7. *Absence of self-confidence among subjects*—Without enough confidence to resist, many people prefer rulers to relieve them of the task of making decisions.

Obedience, however, is not inevitable. It is essentially voluntary, and consent can be withdrawn. In some cases, this leads to gradual reforms. In others, many years of agitation finally culminate in a very sudden withdrawal by large numbers due to triggering events. An example of this was when Milosevic of Yugoslavia attempted to steal an election, and this triggered an outpouring. Sometimes those years of agitation lead to the goal, as when Britain left India. Other times, massive campaigns lead to specific goals that leave governments intact and are intended to, such as the civil rights movement in the United States.

Sharp offers an encyclopedic history of various kinds of successful nonviolent campaigns in the second volume of his 1973 work, and the third volume lays out organizing and strategic dynamics. The entire set is a classic in the understanding of nonviolence. Walter Wink has done calculations on how many nonviolent rebellions there were in the twentieth century and finds that the countries touched by major nonviolent actions cover a population of about 3 billion, or about 64 percent of humanity (Wink, 1998, pp. 116–117). Nonviolent action is not just a theory; it has been put into widespread practice and found to work.

ACTIONS

Training

Symbolic protests that involve little risk, such as marches, rallies, or vigils where the police are cooperative, are frequently done without any particular training of those invited to participate. Training is needed, however, for demonstrations where a violent response is possible or when civil disobedience is expected because high risk is involved. Thorough discussion of contingencies and careful decision making and planning are important.

Role-plays in which people practice are effective. Rituals, religious activities, and trust-building exercises are also used. Written materials are often shared, ranging from full manuals to simple sheets on which agreed-upon rules and advice are given.

Overall, in addition to simple preparation, the training needs to have these psychological effects:

- *Fostering creativity*—providing greater flexibility of thinking
- *Stress reduction*—calming people down as they counter the stress of the unknown
- *Boosting confidence*—building self-efficacy in the situation
- *Conditioning responses*—some operant conditioning when automatic responses are necessary
- *Building group cohesion*—essential for a high-risk group activity

Strategies

The various tactics used in nonviolent campaigns must all use the basic principles, but be selected and adapted to the situation at hand. Gene Sharp (1973) has taken a very detailed look at varying strategies, with nuances from throughout history, in the second of his three-volume work, *Methods of Nonviolent Action*. Here we only consider very broad categories, with a focus on the behavioral and mental aspects of interest to psychologists.

Symbolic Actions

Symbolic actions, such as Gandhi's March to the Sea or various protests that simply make a statement, are often initially regarded with contempt by those at whom they are aimed on the grounds that they are *only* symbolic. It is therefore believed that these actions are not substantive. Their first reaction is that such actions do not constitute actually *doing* something.

Those with this view do not take into account the importance of the psychological components of their power. The symbolic action can reorient the perception of the situation by onlookers, by the aggrieved group, and even by the powerful themselves. Their power rests on a symbolic base—a set of symbols that large numbers of people have agreed to. An alternative representation of the situation can diminish the fragile base on which their power rests.

Remember also the Milgram experiments on destructive obedience to authority. One of the variables that caused a major drop in compliance was the example of one other person in the same situation showing defiance. Since participants were already uncertain as to whether they should go on, the example of another person refusing to do so gave them the information they needed to also refuse.

The construct of social referencing also applies. People look at others to see what it is they are supposed to do. In a novel situation, the behavior of other people is the best reference to figure out how one is supposed to behave. This was covered in the effects violence can have on observers; sometimes they see that others are not reacting, so they do not react either. The same dynamic works in reverse. By seeing others are opposing something, a reference group is set up and people are more likely to behave accordingly.

None of this is magic. Any onlooker who disagrees with the symbolic action remains unaffected by it. A symbolic action on behalf of racial segregation or an unpopular monarchy may simply be regarded with disgust by others. The powerfulness of symbolic actions requires that onlookers are either sympathetic but need to be moved to action, or that they can become sympathetic once they have the matter brought to their attention.

In many cases, time is necessary for this to occur. For example, during the sit-ins of the civil rights movement in the United States, some White people who had nothing against Black people still thought the Blacks were being rude to go where they were not wanted. After some time, it became clearer to them that this was defense rather than rudeness. Of course, those people who were bigoted against Blacks took even longer; they required persistence in the firm, nonviolent, continuous crusade.

The role of the media can be crucial for symbolic actions. Media coverage greatly increases the number of onlookers. For example, the media was often sympathetic to the civil rights movement in the United States and to the movement for home rule in India. They showed violence perpetrated against protesters and commented on how terrible it was. However, similar police and counter-picketer violence against nonviolent protesters of abortion clinics in places such as Los Angeles went generally ignored. Several large demonstrations for peace held in Jerusalem by Israelis and Palestinians together in the middle of intense blood feuding between the two sides went largely unreported. Participants were disappointed, but accustomed to this. The effectiveness of the activity would have been greatly increased if the media had regarded it as newsworthy, rather than focusing on violent acts and belligerent statements.

Civil Disobedience

Civil disobedience may be symbolic actions or may involve noncooperation. In some cases, such as the civil rights movement, the act of "filling the jails" is a strain on the segregation system because unjust laws are disobeyed. In other cases, a trespass occurs by those who ordinarily respect the laws on trespass but find that the target of their protest requires symbolic opposition. As with legal symbolic actions, civil disobedience is most effective when the media covers the action for the wider community.

It has long been one of the major principles of civil disobedience that those who engage in it should be prepared to go to jail and take the legal punishment. No matter how unjust certain laws are, a disintegration of social order based on neutral laws is not helpful. Civil disobedience is meant to promote justice, not lawlessness. When violent revolutionaries succeed and take over a government, it is often true that they have so inspired additional defiance that the only way they can restore a semblance of order is with the continuation of the violence. People they fought with in the revolution can then be subjected to a bloody purge. The foundation on which peaceful cooperation among members of a society is based is sabotaged, and cannot be put back together again so quickly. For this reason, strong advocates and practitioners of civil disobedience such as Gandhi and King have insisted on paying the legal penalty in the form of jail time, and have objected to not being so punished. Peace is not served when lawbreakers in general are not held accountable, and it is not healthy for maintaining a legal system to make exceptions. If the law is unjust, it should be properly repealed rather than ignored and left on the books.

Noncooperation

Gandhi is quoted as saying, "The first principle of nonviolent action is that of noncooperation with everything humiliating." Noncooperation is the essence of the power of nonviolence. From refusal to obey unjust orders or unjust laws, to boycotts and strikes, all the way to alternative governments, opponents in this conflict never see this as failure to actually *do* something. Cooperation with authority is the way authority gets its power, and withdrawing cooperation is basic to the ability to stop illegitimate authority. For a good list of historical actions up to 1973, see the second volume of Sharp's three-volume *The Politics of Nonviolent Action*.

One of the more famous historical pieces of advice on noncooperation, the concept of turning the other cheek, is explained here by a theologian of nonviolence, Walter Wink:

"If anyone strikes you on the right cheek, turn the other also" (Matt. 5:39). You are probably imagining a blow with the right fist. But such a blow would fall on the *left* cheek. To hit the right cheek with a fist would require the left hand. But the left hand could be used only for unclean tasks . . . the only feasible blow is a backhand.

The backhand was not a blow to injure, but to insult, humiliate, degrade. It was not administered to an equal, but to an inferior. . . . The whole point of the blow was to force someone who was out of line back into place.

Notice Jesus' audience: "If anyone strikes *you*." These are people used to being thus degraded. He is saying to them, "Refuse to accept this kind of treatment anymore" . . . By turning the cheek, the servant makes it impossible for the master to use the backhand again: his nose is in the way. . . . The left cheek now offers a perfect target for a blow with the right fist; but only equals fought with fists. . . . This act of defiance renders the master incapable of asserting his dominance in this relationship. He can have the slave beaten, but he can no longer cow him . . .

Such defiance is no way to avoid trouble . . . Such "cheeky" behavior may call down a flogging, or worse. But the point has been made. The Powers That Be have lost their power to make people submit. And when large numbers begin behaving thus (and Jesus was addressing a crowd), you have a social revolution on your hands. (Wink, 1998, pp. 101–102)

Noncooperation can also be creatively done in ways that look like cooperation at first, when in actuality the power of the powerful is countered just as well. For example, the opposite of a strike is having people obey all the bureaucratic rules scrupulously and down to the letter, avoiding the normal cutting of corners that are necessary in getting a large system to work. There have been occasions such as with railroad workers when this technique has thrown a serious monkey wrench into the smooth functioning of the system. It was difficult for administrators to counter this, however, since everyone was simply following the rules.

To extend the example cited above, Jesus further advised people who had been pressed into service to carry a soldier's pack to go a second mile. Impressment into carrying was a heavy burden to poor people of that time. Whole villages would flee to avoid it when Roman soldiers came. Yet, in one of the few areas of more humane policy by the Romans, soldiers could only force people to go one mile; to do more was an infraction of military code. At a time when punishments for infractions were arbitrary and therefore unpredictable, soldiers could be afraid of the consequences if some cheerful Jew went on a second mile. This was also puzzling and disconcerting, perhaps an insult to the soldier's strength. It deprived the soldier of predictability and feelings of superiority over the other. Under the circumstance, it could easily happen that a soldier would plead to have his pack back, or wrest it away from the Jew, and the humor of this outcome was probably not lost on Jesus' audience (Wink, 1998, pp. 106–109).

There are times when overcooperation is a form of creative noncooperation, a way of taking the initiative rather than submitting. It can maintain the dignity of the downtrodden when used with discernment.

Objection to the Military Draft

One of the major forms of noncooperation with the military is with the military draft. This can take the form of *conscientious objection*, sometimes allowed as a category of being legally excused from fighting. Some objectors still participate in battle by serving as medics or other tasks not involved in committing violence. It is not the war to which they object, but they cannot kill. Other objectors do alternative service that is entirely civilian, such as working in hospitals. Governments have so far been able to absorb this form of protest because there have not been enough people taking the option to cause a problem with prosecution of wars.

Another form of noncooperation, a form that is more clearly not cooperating at all, is *draft resistance*. This may mean refusing to register for the draft, or registering but refusing to go once drafted. In some cases, men have fled to another country to avoid being drafted; in others, they have gone to prison. These actions are illegal, and therefore a form of civil disobedience.

One of the differences in the psychological aspects of this form of nonviolent action is that under contemporary conditions it is almost entirely young adults who must face these circumstances and carry through on their decisions. Historically, it has also been an almost entirely male population, but that may change in the future, and the gender differences may also be of interest. Historical circumstances, the level of popularity of the war, its length, and the level of social and practical support for young people who may have to face this in the future—not to mention how those individual young people were raised—will have a major impact in the psychology of the situation.

Documenting

For techniques relying on psychological principles, and which have been labeled as "truth force" (*satyagraha*) in Hindi, establishing in fact what the truth is would be the first step of any campaign. In some cases, it can end up being the totality of the campaign, as exposing factual information causes changes in behavior in those who wished to ignore it or keep it secret. Some nonviolence activists have gone into violent situations and documented acts of direct violence, and others have gone in to document circumstances of structural violence. Publicizing this documentation may require obvious steps or may necessitate some creativity, but there have been innumerable instances in which the scandal that arose has caused those in power to take action to correct the situation. A public education campaign may take years to develop. Yet, at other times, activists are not satisfied with getting out the information, but wish to use additional nonviolent strategies to make a major campaign. They still need to have documented their case first, as a solid foundation to building that campaign.

Interpositioning

Nonviolent interpositioning, also known as protective accompaniment, is an international technique that makes use of a dominant group's position on behalf of oppressed groups. In various countries, native nonviolent activists are in danger of arrest, imprisonment, torture, abduction, street attack, and murder. People from outside the country, especially Americans and Europeans, accompany these activists, under arrangements appropriate to the situation. They have no arms, yet they are bodyguards. The power here comes from the knowledge of potential perpetrators that their violent actions will not be hidden. While the media may ignore the tribulations of the local population, much more excitement is generated if someone from outside is hurt. This does not work perfectly, and people from outside the situation have been hurt. Nevertheless, this does not happen very often. This is a prime case of nonviolent *deterrence*. Current groups active in this include Peace Brigades International and Witness for Peace.

Civilian-Based Defense

Civilian-based defense applies the concepts of nonviolence to defense from foreign invasion or internal coup d'état. At present, it is most effective in a small country that is invaded by a larger country, where the possibility of a military defense is ludicrous. In the case of the coup, the military is the problem, so a non-military defense is necessary. There have been several historical examples of successful or almost successful cases (see Sharp, 1990).

Some propose replacing military-based defense with civilian-based defense, on the grounds that it works better and with fewer casualties. This would replace the idea of *dis*armament with *trans*armament. People would perceive greater safety in not giving up defense but simply switching to a different form. Some small countries have shown interest in this method. The U.S. military has no interest in replacing violent weapons with it, but they have paid some attention to the techniques of noncooperation as supplementary. So far, the historical instances of it have been spontaneous, arising at the time of the invasion or coup. Theorists propose that advance planning would increase the effectiveness considerably, just as it does with military techniques.

Getting the Word Out

Every method of nonviolence requires disseminating information, from documentation of the injustice being opposed to the treatment of those opposing it. An old platitude, that the pen is mightier than the sword, is based on this premise. The power of information, of education, of the press, can by virtue of persuading people cause events that the mere threat of violence would be powerless to cause or to prevent. Information sometimes persuades, and at other times focuses the attention of the already persuaded, inducing them to take some form of action.

Ways of getting the word out can include finding creative methods of getting the media—which already reaches a vast audience—to cover issues or events. This can be done directly, for instance, by sending letters to the editors of prominent periodicals. Holding events for media coverage, with articulate spokespersons, has also become standard in many places.

There are times when the media refuses to cover a movement, and even when it does, it is still unlikely to go into the kind of depth most activists would like. If there are to be events, then there has to be communication to get people to come to those events. If there is action asked of people, such as writing to legislators or boycotting a product, then activists must personally design and put out the leaflets, flyers, brochures, booklets, newsletters, e-mails, and Web pages that inform people.

Some of the important features in such publications are:

Consider the Audience

This is the most important consideration—all else fails if the audience does not care. If the target audience consists of people who work in a particular field, it makes sense to use the jargon of the field. If it is the general public, those jargon words should either be avoided or explained. An older audience will regard certain events, and feelings surrounding those events, as memorable. A younger audience will regard them as history, and may require some explanations the older audience takes for granted. People who are already sympathetic to a viewpoint will be more interested in in-depth information and can be addressed as sympathizers. Those who are potentially supportive can be given information on why they should become completely sympathetic. People hostile to the view can be given entirely different information, and require more with regard to recognition of their opposing concerns. The first step in a communication is to define who the target audience is, so the publication can be tailored accordingly.

It Should Be Neat, Orderly, and Appealing to Read

There are those who believe content is all that matters, and they put all their energies into this. It is indeed important to be very careful with content; however, if the initial appearance is not attractive, it gets no further attention.

The Layout Should Be Easy to Follow and Broken in Chunks

Most commonly, there will be a major catchy headline, and then smaller headlines to present the points more clearly. Lists can be bulleted; quick points in a logical flow are more likely to attract people and keep them reading the material. Since they do not have to make a major commitment to read the next section, they do, and keep reading with each new segment. If there is no time when a section is so large it looks daunting, the continued interest is more likely.

Start with a Hook

The first thing that greets the eye of potential readers should be something that tells them why they should care.

Be Succinct

A publication should get right to the point, and not add too much at once. Sometimes it makes sense to do a series rather than ask people to absorb more information at once. Hyperlinks on Web pages can also be used to expand information. There is a time for extensive philosophical musings, and a book on any subject gives more extensive information than a booklet or newsletter, which in turn gives more information than a leaflet. What it takes to be succinct varies with the needs of a campaign.

Consider Graphics

Well-placed pictures, graphics, and cartoons can add to making a publication appealing to read. Quotations or particularly good sentences in the text can also be highlighted in boxes. When they are related to the point being made, they are at times all that is absorbed by those who will take no more than a quick glance. When the budget allows for differing colors, then this can also be artistically used for appeal and for attracting attention to specific points.

Be Very Careful with Credibility

Facts should be documented. Ideally, the skeptical reader can be sent to books or a Web page for more details. Exaggerations can lead to a loss of credibility that can be permanent. These are especially tragic when the unexaggerated, true information would be impressive enough. Sometimes, the facts are accurate but the horrific nature of the violence or injustice is so amazing that people think they are being fed propaganda. If that is the case, special care must be taken with documentation, and with acknowledging this reaction.

Treat the Audience with Respect

An attitude that castigates people for not having taken action, or for being so corrupt as to allow certain evils to continue, is not likely to lead to an effective publication. More successful would be the approach that people of goodwill wish to be given information, and will either take action or engage in dialog on the subject. It does not matter if people seem to be corrupt and do not care, or they give no signs of wishing to be knowledgeable. If any self-fulfilling prophecy is to be set up, it can consciously be the more desirable one.

In the case of recorded messages such as advertisements, or sound bites on television, or discussions on talk shows, some of these points also apply. Specifically, knowledge about the target audience is essential, and being succinct is especially important. Before interviews, spokespeople can practice short lines, quick ways of making the point, and for more lengthy interviews, ways of saying it that provide a hook for more information. Credibility is essential, and so is a tone of voice and wording that treats the audience with respect.

A skill in the psychology of making publications more likely to be read, or recorded messages or sound bites on television more likely to be listened to, is an important part of the skill of making nonviolent campaigns work. Quality of communication is crucial in any set of techniques that require psychological mechanisms to be effective.

MOVEMENT DYNAMICS AND STRATEGIC CONSIDERATIONS

Negative and Positive Goals

Beyond specific types of nonviolence, there are also psychological considerations of approach. Richard Wagner (1993) points out the difference between negative and positive goals. Negative goals avoid the bad while positive goals achieve the good. Disease prevention or treatment would be a negative goal while robust health would be a positive one. In the same way, prevention of specific forms of violence and injustice are negative goals, while building a peaceful society is a positive goal. Wagner points out these features of negative goals:

1. Negative goals are narrowly defined, with limited assumptions and definitions.
2. Negative goals are more concrete—once the specific thing is avoided or eliminated, the goal is achieved.
3. Because of both these features, negative goals lend themselves more readily to short-term objectives.

This makes negative goals easier to implement. It has the advantage that concrete, specific goals can offer feedback on success and therefore greater satisfaction and avoidance of burnout. Speed of achievement gives reinforcement for efforts.

Advantages of positive goals include:

1. Results are more durable, more easily maintained. An agreement between two groups to stop attacking each other, for example, must be constantly monitored. However, once they come to cooperative arrangements, they do not require the same level of monitoring.
2. Failure to *keep* peace has more drastic consequences—people can die. Failure to *build* peace means that a project that did not work today may work better under a different approach tomorrow.

The disadvantages of positive goals are that they can lead to frustration and a sense of being overwhelmed by the task, while negative short-term goals are more manageable. Negative goals, however, are more difficult to maintain and more fragile. They also focus our attention on the violence that they wish to counter, which increases anxiety.

Efforts for peace have always included both. An awareness of the psychological advantages and disadvantages of each can be considered when planning strategies.

Unseen Problems of Other Groups

One feature commonly found in any social movement is a sense that one's own movement has so many problems, while the opposition runs so smoothly. However, the opposition, similar to one's own group, is not likely to publicize its personality clashes, territorial squabbles, financial difficulties, and insufficient volunteers. The impression can easily arise that the group one is involved with is subjected to this, and other movements have it easy.

This is something of a variant of the out-group homogeneity effect. In this case, it is an out-group unseen-problem effect. The troubles of one's own movement tend to weigh more heavily on the mind. The problems are also widespread and predictable in opposition groups, in businesses and governments, and other social movements one might be sympathetic to but not active in. Even religious groups that stress harmony have them.

People often find it discouraging when they discover such problems and believe their group is uniquely afflicted with them. It is actually quite encouraging to know that this is normal. This is life; it does not distinguish one movement from another. Any movement without such problems is either very small or very short-lived.

Some problems, like a shortage of volunteers or financial difficulties, can be practically impossible to solve. They are bottomless pits. If an organization wishes to simply sponsor an event or provide a well-defined service, then it can have enough volunteers and money. However, if it wants to help solve a major social problem, it will never have enough volunteers or money. The creative mind can always come up with more projects for more resources than are available. The budget could be ten times the current one and quickly be seen as insufficient. In those social movements that have another in opposition, the tendency is to see the other side as having it easy on the finances and plentiful volunteers. It is unlikely that the other movement sees itself this way. Even if they do have more money, they are likely to be more impressed with what they cannot do, and more intimidated by what their opposition does, therefore perceiving that the opposition is rolling in money while they are strapped.

The amount of problems does vary widely. The ability of a group to handle this with conflict resolution techniques can make a difference.

Progress and Gloom

A comparison between social indicators of the year 1900 and the year 2000 show considerable progress in many ways. Life expectancy increased by decades for all demographic groups. High school graduates in the United States went from 6 percent to 85 percent, with similar rises around the globe. The right to vote in the United States in 1900 was limited to men age twenty-one and older, with African American men being effectively blocked from the polls. All over the world, utilities and technology that were unimaginable luxuries in 1900 are commonplace now.

Nevertheless, rhetoric suggesting the world is getting worse is easy to find. Medical care is insufficient in many areas, lowering the life expectancy of the poor—not in comparison to what it was, but what it could be if medical care and nutrition were up to the standards the middle class now expects. If 85 percent are graduating from high school, that means that 15 percent are not. Voting irregularities, with inferior equipment in areas where poor people vote, are still prevalent. New technologies bring pollution problems and are often produced with sweatshop labor.

These are all real problems, but the comparison of the two times still shows that there has been progress. Why is the progress unacknowledged? Is there a reason why a glass that is half full is so often perceived as half empty?

Joel Best (2001) suggests four paradoxes for how greater progress leads to a sense of lack of progress: perfectionism, proportion, proliferation, and paranoia.

The Paradox of Perfectionism

The ideal of social perfectibility is grounded in optimism but has the paradoxical consequence of fostering pessimism. Our efforts in the real world fall short of perfection. Those who hold perfection as a goal perceive the failure to achieve it, rather than the progress made toward it.

To refer to things as social problems rather than social conditions that would not change or social issues that may never be resolved means that problems are meant to be solved. Expecting short-term, correct solutions to problems means disappointment when conditions are such that long-term, incremental improvements occur instead. The incremental improvements are not appreciated as progress because the ultimate goal of a problem solved has not been achieved.

The Paradox of Proportion

When large problems are solved, smaller problems come to weigh more heavily. When medicine prevents many deaths from infectious diseases, then killers like cancer and diabetes are no longer overshadowed and they receive the worrying energy that used to go into the more egregious diseases. When we no longer have widespread lynching and women commonly have the vote, we find more subtle kinds of racism and sexism. When people in general are better educated, there is a different idea of how much education a person can have and still be regarded as insufficiently educated. All of the smaller problems are real problems, but their being ignored previously was not callousness but the fact that there were larger problems with greater urgency. Once the larger problems are solved, the smaller ones become more compelling. The threshold for what constitutes an urgent problem has been lowered. Progress is made, but not perceived.

The Paradox of Proliferation

In the same way, social progress encourages the recognition of a larger number of problems. The contagion of successful social justice movements in one area encourages people to think in terms of social justice and rights in a wide array of other areas. Society is more receptive to listen to additional claims, activists have gained the skills necessary to promote such claims, and the proliferation of cable channels, talk shows, and the Internet accelerate this trend.

The Paradox of Paranoia

Progress not only makes us aware of new problems, but they take on more of a fear of potential catastrophe. Doomsday scenarios abound. Social progress has led to large, intertwined institutions that we depend on. We have ordered our lives thoroughly around certain technologies and feel vulnerable to the dependence. Our higher expectations for institutions inspire greater fears about possible institutional failures.

The danger in these four paradoxes is that people who desire progress toward peace may pronounce the progress already made as trivial and past social policies as ineffective. This is not only untrue, but can thwart commitment to new policies and further progress.

Many believe that an emphasis on how great problems are is the best way to encourage people to take action, but it may have the opposite effect. It is discouraging to think that all the effort put in by so many people in the past has led to only trivial changes or none at all. The assertion that no incremental progress was made with old policies gives ammunition to the arguments of those that oppose instituting new ones. It also dampens enthusiasm from those who might otherwise think they are a good idea. Pessimism and paranoia lead to despair, not eagerness. People are more likely to put effort and energy into further progress if they have a sense that it is worthwhile and if it is acknowledged that the past investment has borne fruit.

Deceit

In an episode of *Star Trek: The Next Generation*, one of the spaceship's officers, Riker, is trying to talk another, Worf, into joining a war-games exercise. They will be on an old, outdated, small ship. Riker informs Worf that they will be badly outnumbered and outgunned, and asks what Worf would use. With a spark in his eyes, Worf replies, "Guile!"

The withdrawal of consent that gives power to those who are weaker is often accomplished without informing the seemingly powerful that this has occurred. This leads to fewer repercussions, which the powerless often prefer. Those in seemingly powerless positions have long enjoyed tales of effective trickery, tales that have the advantages of a sense of ethical superiority compared with violence. They are clever. Deception shares with nonviolence the characteristic of being a way of countering violence without the use of violence.

Deception also shares characteristics with violence. It can be a short-term, efficient solution to a problem, yet have negative long-term consequences and impact on society. For example, the use of deception by some among dominated groups such as women, Jews, and Blacks has helped to establish their image as being conniving, and added to the negative stereotyping of them by those with more apparent power. Thus, although deception has solved all kinds of short-term problems for individuals, it has been no help in establishing long-term justice for any of these groups.

The use of deception in a short-term situation, such as the commonly raised hypothetical circumstance of a madman chasing one's mother with a knife, may be better than the use of violence in that specific dilemma. For long-term effects, however, it is more often counterproductive. The use of deception by a long-lasting, well-organized campaign could easily lead to its destruction. It is dispensing with the power of truth in advancing its cause. The discovery of a deception, which happens frequently, means that any power the campaign could gain by appealing to truth has been lost.

There may be an exception in the case of civilian-based defense, which has more the character of an emergency situation. People have, for example, pretended to help fix broken helicopters and actually introduced delays instead. In this case, the deception was on practical matters rather than on the overall point that an invasion or coup was being resisted. Participants could still deal honestly with soldiers in attempting to get them to switch sides in the conflict.

One conclusion, though, is that the nonviolent campaign that stresses its preclusion of violence may also wish to make a point of emphasizing honesty to its participants. Dishonesty shares features with nonviolence along with practical and ethical disadvantages of violence. It is not the same as violence, but is not normally regarded as a component of nonviolence either. Repudiation of dishonesty in a campaign may need to be mentioned along with the denial of violence, for those who wish to be clear.

Schools of Thought

Several kinds of arguments show up in most large, long-lasting nonviolent social movements. People are often distressed by these divisions, and feel that if there were more unity, the movement would be more successful. Since these show up so consistently, it may be a better approach to expect people to have differing views and work with this point harmoniously. Movements can work with differing schools of thought. These divisions include:

The "Purists" vs. the "Pragmatists"

Purists say that compromise is immoral and detrimental in the long run. Pragmatists argue for an "all or something" approach, believing it immoral to allow violence to continue while waiting for purity.

These two approaches can complement each other. The purists keep the compromises from getting too watered-down, and the pragmatists can use the purists to make themselves appear more moderate.

"Reform" vs. "Root Cause"

There is a parable of the people of a village who awake to find many babies floating in their nearby river. They immediately pull the babies out of the river, dry, clothe, feed, and shelter them. This happens day after day. Finally one person decides to go up along the river to find out why on earth all these babies are being thrown in. This story is often told as an explanation of a radical approach, one that goes to the root. The babies are obviously better off not being placed in danger than they are being rescued.

Nevertheless, while the person is searching for the root cause, the babies are still in desperate need of immediate assistance. What if the person cannot find the root cause or cannot quickly do anything once it is found? Both approaches are therefore needed.

The "Street" People vs. the "Straight" People

Nonviolent "street" people argue that it is immoral to wait for normal legal channels rather than taking direct action immediately. "Straight" people believe respectability is crucial to success. This is not a strict division. Both groups attend legal demonstrations, and those who may engage in civil disobedience might still lobby for a certain bill. Yet, there are usually tensions, as those who are desperate for respectability think that those who opt for the priority of urgency are hurting the movement, and vice versa.

Again, these two perspectives provide for a more holistic movement. Those in the street who communicate urgency can be ignored if they are seen as crazy and not respectable. Those who are respectable can be ignored because the issue is not understood as urgent. There is a greater likelihood that both will be heard if they are both present.

The "Old-Timers" vs. the "Newcomers"

Newcomers to a movement are obviously crucial; it will not grow without them. They also bring in fresh new ideas, enthusiasm, and help avoid ruts. Old-timers of a movement are also crucial; they know what has happened before and have experience of what does and does not work.

Newcomers that are brimming with newfound enthusiasm may also have the impression that nothing has gone on before. They were not there when it happened. They may think that the movement was not doing successful things because it has not yet succeeded. Their contempt for the experience and accumulated wisdom of those who have been working hard for years can be very painful to the old-timers.

The "Single Issue" vs. "Everything's Connected"

A focus on a single issue has greater clarity. It allows more people to work on a problem, since widely divergent views on other issues do not matter. A focus on multiple related issues has greater coherence. It allows for a greater sense of community among people who are concerned with interrelationships in a larger context: various peace issues, feminism, civil rights, antipoverty, consistent life ethic, and so on.

The different approaches are useful in different contexts. Because there are advantages and disadvantages to both, some discernment about what is called for in specific situations is helpful.

INDIVIDUAL SITUATIONS

Melting Meanness

Conflict can be one-sided, caused by bullies or people who tease. Mediation or reasoning is beside the point. Kate Cohen-Posey (1995), a therapist, wrote a book for children on how to deal with such people. This is intended for verbal communication, for painful but otherwise harmless words. Dealing with more dangerous threats of violence is covered in the next section. Many of the strategies are also helpful for adults or onlookers in such situations.

Turn Insults Into Compliments

Ignore the actual words and pretend something nice has been said. This can have the effect of turning the remarks into what the interaction makes them become. Failing that, it at least confuses the bully. Without getting the expected reaction, the bully is not rewarded for using intimidating behavior. Bullies are accustomed to insulting replies; it throws them off balance to hear otherwise. Gandhi called this effect *moral jiu-jitsu*, after the martial art that physically throws an opponent off balance.

Agreeing

Similarly, sometimes a person can find something factually correct in what the bully said and agree with it. If not, some things that are clearly untrue can still be admitted, at least as a possibility. The bully is looking for an argument and simply cannot get one from someone who does not cooperate.

Asking Questions

Bullying is generally not a well-thought-out behavior, but a habit. Introducing any thoughtfulness means responding to a bully not as a victim or another bully, but as a person. Introducing *thinking* into the situation changes its dynamic. On some occasions, asking for thinking can have long-term beneficial effects on the person who is engaged in the bullying behavior.

Golden Nuggets

This combines the above two techniques: keep asking questions with a goal of finding something that can genuinely be agreed upon. Look for something that shows that the person who is teasing or bullying does have some valid concern—even if it does not apply to the situation the way he or she thinks it does. This is not a matter of avoiding arguments, as with the agreeing strategy, but of searching for a connection that shows that the bully is a real person with real feelings.

"I" Feelings Rather than "You" Accusations

Sometimes a person's feelings are too badly hurt to use these methods, which require a certain amount of calm. Unfortunately, people often then lash out. They make accusations ("you should be ashamed of yourself") that simply feed the unthinking dynamic that a teaser is following. On some occasions, it would be more appropriate to admit feelings ("it hurts my feelings because you hit a sore spot"). This depends greatly on the occasion, and there are some people for whom this would not be a good idea. However, the temptation to engage in lectures, accusations, and other forms of lashing out are generally counterproductive. There are times when putting the focus on your own feelings rather than on the other person makes the other person less defensive.

Name Their Feeling

On the other hand, there are times when it is most productive to show an understanding of what they are feeling. If another person is lashing out in anger due to something else, then ignoring the actual words and getting to understand the reason for the anger behind them can be helpful. Giving them feedback gives them permission to be upset, and it means no one needs to be defensive.

Tone Twisters and Disconnected Comments

A tone twister is responding by using the same tone but giving an opposite meaning. This can at least confuse a bully or teaser and at best lead him or her to crack a smile. Both take the wind out of an escalating confrontation. A bully yells, "You can just go to hell!" and a person shouts back "Yeah? Well, you can just go to Disney World!" Similarly, comments that are disconnected can introduce humor and diffuse tension. In general, refusing to take hurtful remarks seriously, yet still being aware of the feelings of the person making them, can on certain occasions be a good way of handling them.

Dangerous Confrontations

The traditional concept when faced with dangerous circumstances from individuals who are not in authority (that is, criminals) is that people possess a "fight or flight" reaction. Fighting in the sense used here is violent. As for flight, removing one's self from a harmful situation has its advantages, and if the threat is from a nonhuman source, machine or animal, it may be the most useful. When it is perceived as cowardice, however, then it can no longer be classified as a nonviolent reaction.

These two options are limited and oversimplified. "Fighting" can also include use of a deceptive trick, or it can include enlisting the aid of others. Grossman (1995) as an army officer adds two other categories of possible reaction: posturing and submission. Posturing is like fighting, but not as extreme. It is an indication that a fight could come, in the hope this will be sufficient to send the other party away—shooting a gun into the air instead of at someone. Submission is a way of trying to convince the other party not to do further violence, as when someone gives a mugger a wallet.

All four of these approaches are not active nonviolence. Both violence and cowardice are contrary to the practice of active nonviolence. Countering violence means not engaging in it, but also not rewarding others when they do.

Two other approaches can be added to these four categories, to allow for a firm resolve to counter violence. Unlike the other two pairs above, these are not opposites. They are *connection* and *changing the script*. Any connecting done automatically changes the script, and if the script is changed, connecting is likely to be involved. They are considered separately because of different perspectives they provide.

Connection means people treating one another as people. Rather than allowing the kind of disconnection necessary for a violent confrontation, the defender thinks of the attacker in terms that reestablish ordinary human interaction. This is more easily done when the attack is threatened but has not yet happened. An illustrative story comes from Japan. A man had been well trained in martial arts. On a bus one day, a large burly man came on, clearly drunk and acting belligerently. The original man thought this would be a chance to use his skills defending other passengers. However, an old man, small and frail, struck up a conversation with the drunken man. It became clear that he was upset because his wife had recently died, and he ended up crying in the arms of the old man. He was no longer a threat to anyone. The man with the martial arts training left, feeling ashamed of himself. The conversation that treated the belligerent man as a real person had done so much more good, for everyone concerned.

Changing the script is an assertive way of refusing to recognize fight or flight or posturing or submission. An attacker generally has a script in mind that expects one of those responses. If the response is something else, the attacker is at least disconcerted. If the changed script is one in which there are other expected responses, those ordinarily expected responses may well occur. For example, a woman awoke in the middle of the night to find an unknown man approaching her. She simply asked him what time it was. He paused to look at his watch and told her what time it was. By the time he had done this, she was able to turn the light on and look him straight in the eye. The attacker script was subverted and ordinary conversation ensued.

Other non-attack scripts are commonly available. Women can use the teacher or mother script, as in this story:

A woman with two children in a disabled car late one night on the New Jersey turnpike looked up to see a man pointing a gun through her window. He ordered her to let him in the car. Instead of panicking, she looked him in the eye and, like an angry mother, commanded, "you put that gun away and get in your car and push me to the service area. *And I mean right now!*" He looked startled, put the gun away, went back to his car, and did as she ordered: pushed her car to the service area. (Vanderhaar, n.d., p. 1)

This hearkens back to the concept of power, which applies in individual situations as well as the larger social ones. It is common to have jokes in which some big, macho man—a soldier, cowboy, Mafia boss—is confronted by a small, frail, gray-haired woman—his mother, grandmother, aunt, old schoolteacher—who makes a demand upon him that he immediately obeys, with remarkable meekness. He would never put up with this from another large, muscular man; there would be a physically matched confrontation. Part of machismo is an intolerance for submitting to implied threats. Yet the authority of the woman comes from someplace other than physical strength. It is not violence backing up her demands; it is legitimate authority. The incongruity in the relative physical power is what makes it a joke, but it is a psychological dynamic that can often be seen in real situations.

CONCLUSION

Psychology courses on aggression generally deal with wide-ranging theories that usually do not consider the possibility of nonviolent aggression. Forms of aggression that are not violent refer to yelling, glaring, and so on. Loving aggression is not normally discussed. A corresponding course in nonviolent action is considerably less common in most colleges and universities. This parallels the history books' focus on wars and other violent episodes and tendency to ignore nonviolent campaigns. Nevertheless, history is full of instances of spontaneous actions of this kind. It is a vastly understudied area in all disciplines.

When assertive nonviolence becomes more studied, when it can be planned and builds on previous experience, its psychological components can change. It might be done with greater confidence and self-efficacy because of its known firmer foundation. Perhaps it will be done with greater effectiveness as people understand what the important components are.

FURTHER READING

Overviews

Gregg, R. B. (1972). *The psychology and strategy of Gandhi's nonviolent resistance.* New York: Garland Publishing, Inc.
Pelton, L. H. (1974). *The psychology of nonviolence.* New York: Pergamon.
Sharp, G. (1973). *The politics of nonviolent action, Part 3: The dynamics of nonviolent action.* Boston, MA: Extending Horizons Books.

Power

Boulding, K. E. (1989). *Three faces of power.* Newbury Park, CA: Sage Publications.
Sharp, G. (1973). *The politics of nonviolent action, Part 1: Power and struggle.* Boston, MA: Extending Horizons Books.

Actions

Proposal for third-party intervention, Nonviolent Peace Force: http://www.nonviolentpeaceforce.org.
Sharp, G. (1973). *The politics of nonviolent action, Part 2: The methods of nonviolent action.* Boston, MA: Extending Horizons Books.

Civilian-Based Defense

Sharp, G. (1990). *Civilian-based defense: A post-military weapons system.* Princeton, NJ: Princeton University Press.

Individual Situations

Cohen-Posey, K. (1995). *How to handle bullies, teasers and other meanies.* Highland City, FL: Rainbow Books, Inc.

Fry, A. R. (1986). *Victories without violence: True stories of ordinary people coming through dangerous situations without using physical force.* Santa Fe, NM: Ocean Tree Books.

CHAPTER 7

Public Policy Issues
of Violence

Public policy is normally divided into issues, and that convention is followed here. In all cases, there are political, sociological, and economic considerations that are also necessary to inform public policy. In this chapter, we deal specifically with psychological contributions to the discussion of what the best policies might be.

The issues are divided into three categories:

- War—the most obvious issues of violence for the psychology of peace
- Crime—forms of everyday violence and how to counter it
- Medical Matters—issues of beneficial services connecting to violence

WAR

Decisions for War

Psychologists can find specific psychological causes for specific wars, with the particular individuals involved and particular historical circumstance. Examples are found in the book *Psychological Dimensions of War* (Glad, 1990).

For more general knowledge applying across many different wars, one concept that has shown promise and needs further exploration is *integrative complexity*. This psychological construct has two features: *Differentiation* is the degree to which people see differences among aspects of, or perspectives on, a particular problem. *Integration* is the degree to which people then relate those perspectives to each other within some coherent framework.

The basic idea is that leaders who take an oversimplified, inflexible approach to any conflict that could lead to war are more likely to end in war. Leaders who are more flexible, willing to compromise, and able to understand the other side's perspectives, are less likely to get into a war.

Studies that have done content analysis of public speeches and similar documents before various wars have shown that a drop in the integrative complexity scores is a good predictor of an outcome of war (Conway, Suedfeld, & Tetlock, 2001). In two-sided wars, the scores drop on both sides as they move to war. In one-sided wars in which one nation attacks another, the scores drop on the attacking side but go up for the defending nation. Defenders are hoping for a negotiated solution avoiding war. In revolutions within a country, analyzed as far back as Cromwell in England, the scores drop as the revolution is successfully taking over. However, if the scores remain low afterward, the new government is less likely to remain in power.

Whether or not it is a cause of specific wars awaits further study. It is possible that the coming of war causes leaders to become more rigid rather than the other way around. Perhaps the rhetoric differs from the actual thought processes of the leaders as they consciously manipulate the public for one outcome or another. However, there are some laboratory studies, in which people do simulations of international conflict, which suggest mechanisms whereby low complexity may be a cause rather than just a symptom. Those who came into the situation with low scores did tend to move to more violent solutions within the same situations as compared to those who came in with high scores. They got frustrated more quickly and lacked the kind of negotiating skills that require integrative complexity.

We would still need to account for why there is a *change* in the scores of content analysis of rhetoric leading up to wars. One idea is the *disruptive stress hypothesis*, that while low or moderate levels of stress can increase complexity, high levels of stress deplete the cognitive resources necessary for complex thinking. Another is the group dynamics of the *groupthink model*, as covered in chapter 1. This applies especially in crisis situations, because the pressure for consensus within groups escalates. Part of this process is that individuals must lower the complexity of their thinking. Studies of those in historical situations that are classified as groupthink scenarios back this up. They also find that groups of individuals who are lower in complexity to begin with seem to be more likely to get into groupthink situations. Finally, the characteristics that individual leaders bring into the situation vary. For example, Gorbachev had higher complexity scores than previous Soviet leaders.

There is some similarity in the idea of lowered integrative complexity and the "mythic mode" of thinking, the war hysteria discussed in "Passions of War" in chapter 1. The major difference is that war hysteria applies to the general population, while the lowered integrative complexity is a concept applying to policymakers. The similarities are great enough that the above three suggestions for causation may also apply to some extent to the case of war hysteria.

Arms Races

There have been a large number of arms races throughout history. The psychological logic is clear: each side has a clear perception that they are endangered unless their weaponry is superior. Accordingly, one side makes their armaments superior to the other's. Then the adversaries do the same. The first side has to do it again, and a race continues. Throughout history, most such races have ended in war; a few have instead ended in economic collapse.

The idea is that better weaponry has a psychological deterrent effect by making an opponent afraid to attack. This is difficult to establish empirically because it is trying to prove a negative. One can document when deterrence failed because an attack nevertheless occurred. If an attack does not occur, however, it could be due to all kinds of reasons—including that the opponent never had any intention of attacking. Empirical validation, however, is not usually the first thought on the minds of those who practice the technique.

The most famous arms race is the nuclear arms race of the Cold War. Contributions by psychologists early in this race include the concept of the *mirror image* (Bronfenbrenner, 1961). It was found that citizens on both sides, American and Soviet, had remarkably similar views of the other. For example, experimenters showed a picture of a street lined with trees, told participants their own government had planted the trees, and then asked why. Answers included such things as providing shade and preventing soil erosion. However, when people were shown the same picture but told the other country's government had planted the trees, the answers included such motives as to hide tanks.

Some of the specific beliefs both sides held about each other were:

- They are the aggressors.
- Their government exploits and deludes the people.
- The majority of their people are not really sympathetic to the regime.
- They cannot be trusted.
- Their policy verges on madness.

These beliefs tend to be self-confirming. When one sees actions as unfriendly, one responds in an unfriendly way. The other side perceives this as unfriendly and responds in kind. A cycle continues.

A classic on how to deal with the arms race was Charles Osgood's 1962 Graduated and Reciprocated Initiatives in Tension-Reduction (GRIT). This idea was to defuse international tensions by essentially running the race in reverse. Each side would take turns at initiating tension-reduction actions. Amitai Etzioni in 1967 identified steps taken by both sides under Kennedy and Khrushchev that appear to have been based on this model, culminating in the Partial Test Ban Treaty. In current conflicts, the concept of "confidence-building measures" is used similarly in diplomacy.

Economic Sanctions

A boycott is a form of economic sanction that can be effective against large corporations when they engage in harmful activity for profit. Because the boycott lowers their profits, it directly impacts the behavior. Boycotts fit under the idea of withdrawal of consent, since corporations only profit with the consent of customers.

However, when comprehensive economic sanctions are used against an entire country so that widespread poverty and disease result, this is no longer a nonviolent action. The violence is worse than an attack with weapons—it targets innocent civilians. This does not impact, and sometimes even benefits, the guilty ones in power and the combatants.

The concept of economic sanctions is a modern phenomenon. The cooperation from other countries and intense interdependency of countries are also recent. The strategy, however, has been used since ancient times as a tool of war—it is called a "siege." This generally has been done by cutting off supplies into a city and causing surrender after a few months without danger to the surrounding soldiers. Economic sanctions are a more sophisticated, modern version.

The reaction of the besieged population is the psychological response that would be expected from victims of an act of war. People pull together, their group identification increases, and they stand stalwart against the common enemy. This is predictable as a response; it is the normal social psychological reaction to being attacked. It can be clearly seen in places such as North Korea and Cuba, which have undergone sanctions for several decades, and Iraq, which had very stringent sanctions for more than a decade. Poverty and disease were rampant, but dictatorships were not weakened. The expectation was that material deprivation would cause a popular uprising from people who wished to better their material conditions. Instead, people perceive a common enemy, they see their dictator as standing up to that enemy, and the dictatorship can be strengthened.

Economic pressures can be used if they are part of a conflict rather than an all-out attack. Sanctions that cause discomfort rather than pain can have an effect under the right circumstances, when they are nudging policy rather than demanding that people give up their self-respect. Serbia did turn Milosevic over to the War Crimes Tribunal, and South Africa's move to end apartheid may have been accelerated. Depriving innocent people of luxuries they could otherwise have is different from depriving them of necessities, and can be expected to have different psychological ramifications. As with any method of dealing with conflict, any use of economic pressure should be considered carefully, and not done with stereotyped or dehumanized views of the other side.

Genocide

While *homicide* means the deliberate killing of an individual, *genocide* means the deliberate destroying of an entire people or culture. Genocide is commonly done by killing people who are members of the targeted group, but there are other elimination methods that can also be used. One is to forbid the culture itself, by forbidding members of the group to speak their own language, wear their distinctive clothing, practice their own religion, tell their own culture's stories, or play their music. Removing the means of maintaining a culture, such as depriving a farming culture of farmland, can also apply. Another method is to sterilize massive numbers of the population, by force or with intense economic pressures, so they cannot reproduce well and the culture dies. These methods can seem less vicious since they involve no bloodshed, and that makes them all the more likely to be practiced.

Psychological principles to explain genocide can be found in those behind all ethnic hatreds and long-standing conflicts, as considered in "Chronic Conflict" in chapter 5, and in the discussion of hate crimes in the next section. Most of the psychological causes of violence mentioned in chapter 1 particularly apply here. The victims are blamed, scapegoated, and very strongly dehumanized. Euphemisms are used to describe the actions taken against them. Obedience to authority is especially strong— the very reason the Milgram experiments were set up was in response to the Nazi's recent genocidal activities against the Jews. Beliefs are constructed to suggest that the elimination of this group is necessary to solve problems.

One important feature of massive genocides in particular is the slippery slope. It is rare if ever that a genocide pops up suddenly. Generally, there is a set of sequential steps whereby more minor things are done first, a buildup before the explosion of major genocidal activity. This means that there is also a possibility for *early warning systems* in which knowledgeable people can monitor international situations to see when the marks of an oncoming genocide seem to be developing. Interventions can then be offered quickly.

It is difficult to know which interventions are the most successful. If interventions occur and a genocide never materializes, there is no way to know if it would never have materialized anyway. It often does not. However, we do have knowledge of countering violence at least in other situations. Preventing smaller incidents of violence that might have occurred even if a genocide never did is also worthwhile.

Terrorism

The word "thug" comes from ancient Hindu militants, "zealot" from ancient Jewish militants, and "assassin" from ancient Muslim militants. The use of violence for the purpose of instilling terror in a civilian population is more ancient than the Roman execution method of crucifixion and as modern as the death squads of Latin America. Organizations that explicitly wish to cause fear in specified groups range from al-Qaeda to the Ku Klux Klan.

The idea of Mutually Assured Destruction (MAD) as a deterrence strategy during the Cold War was called the "balance of terror." The very concept of deterrence is to terrify people out of attacking, yet the term "terrorist" is rarely applied here. There is not a clear definition that unambiguously distinguishes this form of violence from others. There is much controversy. Arabs and Israelis, for example, have argued over whether groups fighting for Palestinian independence are resisters of unjust aggression or terrorists, and whether Israeli reprisals are legitimate self-defense or governmental terrorism. How does one distinguish freedom fighting or self-defense from terrorism? If the answer is that in one case one approves of the violence and in the other case one does not, then the term is not being evenly applied in a way suitable to social science.

In modern usage, the term "terrorist" is normally limited to nongovernmental but well-defined organizations whose fear-causing violence is motivated by political or religious policy goals, not simple greed. Terrorists are accordingly people who believe they are engaged in fighting against injustice or in self-defense. If the term is expanded to include violence by decentralized groups aimed at military targets with a military strategy in mind, rather than a goal of causing terror in civilians, then the term covers guerrilla tactics and becomes an emotional term used by repressive governments to stigmatize their violent opposition. At times, they also use it to stigmatize their nonviolent opposition. Even more than the previous terms of "anarchist," "Papist," and "Communist," terrorism has stigmatization properties without a need for definitional accuracy.

In search of a distinguishing definition, it may be useful to think in terms of the difference between *instrumental* and *expressive* violence. Instrumental violence is aimed at a specific goal. Many see the violence as legitimate if the goal is legitimate, as in self-defense. However, if the goal is not perceived as legitimate, as in committing theft, then the violence is seen as illegitimate. Military strategy normally relies on instrumental use of force. When terrorizing is the goal, the underlying emotions tend to be hatred and rage, and the violence is expressive rather than instrumental. This is why commentators often express puzzlement as to what the actual goals of the terrorist actions are.

The next question becomes the psychological study of prevention. Are terrorists mentally deranged people, or are they following a form of military logic that takes their resources and position into account? As with most military structures, there may be some with clinically diagnosable disorders, but an overview of the literature shows that "the only real difference between terrorism and conventional military action is one of strategy. Terrorists lack the necessary resources to wage war in furtherance of their political goals" (Ruby, 2001).

Some argue that the acts of violence themselves are dysfunctional, and if clinical psychology does not see the perpetrators as suffering from a disorder, it is because psychological phenomena like fanaticism are not regarded as disorders. *Fanaticism* is excessive and irrational devotion to a belief, often paranoid and involving a distortion of reality or of a religious belief system. Its major feature is an utter imperviousness to counter-arguments. Fanatics are people who cannot be reasoned with.

Fanaticism may be commonly observed in terrorist groups, but it is also common in military groups and certainly in governments maintaining a dictatorship. It can therefore be regarded as a feature worth investigation in terrorist groups, but not one that distinguishes terrorism from other forms of violence. There are those who would regard fanaticism as definitional for terrorism, but as stated above, a clear-cut definition of terrorism distinguishing it from other forms of violence is still evolving.

Some of the features that may be common in the organized nongovernmental groups that use fear-inducing violence include:

- Their expressed reasoning involves abundant anger and rage. Speeches detailing the reasons for this are frequent, belligerent, and motivational.
- Scapegoating a group other than those who cause the actual problems is common.
- Groups are in a permanent state of war hysteria; the ideas other people must shift to in order to prepare for war are ever-present.

The perpetrators of violent acts receive the most attention, but the instigators, who do the recruiting and planning, are a psychologically separate group (Mandel, 2001). They tend to be more powerful, less interchangeable, more likely to be wealthy, and less likely to risk their own lives—the difference between someone like Osama bin Laden and the nineteen hijackers who carried out the September 11 attacks.

The victims of the violence are also receiving substantial research attention and therapy intervention. Psychologists already know a great deal about suffering from trauma. Therapists have certainly rushed into situations of massive violence to help the victims in well-known forms of posttrauma stress. When the violence is against a large portion of a community, there are more community-oriented responses. When people suffer the individual murder of a family member, members of the community may be sympathetic but did not suffer the loss themselves. When it is easy to find other people who suffered a similar loss, when the whole community was convulsed by the trauma, then the supportive actions and organization of help along with the emotional responses have some differences.

There are also some differences to be noted when the massive violence is done in a clandestine way. The streets of New York City were lined with pictures of the missing after the World Trade Center attacks of 2001, and this was similar to the outpouring of pictures of the "disappeared" in Argentina of the 1970s when family members put large numbers of photographs of loved ones on display. When violence against a community is done out in the open, in a war in which the enemy is clearly known and identified, then people can engage in the kind of thinking and behavior that goes with being victimized by war. When the masterminds of the violence are hidden, there are some different typical responses.

These are preliminary ideas. The study of the psychology of terrorism is still in its early stages. Events have certainly conspired to make it one of the major areas for the current study of peace psychology.

Defense

Are there times when *failing* to use violent force can result in *more* violence? Augustine of Hippo in the fourth century thought so, and detailed a "just war" doctrine with stringent requirements for war defending innocent people and being conducted strictly for that goal. The Koran also states that proper wars are for defense only. Even Mohandas Gandhi, as a pacifist, held that violent action for defense of others was better than apathy or cowardice.

In Gandhi's case, he believed superior nonviolent means were available, and that violence was only necessary when these had not yet been found. Alternatives range from diplomacy to nonviolent force of the kind used by social movements. There are nonviolent technologies, such as nonlethal crowd control for riots or the Berlin airlift that circumvented a ground-based blockade. Civilian-based defense, which uses well-planned noncooperation techniques, may be the only defense available for small countries invaded by larger ones or when a coup d'état is inflicted by the military itself. It may be developed for more sophisticated uses as well (Sharp, 1990). One of Augustine's rules of a just war is that nonviolent alternatives should be tried first, but many people are not as convinced as Gandhi that such alternatives can always be found.

The fact that waging war for such reasons as gaining territory, revenge, or political advantage has become more commonly perceived as unjustified is progress toward peace. Defense as a reason for war has the advantage of being more sensitive to the harm violence does. It has the disadvantage that people have become adept at applying the concept so well that it is currently used on both sides of almost all wars.

The mention of defense is so prevalent in the rhetoric justifying violent actions that such rhetoric is unlikely to be useful in an objective evaluation of whether the concept reasonably applies in a given case. Would third parties, knowing the circumstances but uninterested in the issues involved, also perceive the actions as defensive, or is this perception limited to those who agree with those who took the violent action?

Philosophical and political debates apply to specific situations, but psychology offers some further suggestions. Danger signs that "defense" is a moral disengagement mechanism of justification rather than a measured response to aggression include the groupthink dynamic, stereotyping and dehumanization of the targets of violence, and oversimplified and unrealistic views of complicated situations. Even when violent force could be judged as clearly defensive by disinterested third parties, the presence of these psychological phenomena could interfere with sound tactics within a campaign or lead to excessive violence that is unnecessary to the defensive goal. The discussion in "Hoped-for Achievements of Violence" in chapter 2 contains a more extensive list of possible problems when defense is the hoped-for achievement.

The concept of defense is not limited to confrontations against the violent. It has also been commonly applied to preventing violent situations from arising. A slave rebellion will not happen when no one is held in slavery. To the extent that, say, poverty or frustrations over discrimination lead to violence, developments that prevent poverty or discrimination will also prevent that violence. The idea that economic development is connected to prevention of civil unrest, guerrilla war, and terrorist attacks was behind the successful Marshall Plan after World War II. U.S. presidents ranging from liberal John F. Kennedy to conservative George W. Bush have recommended the idea.

While some situations arise suddenly, and others are ignored until they become a crisis requiring attention, there are also situations that never reach an explosive level because preventative measures were applied in advance. When such measures benefit the people involved, the goals of defense and of peace are the same. Difficult decisions on use of violent force need never arise.

This is why the area of peace psychology can be expected to cover much more than the times when wars arise. Addressing the root causes of war goes much deeper.

CRIME

The Death Penalty

The use of executions to punish crime has a long history, and was once widespread and prevalent. It is much less common now. Capital punishment has been abolished for all crimes other than murder and treason in some countries, and it has been eliminated entirely in most industrialized countries. The restriction to murder and treason is severe compared to centuries past, when pickpockets and heretics were commonly executed. The move toward a life-affirming approach has also been evident in the current debate in the United States. Those who favor it argue that it saves lives by deterring criminals from committing murders. The ancient attitude that the condemned deserve the fate is not absent but not as prevalent, and the assertion of a life-saving function means at least that people are concerned that there needs to be such a justification.

This is a specifically psychological question: Do executions deter murder? Since societies with extensive executions continue to have murders, we know it is not a complete deterrent. The argument is over whether it has a statistical effect. Are there fewer murders than there would be otherwise?

Empirically, deterrence or its lack would be difficult to establish. We are trying to measure what did not happen. Murders that might have occurred but did not are impossible to count. Nevertheless, since many countries have at different times abolished the death penalty altogether, one can test the deterrence hypothesis by looking at the homicide rate in the year before abolition and the year after, as was done by Dane Archer (1984, pp. 118–139). If capital punishment were indeed a better deterrent than long imprisonment, the homicide rate should have risen in these countries. In some countries, it did—but more often, it *decreased*. The evidence contradicts the hypothesis.

There is an alternative hypothesis, that executions have the opposite effect and encourage murder by example. If the *legitimation of violence model* remains the most plausible explanation for a rise in homicide rates after wars (see "Cycles and Goals" in chapter 2), perhaps it also applies to executions.

The concept of deterrence is based on the premise that potential murderers, upon seeing an execution, identify with the person being executed. This leads them to realize that they could be in the same situation if they commit a similar deed and therefore refrain from murdering to avoid the fate. This view does not take into consideration the human propensity to avoid identification with evil, and to instead identify with good. In other words, the potential murderer perceives the executed as a villain just as others do. This person is more likely to identify with the one perceived as the purveyor of justice—the executioner. Wishing to perceive themselves as purveyors of justice, they have just been given instructions on how to deal with individuals they see as villains in their own lives.

The evidence from Archer and several other studies is unable to find a deterrent effect in homicide rates. If the two hypotheses were set up as alternatives to be tested, the evidence is more consistent with the hypothesis of increased homicides associated with capital punishment. However, the studies are still ongoing and argued.

There is also a hypothesis that the form of punishment—death versus long imprisonment—does not have much of an impact at all on people who expect not to get caught or who are acting in the heat of passion. This can also be consistent with the evidence. There are presumably fewer murders because there are severe legal penalties, and no country has been willing to experiment otherwise. However, the deterrent hypothesis for executions as opposed to other legal penalties so far has very weak support in the empirical data.

On another point, as mentioned in chapter 2, there is evidence of post-trauma stress symptoms in those who carry out executions. Death row is itself a traumatic experience for those confined there. In addition, those who are guilty may have posttrauma symptoms from the crime itself. They very frequently were long-time victims of abuse. The extent to which this might impact public policy is yet to be ascertained. While many would have no sympathy for the guilty having symptoms, and most would feel sympathy for the condemned innocent whether or not there were symptoms, many people have not thought about the question of posttrauma symptoms in those whose job it is to carry out the executions. If they think more about this question, it may or may not influence their thoughts on the death penalty in general. Studies in all these areas are still ongoing.

Many people support the death penalty because they feel special sympathy for the victims' families. The psychological impact on these families requires much more study. It is clear from journalistic interviews that this group varies widely in its attitude toward the death penalty. Some argue that they need it to get a psychological sense of closure. Others say it compounds their own suffering with another death and in creating another grieving family. Do those who seek a sense of closure get this in the long run? Do those who wish to and are allowed to witness the execution benefit from greater mental tranquility afterward than those who do not? People who support the death penalty because of sympathy for victims' families deserve empirical answers to these questions.

The Drug War

As far back as the eighteenth century, a Quaker abolitionist noticed and analyzed a social dynamic that could be updated and applied to current events. This comes from *John Woolman's Journal*, written in 1761:

In conversation with him I perceived that many white people do often sell rum to the Indians, which I believe is a great evil. First, they being thereby deprived of the use of their reason and their spirits violently agitated, quarrels often arise which end in mischief, and the bitterness and resentment occasioned hereby are frequently of long continuance. Again, their skins and furs, gotten through much fatigue and hard travels in hunting, with which they intended to buy clothing, these when they begin to be intoxicated they often sell at a low rate for more rum; and afterward when they suffer for want of the necessaries of life [they] are angry.... And while my mind this evening was thus employed, I also remembered that the people on the frontier, among whom this evil is too common, are often poor people who venture to the outside of a colony that they may live more independent of such who are wealthy, who often set high rents on their land. (Moulton, 1971, p. 126)

The selling of illicit drugs today has similar deleterious effects on those who use them, especially those who are already poverty-stricken. Yet those who do the selling also often come from the ranks of those who would be suffering material deprivation if they did not sell or grow drugs.

It has also become clear that current drug practices are connected with high amounts of violence. Drug users commit crimes to raise money to buy drugs, or they do so under the influence of intoxication. Drug dealers are gang-connected and have turf wars with each other. As was pointed out in chapter 2, substance abuse can be the result of having been a victim or a perpetrator of violence. This is another of the many mechanisms of how violence begets further violence.

Several governments use military techniques to try to stop the flow of drugs in the illicit market, using weapons and prisons as tools in a punitive approach. While the "war on drugs" might seem to many to be a metaphor, there is enough actual violence that some could regard it as an actual war. The assumptions underlying this approach have rarely been given empirical scrutiny. Assertions of its effectiveness have generally not received, or even tried to receive, sound psychological grounding.

On what is called the "demand side," both educational and treatment programs have the clear advantage of being nonviolent and peaceful techniques. Studies to make them more effective, therefore, use nonviolent techniques to counter harm and violence. This would be a *public health approach* to solving the problems of excessive substance abuse, usable for both illicit drugs and legal alcohol.

Family Violence

Violence in the home has been a major problem for millennia. Child abuse has been practiced and historically socially approved in the form of beatings for discipline and infanticide for female and disabled babies. Abuse of wives has been regarded as a husband's right, and abuse of elders when they become dependent has ranged from beatings to deliberately causing death as "euthanasia." Such forms of abuse are now illegal in most places of the world, and the practice has become less widespread accordingly. However, domestic abuse is still widespread—physical abuse, sexual abuse, or neglect of those dependent on care. Causes include the moral disengagement mechanisms discussed in chapter 1, including blaming the victim, minimizing the detrimental effects, and justifying the behavior.

One of the explanations especially characteristic of this specific form of violence is the idea of *intergenerational transmission* of physical abuse. This hypothesis is that patterns of violent behavior are passed from one generation to the next. In other words, children learn that violence is the way to deal with anger or frustration, so when grown they do what they have learned. Additionally, they would have suffered trauma by virtue of having been physically abused, or watching others be abused, and therefore have more anger and frustration and numbing once they are adults.

Kaufman and Zigler (1987) tested the hypotheses of intergenerational transmission in looking at a number of studies. They found that approximately 30 percent of parents who had been abused as children went on to abuse their own children. The overall societal rate is more in the range of 2–3 percent. Having been abused can make it about ten times more likely that one will abuse one's own children. Nevertheless, 30 percent is still well below the majority. Furthermore, when put the other way around, research also shows that the majority of those who abuse their children were not abused in their own childhoods (Widom, 1989). The hypothesis clearly accounts for some of the problem, but not for most of it. As is common for explanations in social science, it will be only one of many explanations for the problem, only one piece of the puzzle. In the case of elder abuse, it does not seem to apply at all (Wolf & Pillemer, 1989).

Another psychological explanation to be added is still in dispute. People on each side of the abortion controversy claim causation in physical child abuse. Proponents of abortion availability believe that when children are unwanted, they are more likely to be abused. Therefore, when we prevent unwanted children from being born, we lower the rate of abuse. Opponents of abortion believe that abortion itself is child abuse, since in their opinion the fetus is an unborn child who is being killed. They believe it also follows that abortion removes a taboo against hurting children, it teaches violence as a way of dealing with children, and that any lesser violence against children seems mild by comparison when parents reflect that they could have aborted this child and did not.

If one took each of these positions as a prediction of what would happen to child abuse if abortion were legalized, that it would decrease or increase dramatically, then a test is readily available. Legalization was very sudden in 1973 in the United States. The prediction, which was confirmed, was the dramatic upsurge in child abuse. According to the U.S. Department of Health and Human Services, cases went from 167,000 in 1973 and 785,100 in 1980 to 2,025,200 in 1987.

This has the same problem all studies based on statistics from the population have. Many other things were going on at the same time that could account for this. People were becoming more sensitive to child abuse and it may have been reported more. Perhaps rates would have gone up even more dramatically if it had not been for the abortion legalization. Some data does report that women who have had abortions are more likely to abuse their children (Ney, 2001), but the researcher is an abortion opponent who would have a bias in this case. More research in this area is clearly needed.

As with many other forms of violence, causation for domestic violence and efforts to counter the problem are varied and complicated. They include individual and group therapy; treatment for related problems such as substance abuse; and community support services that enable parents, battering spouses, or adult children taking care of elderly parents to get needed services. Training in skills includes anger management, coping with stress, resolving conflict, using positive discipline for children, getting jobs, and educational and career development. Much research has shown positive results from the intensive, multipronged approach, and current studies can be expected to uncover more about the most effective ways to deal with various kinds of family violence. Many people working in this area also believe that society-wide attitudes on the acceptability of the use of violence can be expected to have an impact.

Hate Crimes

Hate crimes are defined as those crimes of expressive violence that are motivated by a bias against the victim's group, such as race, gender, or religion. Hatred against a specific individual can bring about crimes of revenge, but are categorized as a different form of crime. In public debate over legislation, the term "hate crimes" normally refers to crimes that target people for who they are, with any member of their group being just as vulnerable. The violence is expressive, not instrumental—for example, synagogues are vandalized, but not looted.

The U.S. Surgeon General (2001) has reported that racial hate crimes can put victims at greater risk of Posttraumatic Stress Disorder (PTSD) and similar posttrauma problems. Other victim categories besides race are likely to be impacted in the same way—victims suffered because they were members of a certain group. Being a victim of a theft is bad luck, but becoming a victim because someone hates your group is much more chilling.

There has been a suggestion that hate crimes go up due to economic circumstances, but empirical data does not bear this out. For example, there was no significant correlation between lynchings and cotton prices in the American South, or between bias crimes and unemployment figures in New York City (Green, Glaser, & Rich, 1998). Racially motivated hate crimes erupt most often when a racially or ethnically homogeneous neighborhood begins rapidly to have people from other racial or ethnic groups migrating in. Already integrated neighborhoods tend to have lower rates of hate crime (Green, Strolovitch, & Wong, 1998). Interviews with White supremacists indicated the main thing that distinguished them from the general public was not any evaluation of their own economic circumstances, but a visceral sense of discomfort with social change (Green, Abelson, & Garnett, 1999). According to this research, the most critical time to monitor and intervene for hate crimes is when there is a rapid influx of people or new ideas into a place that previously had been stable without them.

Psychologist Edward Dunbar has been studying perpetrators of hate crimes by profiling them through the Los Angeles Police Department (DeAngelis, 2001). He and graduate students interviewed hundreds of these criminals on motivation, childhood histories, and levels of pathology. Those interviews found:

- There was not much by way of diagnosable mental illness, such as schizophrenia or manic-depressive. They are mainly not psychotic.
- They nevertheless do have high levels of aggression and antisocial behavior and are very troubled.
- Childhood histories show high levels of abuse by parents or caretakers, along with a use of violence to solve family problems. For all violent hate crimes, this is about in the range of 30 percent, similar to perpetrators of family violence, as mentioned above. This is not a majority, but still several times higher than the general public. For those who committed homicides, the portion was much higher; about half had files with previous notations of being abused as children.
- They tend to deliberate on and plan their attacks, and may travel distances to find the people they wish to target. These tend to be premeditated rather than spontaneous crimes.
- They tend to show a history of such actions, beginning with smaller incidents and moving up to more serious crimes.
- Only about 5 percent identified themselves as members of organized hate gangs or associations.

Their hostilities are most likely to be aimed at groups that society as a whole is against. They get more permission to commit violent acts when social sanction seems to be available. Thus, such crimes against African Americans were at their height during slavery and Jim Crow law days, and similar offenses against Jews were heightened during the 1930s in Germany. Japanese Americans were subject to higher amounts in the aftermath of Pearl Harbor, which persisted as the government continued to discriminate against them. Muslim Americans, along with Muslim guests, Sikhs, and people of Southern Asian origin were subject to a surge of such crimes immediately after the September 11 attacks. In this case, however, government officials at all levels immediately expressed strong disapproval publicly and law enforcement often investigated right away, so the surge subsided. In short, one of the major contributors to hate crimes is the attitude of the larger society. Such crimes still occur with social disapproval, but not as often.

One solution to hate crimes, then, includes projects that cause the society as a whole to disapprove. Those crimes that are more likely to be fed by social approval will then be less likely to occur. More knowledge about the out-group seems to have this effect, as people learn to understand their members as individuals rather than as stereotypes and a sense of community is expanded.

Another of the solutions to hate crimes includes any projects that reduce family violence. For those occasions when these painful experiences have not been prevented, efforts at healing those affected are crucial. Ideally, these can be caught when hateful incidents are at their beginning phase and more minor, before they have escalated.

All of these things have merit aside from their effect on preventing hate crimes. More research is being done on causes and prevention. This is naturally a field of intense interest to social psychologists.

School Violence

Violence prevention programs in schools include conflict resolution and anger management training, as was covered in "Peace Education and Research" in chapter 3. For more extreme cases of violence, when students engage in serial shootings, efforts at predicting which individuals need intervention have proven to be nearly impossible, in part because the sample of those who go to such an extreme is so small. Attention to the overall school environment is probably the best preventative, where problems are not tallied with a scale but discussed, and there is a focus on positive relationships among students and with school personnel (Mulvey & Cauffman, 2001).

Bullying is a form of violence that is especially associated with schools. It is not only distressing at the time of schooling, but can lead to negative reactions and long-lasting traumatizations. Many of the school shooting incidents have been traced to outbursts by victims of bullying. Timothy McVeigh claimed this as part of his motivation for the Oklahoma City bombing. Victims of bullying are more likely to, at the least, avoid school.

Nevertheless, for later crime, the biggest danger is from the bullies themselves, because they have higher-than-average criminal records, while victims are average or below average in theirs. A follow-up of bullies in one study showed about 60 percent of boys identified as bullies in Grades 6–9 had at least one conviction by the age of twenty-four and more than a third had three or more (Olweus, 1991). Another sample reported that bullies who are identified early in school had a one-in-four chance of having a criminal record by age thirty (Eron, Huesmann, Dubow, Romanoff, & Yarnel, 1987).

A review of studies on bullies (Batsche & Knoff, 1994) has found the parents of bullies to have these characteristics:

- prefer physical means of punishment
- are sometimes hostile and rejecting
- are inconsistent, being hostile at some times and permissive at others
- have poor problem-solving skills
- teach their children to strike back at the least provocation

The bullies themselves have a strong need to dominate others, impulsivity, and little if any empathy with victims. There have been theories that bullies are acting out of insecurity, are anxious, and lack self-esteem. However, empirical evidence for these characteristics has been looked for and is lacking. Bullies like being bullies; they perceive their actions as justified.

Behaviorally, they are reinforced for their actions. They have positive reinforcement by attaining their goals, and negative reinforcement by removal of threats. They desire, expect, and receive control through physical strength, and are unaffected by the possibility of inflicting suffering. Bullies process information about victims in a rigid and automatic way. In line with Bandura's moral disengagement mechanisms as detailed in chapter 1, they believe they pick on their victim because he or she provoked them or otherwise deserves it. Their primary emotions about bullying incidents are either to be happy because they were in control and did what they wanted, or to be angry because the victim made them that way.

Factors that have been considered and found to have no effect on rates of bullying include size of school, size of class, ethnic mix, and socioeconomic level. There is also no effect for any physical characteristic of the victim other than physical weakness. Boys are more likely to be bullies and victims of bullies than girls, though both are involved. Younger children are more vulnerable to older children, which goes along with their being physically weaker, but the incidence of direct physical bullying goes down as children get older. The aggressive verbal form of bullying, however, does not decline.

Features of preventative intervention programs include having accurate information about bullying in general and a schoolwide assessment of the current situation in particular, dispelling beliefs about combative behavior being normal, providing counseling services for both bullies and victims, involving parents, and implementing strategies known to work with aggressive children. Those training strategies include behavior management, self-control strategies, social skills training, information processing, and cognitive perspective taking.

With prevention at an early age, much later crime can be avoided, along with current suffering of other children. The question of how the bullying personality fits into drives to go to war has not yet been thoroughly considered in either the studies of bullying, or on psychological dimensions of war. It would seem the bullying paradigm fits many war situations. Victims of attacks often say so outright. A form of violence that is so prevalent among children as they are developing could well have an impact on decision makers and populations, especially if the adult world magnifies the size of the consequences.

Gun Violence

A classic study on the psychology of guns found that even having a gun in the vicinity seemed to have a priming effect in causing more aggressive behavior (Berkowitz & LePage, 1967). It was the presence of the gun, not having it in one's hands, that caused the effect. Replicating studies, though not entirely consistent, for the most part back up this finding (see reviews in Turner, Simons, Berkowitz, & Farodi, 1977; and Carlson, Marcus-Newhall, & Miller, 1990). One study has shown that even pictures and names of weapons can have this aggression-increasing effect, suggesting it is not the gun alone but the priming effect of the idea that causes the effect (Anderson, Arlin, & Bartholow, 1998).

Of course, if it is someone else who pulls out a gun, then this priming effect means little. Those who oppose gun control argue that it is necessary for self-defense, that guns represent the democratization of the use of force, and problems such as accidental shootings and children getting guns are best dealt with by gun safety education rather than bans. Gun control proponents argue that guns are more frequently used in causing homicides in the home that would not have occurred otherwise, they result in many tragic accidents, especially with children, and they are more likely to give criminals access to guns than to be a defense.

The scientific approach to answer these questions is more difficult than the question of priming, which can be tested in lab experiments. What cannot be done as a lab experiment must be figured out with the statistics of what happens in the real world; however, there are many confounding variables and complications in doing that. For example, it may be true that more people are shot with guns in their own homes than there are burglars shot—but how many burglars were scared away without being shot? How many people did not attempt to burglarize a house because they thought there might be a gun there? The question of whether or not guns work as defense, and even more so deterrence, requires the counting of what did not happen. This is difficult. A comparison group of people who dealt with threats in nonviolent ways may also have a success rate, or failure rate, that goes unreported.

Cruelty to Animals

There are many who would regard violence to animals as being a threat to peace, no matter what the impact is on violence toward humans. Nevertheless, most recent studies are showing there is a strong connection between children being cruel to pets as a pattern and building up to a pattern of violence against other human beings (Miller, 2001). Even the U.S. Federal Bureau of Investigation has said, "investigation and prosecution of crimes against animals is an important tool for identifying people who are, or may become, perpetrators of violent crimes against people" (Lockwood & Church, 1996, p. 211).

Reasons for this may include the priming effect of violence, the lack of empathy necessary to be cruel, and the habit and conditioning that comes with systematic desensitization to violence. *Systematic desensitization* is used well by behavioral therapists in clients with phobias. Clients gradually get used to small things, followed by things closer to what they are afraid of. They relax themselves as a practice, and eventually the phobia is gone. In this case, however, if children are cruel to pets and it is not regarded as a serious problem, then they can become quite acclimated to what would normally be considered repulsive, and the next step to cruelty against people is not so large. As with the sequential steps allowing people in the Milgram experiments to give greater shocks than they would have without the previous more minor steps, cruelty to pets serves as a stepping-stone to targeting humans.

For adults, violence to animals can include blood sports such as cockfighting, fox hunting, and bullfights. Blood sports vary in how much they are legal or approved of. Do the more socially approved methods of violence to animals have similar effects as cruelty to pets? This is a question that has not been studied well.

Another group of adults are those who experiment on animals in a way that harms them. These people are markedly different demographically. They are professionals who insist that such experimentation is necessary and beneficial. This is the position of the American Psychological Association, for example. Yet there is some evidence that experimenters do have stress. They also have an aversion to this being mentioned, for fear the idea they are bothered might reflect on the work (Arluke, 1991). There is a need for much more research in this area, research that is rigorous and scrupulous enough to find true answers without a bias in favor of either side of the debate.

Factory farms involve massive cruelty to animals. Slaughterhouses have assembly-line killing to make animals into meat. The effect of this on workers in both places is inadequately studied. Whether those involved have greater propensities to violence, in the form of domestic violence or barroom brawls, also has yet to be published in an accessible way. Working with animals for the purpose of making them into meat may have an entirely different psychological effect from choosing to be cruel to pets for pleasure. The distinction could make the causation of cruelty to pets more clear.

There is very little work in the first few decades of psychology on the psychological impact of cruelty to animals because the fate of animals was not regarded as being serious. With peace psychology, concentration has been more on international relations and it is more recent that violence in the domestic sphere has been added. More interest is building now, and a literature search on the subject is likely to bring up many more findings as time goes on.

Prisons

The Stanford Prison Experiment, covered in chapter 1, showed how prisons can become dehumanizing places, occasionally encouraging violent behavior—even when prisoners and guards were randomly selected, screened to preclude pathologies, and for only a few days. Real-world prisons attract certain types to be guards and to be prisoners. There is no screening for pathologies, the time is longer, and there are no provisions to shut down the situation if it gets out of hand.

The process of imprisonment has the following effects:

- Statistically speaking, it is selecting out of the general population those who are least likely to maintain moral principles under trying circumstances.

- These people are then socialized with other criminals. This can bolster criminal attitudes and allow learning practical criminal skills.

- Many are then let out with few practical noncriminal skills, with convictions that make it more difficult to find jobs.

In short, if people with psychological knowledge wished to set up the most effective system for increasing crime, they would be hard-pressed to do better than the current prison system. When restorative justice techniques are practical and appropriate, they tend to lead to less recidivism (see "Public Policy" in chapter 5). The schooling effect is different.

Hickey and Scharf (1980) also found that the biggest predictor of how well specific inmates did after prison was the level of social support they found from friends and family. Those remaining in unhealthy relationships were more likely to reenter prison. Those with people aiding them in their postprison adjustment benefited more from in-prison rehabilitation programs.

Rehabilitation efforts have included psychodynamic therapy, behavioral therapy, and moral development processes. Psychodynamic therapy finds subconscious causes for behavior and changes the behavior to make it conscious. Behavioral therapy uses reward and punishment techniques to more mechanically change a prisoner's antisocial behavior. Moral development uses a Socratic dialog technique to develop inmates' moral reasoning capabilities. Various efforts at using the building of community in prison are being developed (Hickey & Scharf, 1980). One ongoing program, the Alternatives to Violence Program, takes the approach of teaching intensive workshops in nonviolence problem-solving skills.

MEDICAL MATTERS

The Impact of War on Medical Staff

There has always been a strong direct relationship between the medical field and war, since battle leaves people in foreseeable need of medical care. The military usually makes arrangements for medical care near the battle lines as part of their preparations for war.

While the medical staff takes action to benefit patients, the larger violent context brings peculiar psychological distresses, such as the trauma that all those close to battle can suffer, and intimate contact with those who are suffering trauma and dealing with psychological aftermath. Ordinary medicine deals with these, but it is more intense in war.

Another distinction from ordinary medicine is that some doctors and nurses may ask themselves the vexing question: Does it benefit patients to make them well enough to put themselves in danger again? What if they get killed after being treated, and would not have been killed had they not been treated so well?

Some psychologists have the same relationship with war that many medical doctors have—repairing the damage done to the people doing the fighting. In many cases, they give therapy to those distressed by battle to get them back into battle. Questions of how therapeutic it is to prepare people for a situations in which they may kill others, see friends killed, or be killed themselves are issues such psychologists themselves must deal with.

Exploiting Medicine for Nonmedical Goals

Jabbing people in the arm with a needle or knocking them unconscious with drugs and then cutting their bodies would be violence, if done without medical intent. With medical intent, however, shots and surgery are beneficial, and applying these abrasive terms to them would strike most people as bizarre. Actions that would be abusive outside a medical context are helpful services within it. In fact, failure to do such things can be medical neglect, and this could be a form of violence. If doctors tend to the needs of rich patients but leave low-income patients in a corner to fester, then both those patients and the principles of peace suffer.

There are times when medicine is practiced badly, and then the patient has suffered destructive behavior. Opposition to this is not a matter of controversy, and psychological details of how best to avoid medical malpractice would most commonly be covered under health psychology.

However, to learn medicine properly, medical personnel must become desensitized to a certain extent. A nurse whose job it is to continually give children inoculations does this with the knowledge that they will benefit in the long run and must therefore become inured to their obvious distress. The situation appears to be violence to anyone who does not understand the benefit of the shots, which includes the small children getting them. A certain amount of numbing to the reality in front of one's eyes is necessary for medical personnel to do their jobs.

This puts medical practitioners in a peculiar position. They are trained to be desensitized to pain in others and have high prestige for successfully doing so, as long as they take actions necessary to reduce pain, disease, or injury. Most of the time, they simply do their jobs well.

On some occasions, however, this mechanism can go awry and there is no real benefit. An extreme example is the Nazi doctors, whose job it was to arrange for euthanasia of the disabled and later to extend the label of "disabled" to groups such as Gypsies, homosexuals, and Jews. Their understanding that this benefited the disabled to not be burdened with life and it benefited society to be rid of them, was a mechanism of moral disengagement rather than actual medicine. The aura of medicine gave the beliefs legitimacy in their minds and the minds of others (Lifton, 1986).

It is in part the emotional numbing necessary to the job that allows this, and in part the high prestige in which medicine is held precisely because it is so beneficial to health. People who wish to use violence to achieve certain goals therefore frequently use medical metaphors for what they are doing. Medical personnel are used for what are actually nonmedicinal goals. Medical metaphors are used as euphemisms for war, genocide, and other violence: surgical strikes in war, racial hygiene, removal of a diseased appendage from the body politic. Battle campaigns are called "operations."

Medicide

Some propose that medicine can be used intentionally for causing death. This has been called *euthanasia* from the ancient Greek practice, a word meaning "good death." It has also been called "hastened death" and "mercy killing." When a physician helps by offering assistance but not directly causing death, it is commonly called "physician-assisted suicide." The term "medicide" is taken from the title of a book by Jack Kevorkian (1991), one of the major proponents of the practice, who refers to it as the goodness of planned death.

Several of the considerations for peace psychology are:

• How much can the practice be used as a euphemism for the elimination of people who have been dehumanized after the normal custom for those targeted for violence? It would naturally seem more desirable to say they themselves desire this death, or would if they were reasonable. It would seem more kind to say it benefits them than to say that other people desire their elimination. There was an influential book published in 1920 in Germany by two doctors, Karl Binding and Alfred Hoche, called *Permitting the Destruction of Unworthy Life,* which made that argument on behalf of euthanasia, and the results that followed in the next two and a half decades in Germany serve as a cautionary note.

• How quickly does a "right to die" become a "duty to die"? Once medically planning death is an option, is it subject to the kind of slippery slope of minor violence leading to major violence? Can those who do insist they wish this kind of death acclimate people so well to the idea that it will eventually apply to the more ambivalent, then the reluctant, then the clearly opposed?

• What is the role of depression in requests to die? If depression is the reason for the request and the request is granted without the depression being treated, is this nontreatment a form of medical neglect?

• If there are people with a bigotry against people with disabilities, is this a way for them to express it without realizing that it is bigotry? It would seem to be a very severe form of discrimination to say that people are better off dead, and they ought to recognize this. This is why a disabilities-rights organization has begun, called Not Dead Yet, for the purpose of fighting the proposals they feel are aimed at their community.

• There are long-standing traditions of regarding women, racial minorities, and people in poverty as being of less value. Will they then be subjected to the cheaper alternative of planned death when more expensive options are reserved for those deemed more valuable?

• What is the impact on more general suicide prevention efforts? If a frail elderly woman is encouraged to die deliberately to avoid having to face problems, how do we tell her healthy teenage granddaughter the importance of facing hers? The distinction in tolerability between one set of problems and another may be lost on the granddaughter.

• Should we provide counseling for suicide prevention to one group of people and not to another? Can the distinction between who gets help and support and who does not be based on reasonable criteria rather than traditional forms of discrimination?

• A husband who is motivated by a desire to receive a disabled wife's estate could be perceived as more violent than one motivated by a desire to relieve her suffering. The psychology of each situation would be likely to have different features.

• How quickly will those who run managed care, insurance companies, or socialized medical care notice that death costs less than continued care? Will they then encourage doctors to take this cost containment into account? Would it be a form of structural violence if they did?

• What are the psychological effects on the medical staff members who carry out planned deaths? Do they have the same psychological consequences as those who kill (as detailed in "Effects of Direct Violence on Perpetrators" in chapter 2), or do they respond as people practicing medicine and mercy?

• What would be the effect of habituation on those who carry out planned deaths? Would the sensitivity of the first case continue in later cases?

• One of the major motivations for euthanasia has been the cold, bureaucratic hospitals' treatment of patients as biological units to be kept functioning rather than as human beings with emotional needs. The use of burdensome, futile care is against the Hippocratic oath and can be regarded as a form of violence itself. A rebellion against this does not necessarily lead to deliberately taking life as the only alternative, as if we needed to choose which form of violence we prefer.

• Alternatives that are unambiguously not violent include hospice care, pain management, and family support. The creativity of the foreclosed option, as discussed in "Positive Impact on Participants" in chapter 4, can come into play here especially: If deliberately hastening death is not an option, then improving comfort care and innovating more medical cures become essential.

Some see euthanasia or assisted suicide as being merciful and as being a matter of choice and autonomy. Others see these as being another form of killing, and therefore violence that should never be contemplated under any circumstances for human beings. What can be discovered about the psychological processes of hastening death that can help establish whether it is indeed merciful or violent? Are there certain factors that can make it different in specific cases? Would a screening process take care of the above objections, or are they too formidable? Much debate is likely to continue for some time, but the insights of psychology in general and peace psychology in particular can add much to the debate.

Back-Alley Butchers

One form of violence commonly recognized as medical is the doctors who do abortions in a way that leaves women injured or dead. The slang term for such less-than-competent doctors is "back-alley butchers." The best way to solve this problem has been a subject of debate. One side believes the problem is caused by abortion being illegal and the solution is simple: once abortion is legalized, women are no longer forced to go to the incompetent. The other side believes the problem of incompetence is more complicated, caused because abortion is violence to both an unborn child and to the pregnant woman. They say doctors know this, at least subconsciously, and so even those who support abortion availability frequently do not perform them, but send women to specialists. This side argues that the specialists attracted to do abortions tend to be the less than competent, who are unable to work in more respectable medicine. Further, doing abortions erodes medical competence as the practice leads to the kind of emotional numbing and callousness common to committing violence. Accordingly, they argue, the solution is not to legalize abortion but to recognize it as violence, educate about this, provide pregnant women with community support and services as an alternative, and recognize the circumstances that put women under pressure to get abortions as injustices against them.

Some have argued that compelling women to give birth merely because they are pregnant is itself a form of violence, and therefore defend the availability of abortion as necessary for peace. Others argue that negative psychological aftermath is still common. The study of the actual psychological impact of abortion on women, whether it is beneficial or harmful, therefore becomes crucial to answering this question. There is quite a large literature on this subject; however, it has not yet coalesced into clear answers accepted by both sides. Each side accuses the other of preferring those studies that back up its position. Each side has a large number of women who have experienced abortions.

Whether or not those who carry out abortions are themselves subject to the kinds of psychological consequences common to those who kill has barely been studied. Two studies by those of pro-choice beliefs suggest it as a possibility (Roe, 1989; Such-Baer, 1974). Far more study must be done before any conclusions can be drawn, with more discussion on what those conclusions mean.

If abortion is beneficial medicine, then its only place in peace psychology is the impact of its deprivation, just as the withdrawal of other forms of beneficial medicine can be a form of structural violence. If it is a form of violence, then its role in peace psychology would be due to its presence rather than its absence.

The worldwide debate over abortion is likely to continue for some time, including within the peace movement. Groups such as the War Resisters League and *The Progressive* magazine, for example, take the position that abortion is necessary medical care. A group called Consistent Life instead advocates a *consistent life ethic*, the concept that all issues of socially approved killing are connected and that abortion is in that category along with war, the death penalty, arms buildup, euthanasia, poverty, racism, and so on. While this political debate continues, the concepts and research of psychology in general and peace psychology in particular may add insight.

Coercive Limits on Fertility

Methods of controlling fertility generally fall under the umbrella of medicine—contraception, sterilization, and fertility awareness techniques. Such control is often desired. However, when the limit on fertility is imposed on people against their will, it may still carry the prestigious luster of medicine but can reasonably be perceived as violence. Actions are taking away something people regard as precious to them, which can be highly traumatizing to victims.

Eugenics is one of the reasons these limits have been imposed. This was a popular idea in the 1920s and 1930s, with thousands being involuntarily sterilized in the United States and causing even more major problems in Germany. These practices are now generally held in disrepute. The history of eugenics, the idea of improving the human race by discouraging the "unfit" from reproducing, is generally seen as a history of brutality against those with disabilities. Those who still hold the ideas are more circumspect in expressing them.

Another reason limits are imposed, one even more clearly fitting under peace psychology, is beliefs on strategic military interests for the militarily and industrially powerful. This is illustrated by a quotation from a U.S. Army Conference on Long-Range Planning paper, which details population growth in developing countries in contrast to the stabilization or decline in developed countries and then notes:

Such trends speak to pressures for a systematically diminished role and status for today's industrial democracies. Even with relatively unfavorable assumptions about Third World economic growth, the share of global economic output of today's industrial democracies could decline. With generalized and progressive industrialization of current low-income areas, the Western diminution would be all the more rapid. Thus, one can easily envision a world more unreceptive, and ultimately more threatening, to the interests of the United States and its allies. The population and economic-growth trends described could create an international environment even more menacing to the security prospects of the Western alliance than was the Cold War for the past generation. (Eberstadt, 1991)

For another example, the Center for Strategic and International Studies in its *Washington Quarterly* (spring 1989) concluded that elements of statecraft for defense included "development assistance and population planning every bit as much as new weapons systems."

Elizabeth Liagin (1996) documents that this has led to practices of coercion and manipulation throughout developing countries. While sincere efforts to explain to people why smaller families are a good idea can be done in good faith, and are done by well-meaning people, there are programs that have been sabotaged simply by giving out accurate information in the target country about exactly who is sponsoring the program and what the sponsors are saying in their private memorandums. Many people who might be interested in having fewer children for their own reasons are not interested in doing so for the military goals of another nation.

A third reason is commented on wryly by Charles Dickens in *A Christmas Carol* when Ebenezer Scrooge says that if the poor would rather die than go to poorhouses, "perhaps they had better do it, and decrease the surplus population." Ideas were common in the upper class in Dickens's day that the poor were poor because they were overbreeding, not because the rich were exploiting them. Scrooge used this line as an excuse not to give to charity, yet when it was later repeated about a specific person, that person was the son of his own underpaid employee. Dickens was a sharp social critic, and his ideas still apply in some places today. Some of those running large corporations seeking cheap labor in developing countries prefer to blame employees for having children rather than pay them a living wage to support them.

A final reason for imposing fertility limits is a desire for genocide, diminishing or eliminating entire groups of people. Keeping people from ever being born seems like a gentler way of eliminating them than killing them. It can give every appearance of not being violent, especially under the aura of medical care. The psychology of these more hidden forms of violence is another area where much more research would be helpful.

CONCLUSION

This chapter deals entirely with public policy issues of violence. Policy considerations of nonviolence were covered in chapter 5, under conflict resolution, with a little more on government using nonviolent action for defense as civilian-based defense in chapter 6. Public policy on education to encourage citizens to be more nonviolent is covered under "Peace Education and Research" in chapter 3.

In chapter 8, we turn away from the public and more to the private. Lifestyles and culture have an impact on public policy and vice versa. As usual, lines in reality are not clear-cut, but imposing an organization on ideas can help us to understand them better.

FURTHER READING

Integrative Complexity

Conway, L. G., Suedfeld, P., & Tetlock, P. E. (2001). Integrative complexity and political decisions that lead to war or peace. In D. J. Christie, R. V. Wagner, & D. D. Winter (Eds.), *Peace, conflict, and violence: Peace psychology for the 21st century.* Upper Saddle River, NJ: Prentice-Hall, pp. 66–75.
Raphael, T. D. (1982). Integrative complexity theory and forecasting international crises: Berlin, 1946–1962. *Journal of Conflict Resolution, 26,* 423–450.

Arms Races

Bronfenbrenner, U. (1961). The mirror image in Soviet-American relations: A social psychologist's report. *Journal of Social Issues, 17,* 45–56.
Etzioni, A. (1967). The Kennedy experiment. *Western Political Quarterly, 20,* 361–380.
Milburn, T. W. (1961). The concept of deterrence: Some logical and psychological considerations. *Journal of Social Issues, 17,* 3–11.
Osgood, C. E. (1962). *An alternative to war or surrender.* Urbana, IL: University of Illinois Press.

Genocide

Chirot, D., & Seligman, M. E. P. (2001). *Ethnopolitical warfare: Causes, consequences, and possible solutions.* Washington, DC: American Psychological Association.
Staub, E. (1996). Preventing genocide: Activating bystanders, helping victims and the creation of caring. *Peace and Conflict: Journal of Peace Psychology, 2,* 189–201.

Terrorism

Analyses of Social Issues and Public Policy, Vol. 2, No. 1, at www.asap-spissi.org.

School Violence

Burstyn, J. N., Bender, G., Casella, R., Gordon, H. W., Guerra, D. P., Luschen, K. V., Stevens, R., & Williams, K. M. (2001). *Preventing violence in schools: A challenge to American democracy.* Mahwah, NJ: Lawrence Erlbaum Associates, Inc.
Rubin, I., & Pepler, D. (Eds.). (1991). *The development and treatment of childhood aggression.* Hillsdale, NJ: Erlbaum.

School Psychology Review. (1994). Vol. 23, No. 2. Miniseries on School Violence, pp. 139–262.

Cruelty to Animals

Lockwood, R., & Ascione, R. R. (1998). *Cruelty to animals and interpersonal violence: Readings in research and application.* West Lafayette, IN: Purdue University Press.

Web site for Psychologists for the Ethical Treatment of Animals: http://www.psyeta.org.

Abortion

Because there is a controversy over whether abortion or the lack of abortion constitutes violence, we list here good psychology resources on each side of the debate.

Pro-choice

Beckman, L., & Harvey, S. M. (Eds.). (1998). *The new civil war: The psychology, culture, and politics of abortion.* Washington, DC: American Psychological Association.

Pro-life

Web site for the Elliott Institute, which focuses on psychological aftermath for women: http://www.afterabortion.org.

Web site for the Feminism & Nonviolence Studies Association, an interdisciplinary journal: http://www.fnsa.org.

Euthanasia/Assisted Suicide

Hendin, H. (1997). *Seduced by death: Doctors, patients, and the Dutch cure.* New York: W. W. Norton and Company.

Coerced Limits on Fertility

Web site for the Information Project for Africa (which covers the world, not just Africa): www.africa2000.com/INDX/indx.htm.

CHAPTER 8

Gentle Lives and Culture

Personal practices share with public policy the ability to have long-lasting impact on how peaceful the world becomes. They are different from the public policy since people can take private actions without being required to influence government or other large institutions to do it for them.

The distinction is not clear-cut. Private actions are more effective if done by large numbers, and most are easier to do if there are societal arrangements for them. As has been mentioned throughout this book, links are common, things are all connected, and the division of things into categories is done for aid in understanding, not because reality neatly divides them that way.

The humor, optimism, and creativity covered in chapter 3 could easily apply here, along with character-building virtues such as integrity, simplicity, patience, and temperance. Understanding and avoiding burnout, and helping colleagues to do the same, could easily fit this chapter. Knowledge of conflict resolution for everyday situations and of nonviolent ways to deal with bullies or with dangerous situations is another area that can belong under "gentle lives." Many aspects of this topic have already been addressed.

Art and literature are also ways of coping with violence and fostering nonviolence. The psychology of art that is used to cope with war, nuclear anxieties, and poverty, as well as to build peace, rounds out the chapter.

This chapter examines:

- Personal Practices—points of private lifestyle
- Coping and Healing through Art—the use of art as a way of dealing with violence

PERSONAL PRACTICES

Community-Based Social Marketing

There are actions individuals can take in their personal lives that would have the effect of lowering the amount of violence in the world. These include ecological practices; boycotts of those who exploit workers in poverty; avoiding products made by companies that manufacture weapons, abuse animals, or pollute; and so on. One of the most common ways to get people to engage in these practices is to give them more information about the problem and the solution, with the idea that this impacts their behavior. Unfortunately, studies have shown that this alone does not seem to work well.

A more effective approach is *community-based social marketing*. This is originally designed for encouraging ecological behavior, but it can also be used for encouraging individuals to take just about any action. It has four steps:

1. Selecting behaviors with three questions:
    a. What is the potential impact of the behavior?
    b. What barriers, internal or external, are there for the behavior?
    c. Do resources exist to overcome the barriers?
2. Design strategies
3. Run a pilot project
4. Evaluation

The first step is to select a behavior for the research, taking care that it will have a desirable impact if large numbers of people engage in it, since the project will take much effort. The next strategy is to uncover the barriers to engaging in that behavior. Some barriers are external, such as inconvenience or lack of available alternatives, and others are internal, such as a desire not to look eccentric to others. These barriers can be found with focus groups, observational studies, or surveys—techniques well-trained psychologists do well. Once barriers are known, the next step is to determine if there are ways around them. Things can be made more convenient or more seemingly normal, and alternatives offered.

If resources exist, the strategies can be designed for putting them into place. Since these strategies are often a major expenditure of resources, it makes sense to do what is normally done before a large research project is undertaken: run a pilot study. This is an undersized version of the strategy that uses a small, easier to handle set of resources on a smaller group of people. This is done before broad implementation to see if the program is effective. Sometimes the program can be dropped before major time and energy is wasted on it. Frequently, some modifications are required to improve the strategy before it is tried on a large scale.

Finally, a method of evaluation should be in place, both for the pilot project and for the larger project, to see if it had the hoped-for impact. There should be a direct, quantifiable measure of the behavior itself, or of its consequences. Taking a survey and asking people for self-report may be useful in some areas of study, but is not as effective for this kind of project. Researchers want to know what actually happened, rather than marking down what people knew they wanted to hear and were polite enough to say. Therefore, additional ways of observation should be added to the surveys to get more accurate results.

Listening Skills

Developing good listening skills is one of the most important personal practices for establishing peaceful conditions. The following are the most common reasons for this.

Conflict Resolution

As covered under "Principles" in chapter 5, finding the interests underlying the positions and being creative about finding a win-win solution requires more than merely putting forth one's own view articulately. It requires listening well to the views of others.

Nonviolent Action

The psychological tools of the conflict cannot be employed at all unless both opponents and onlookers are listened to.

Open-Mindedness

Understanding other people's points of view has more value than the ability to better manipulate situations. A bountiful repertoire of views can enrich one's own thinking and it cuts down on arrogance and closed-mindedness.

Group Decision Making

Groups can make decisions in several ways: (1) one person makes decisions and everyone else follows; (2) the entire group votes so the majority rules, and everyone else follows; or, (3) in consensus, not everyone necessarily agrees but everyone is at least agreeable to a decision, which accordingly takes some time to work out. There are advantages and disadvantages to each method, but any of them will bring better decisions and leave the group more satisfied if the people involved have good skills of listening to each other's ideas and concerns. Listening skills can make a difference in whether decisions are imposed or are instead more peacefully composed.

Everyday Therapy

Listening can be a healing art. Therapists, pastors, and other kinds of counselors know this well. In some cases, people are in such a traumatized condition that they need to go to experts of this kind. Most of the time, however, they are simply in need of basic friendship. Everybody has enough trouble in his or her life to require good friends to listen. In some cases, strangers at the bus stop will do. Bartenders and workers at the beauty shop have long filled this function.

Child Rearing

Children who are listened to feel, and are, more respected. They are more likely to develop listening skills in turn.

Parenting

Most of the work on raising children to be more peaceful adults is practically the same as how to raise children in healthy and developmentally sound ways. One of the common approaches in this area is to look at three different *socialization styles* parents have:

Authoritarian

Rules are strict and rigid, and punishment is severe and sure. Children tend to be more anxious and rigid themselves. The use of the same word as the authoritarian personality is not coincidental.

Permissive

Rules are lax, and punishment is low and not consistent. Children tend to have unrealistic expectations and an inability to use the discipline necessary to get things done or get along with other people.

Authoritative

Rules are firm, but negotiable when appropriate. Enforcement is warm and takes the thoughts of the child into account. Discipline is explained.

Children raised this way tend to be more secure and clear about what to do and how to relate to others.

As with most typologies, some people clearly fit into one of these categories, and most tend toward one more than the others. Results vary accordingly. Children are also quite capable of having minds of their own and varying from the normal characteristics associated with the way they were raised.

There is a parallel here with approaches to dealing with conflicts. Violence as a problem solver is parallel to the authoritarian style. Cowardice or submission has a parallel to the permissive style because problems are permitted to continue in either case. The use of nonviolence is firm, countering violence without backing down. It is therefore parallel to the authoritative approach. People often think that violence is necessary because they believe the option of submission or cowardice is worse, and that those are the only alternatives. Conversely, some people believe submission is better as they contemplate the horrors of committing violence. In either case, they are not considering the possibility of a third way—a firm way of nonviolence that is neither brutal nor timid. In the same way, many are authoritarian in style because they see what is wrong with being too permissive, and many are permissive because they see what is wrong with being too authoritarian. There is the third option, one that avoids the disadvantages of both. Though the psychologists working in this area have not commonly mentioned this parallel, they have done quite a bit of research showing the merits of that third option.

The use of the authoritative style, which is so clearly preferable in outcome, is studied in greater length in the concept of *positive discipline*. The methods are both nonpunitive and nonpermissive, kind and firm at the same time. They show respect for both the child and for what needs to be done. The three criteria for a discipline that teaches are: Is it respectful? Is it effective long-term? Does it help children develop valuable life skills for good character?

Violence in the Reel World

Entertainment is a major part of many people's lifestyles, and in many cultures, television and movies are a major part of entertainment. The question of whether the fictional or actual violence portrayed there has any influence on violent behavior has been a matter of heated dispute and study for decades.

The scientific answer to the question is clear. More than a thousand studies say that violence in the media is connected to aggressive behavior in some children (*Joint Statement*, 2000, p. 1). All overviews of the studies find positive correlations. There have also been meta-analyses done; a meta-analysis is a study of studies, research that takes the studies and puts them all together. The largest meta-analysis on this subject, 217 studies, shows a remarkably high correlation of + .31 (Paik & Comstock, 1994). Several psychological and medical professional organizations have said that, as with tobacco, we have now reached the standard of proof that there is not a reasonable doubt about this. The point at which the evidence was strong enough for the U.S. Surgeon General to issue a statement in the case of tobacco was 1964. For media violence, it was 1972 (Surgeon General's Scientific Advisory Committee on Television and Social Behavior, 1972).

The argument has been made that violence in the media is not a cause but a reflection of violence within the society. One film critic comments on this idea by saying:

If this were true, then why do so few people witness murders in real life but everybody sees them on TV and in the movies? The most violent ghetto isn't in South Central L.A. or Southeast Washington D.C.; it's on television. About 350 characters appear each night on prime-time TV, but studies show an average of seven of these people are murdered every night. If this rate applied in reality, then in just 50 days everyone in the United States would be killed and the last left could turn off the TV. (Medved, 1995, pp. 157–158)

Bushman and Anderson (2001) develop an analogy of the studies on media violence to the case on tobacco:

- Not everyone who smokes gets lung cancer. Not everyone who gets lung cancer smokes. Similarly, watching violence does not always lead to aggressive behavior, and human history has certainly shown aggressive behavior is quite possible without violent media at all.
- Smoking is not the only factor causing lung cancer, but it is an important one. Violence in the media is not expected to be more than one factor in the cause of aggression.
- The first cigarette can be repulsive, but repeated exposure reduces the sickening effects. Smokers over time can start craving more. The first exposure to violence can make a person anxious and fearful, but repeated exposure leads to desensitization. Some viewers can start craving more.
- Short-term effects of smoking are not a big problem. The effects can melt away fairly quickly. Watching one violent show is not likely to cause problems, and any aggressive tendencies fostered can be gone before much time has passed. It is a long-standing pattern, not individual instances, that is the problem in both cases.
- Long-term cumulative effects can be severe. It takes many years of daily smoking, or viewing of violent media, to cause the health problems from tobacco or the likelihood of becoming a habitual violent offender from viewing the media.
- In both cases, there is a powerful industry that makes money by

having people consume its product. The industry has argued it is not so harmful and has sought to hide or counter the accumulating scientific evidence.

One major difference, however, is that while journalists generally no longer portray health problems from tobacco as being in dispute, they still treat the issue of violence in the media as if it were. While the empirical data has been accumulating, news reports have gotten weaker in relaying this information to the public (Bushman & Anderson, 2001). Journalists are financially connected to those putting out fictional violent media; a major part of their revenue comes from advertisements for such shows. Many journalists also commonly portray real-life violence themselves, and hope for higher ratings.

This has clear public policy implications, if there are efforts to encourage media people to be more responsible. This would not necessarily be done through government since there are freedom-of-speech considerations. The media is itself a large institution and can be subject to the same kinds of actions. Researchers can be clearer about communicating, through the media itself and through other forums such as the Internet. Organized groups can also take public actions.

The actions of private individuals apply here. As with all actions of private lifestyle, it has more impact if done by large numbers, but being done by small numbers is often a necessary prelude.

This does leave one question unanswered: what about the context of the violence? When the hero uses violence to solve a problem, then the desensitization and modeling mechanisms can be expected to apply. When the violence *is* the problem, and the hero uses nonviolent techniques to counter it, then a different psychological impact can be expected. The sympathy of the audience is with the victims in that case, not with the perpetrators. In the movie *Gandhi*, for example, there were several instances of violence, including a massacre in India. Movies such as *Schindler's List* and *The Scarlet and the Black* show Nazi violence, with heroes doing what they can to counter it, using creative methods with no violence. The use of violence as a problem to be solved nonviolently in a story is generally not covered under the many studies, which are primarily considering the use of violence as a problem solver or source of amusement. Active nonviolence in a story is fairly infrequent in television and movies. The impact of its presence on subsequent behavior is one area that has not been nearly as well studied.

Vegetarianism

Former Beatle Paul McCartney has said if slaughterhouses had glass walls, everyone would go vegetarian. Among vegetarians there is a widespread attitude that their diet is a form of nonviolent action on behalf of animals that are otherwise treated cruelly in factory farm conditions and then brutally killed. Slaughterhouse workers also have very high rates of injurious accidents and turnover. There are environmental effects, with meat production being second only to cars in amount of ecological damage caused. The production of meat uses up so many resources it would be impossible to sustain the current world population on the current American average consumption of meat, yet the earth could easily feed several times its current population on a vegetarian diet. The meatless diet also serves as disease prevention (Messina & Burke, 1997). Vegetarians have argued that while other problems of violence are difficult and perhaps dangerous to solve, with little that ordinary people can do as individuals, the vegetarian diet is an everyday peace action that is remarkably straightforward in its ease and its peaceful effects.

Some vegetarians have put forward as a hypothesis the psychological point that consumption of meat makes individuals more prone to violence, and lack of consuming meat makes people less so (for example, see Adams, 1990). Empirical testing of this is difficult. There is a correlation between being prone to violence and assertive meat consumption. However, when meat is regarded as a luxury, privileged men eat more of it than poor men or women. The fact that powerful men may be more prone to violence than the men or women they dominate is already explainable without taking note of meat consumption.

Furthermore, if vegetarians are less inclined to violence than others, this can be explained by self-selection, by greater reflecting on peacefulness. Even those who become vegetarian for health reasons are more thoughtful about their habits and may therefore be more mindful about not using violence in a street brawl or domestic arguments. There is certainly no evidence that vegetarian advocacy organizations are less argumentative than those of other social issues.

Research on this would be exceedingly difficult to do. Most people are disinclined to use violence much in their personal lives in any event, and those who do have lifestyles in which violence is common have far too many confounding variables. Creative methods of testing the hypothesis may yet arise, however.

There has also been some psychological study of the imagery involved in using metaphors of meat or of slaughter of animals in other situations of violence. For example, Carol Adams (1990) applies this at length to violent male domination of women. The very use of the word "slaughter" to describe battle is an illustration of this phenomenon.

Work

Practically all organizations working to prevent or remedy various kinds of violent action require volunteer work. All need fund-raising and administrative work. Some provide services such as shelters for victims of domestic abuse, assistance for women in problem pregnancies, treatment programs for ex-convicts, and emotional support for the aftermath for those who have been involved in combat, abortion, or crime. Others provide education in an attempt to help people better understand issues, which affects either their lifestyles or their input into public policy. Many provide training, art, practical support, and research.

The fine art of motivating volunteers is not necessarily easy. They need to have a sense that their contribution is substantial, needed, and esteemed. Knowing the different types of volunteers is also crucial to anyone trying to coordinate them. There are those who say they will get something done by next Thursday and they really mean a week from next Thursday; some who say next Thursday but they will actually get it to you the previous Tuesday because they like to overestimate to be sure; some who will never get it to you at all; and, of course, some can be relied on to get it done by next Thursday. Some work well alone and others need more supervision. Some cannot say no when they really should, and of those, some will simply not do the task and others will do it but with seething resentment. Some need to work in groups. All need to feel appreciated.

As for paying jobs, there is a campaign in colleges to have graduating seniors take a pledge to consider the social and environmental aspects of any jobs. The pledge is: "I pledge to explore and take into account the social and environmental consequences of any job I consider and will try to improve these aspects of any organizations for which I work." Students define what being "responsible" means to them. Graduates who voluntarily signed the pledge have turned down jobs they did not feel morally comfortable with and have worked to make changes once on the job. For example, some have promoted recycling at their organization. In one case, a graduate helped to convince her employer to refuse a chemical weapons contract.

Entrepreneurs in small businesses are a form of economic activity preferred by some as a way of being essentially their own bosses. Compared with large organizations, small businesses can have quicker flexibility for ecological concerns and more individualized arrangements for employees. They also do not have the desire or capability to engage in the kind of massive violence large corporations sometimes do to protect profits. From small farmers to mom-and-pop stores to cooperatives, many who wish to avoid giving business to objectionable large corporations select smaller businesses instead. Some people contemplating employment find the more ethical climate and the closer relationships more desirable.

A knowledge of burnout and its prevention, as covered in chapter 3, is also crucial to anyone working. Not everyone is aware of this psychological danger. Those directing volunteer work need to take burnout prevention into account when making arrangements, and those in paying jobs need to pay attention to how well the workplace accommodates the need to avoid this problem. Knowledgeable people can educate volunteers and coworkers.

Religion

The fact that there have been religious underpinnings to many wars makes some psychological sense, for several reasons:

- People wish to see themselves as good people, and use reasoning that explains why they are.

- To move to war rather than talking out a problem, the issue at hand needs to have cosmic significance, not be some ordinary run-of-the-mill difficulty.

- Some rulers cynically use religion to manipulate their subjects into violent confrontations that are actually designed for their own material benefit. Others do the same by rationalizing a religious motivation, even to themselves.

- Ethnic conflicts are often presented as religious conflicts. The different ethnic groups want to establish their superiority in terms other than mere ethnicity.

- Religion helps establish group cohesion, which is essential to the success of any violent social enterprise.

On the other hand, religion has also clearly been part of the motivation for nonviolent campaigns. The civil rights movement of the 1960s, for example, was organized out of the African American churches. The cosmic significance of the struggle is every bit as important to those who must make sacrifices for its achievement. The group cohesion needed for successful wars is also essential to campaigns of peace.

Thus, religion is a major factor in the study of war and peace, and it goes both ways. Religion based on dogma and a sense of justice that precludes mercy and justifies one's own social group at the expense of others is called upon to assist violent enterprises. Religion based on compassion and a sense of justice that includes mercy and expands to all humanity is called upon to assist various forms of effort for human betterment.

This is why one of the first of the ancient literatures to assert the need for peace was by ancient Hebrew prophets, who also railed against what they perceived as the misuse of religion. They argued against the use of ritual blood sacrifices. They were outraged by priestly cover-ups of the oppression of the poor. They denounced continued use of idols that would tell the rulers what they wanted to hear, that conquering was good. They established the idea that ethical behavior had a standard that was not simply what the king decreed it to be. They helped develop the concept that there were universal standards for behavior that apply to all. This concept is crucial to the development of nonviolent campaigns by oppressed groups that appeal to conscience.

Every major and most minor contemporary religions have a tradition of nonviolence to draw from. They also all have traditions of violence. Archbishop Desmond Tutu of South Africa gives an explanation of how religious belief works in violence and nonviolence:

> The perpetrators of apartheid . . . read the Bible, they went to church, and how they went to church! . . . Many times our people were left perplexed by this remarkable fact, that those who treated them so abominably were not heathen but those who claimed to be fellow Christians who read the same Bible . . . The Bible they read and which we read is quite categorical—that which endowed human beings, every single human being without exception, with worth, infinite worth, is not this or that biological or any other extrinsic attribute. No, it is the fact that each one of us has been created in the image of God . . . each one of us is a God-carrier, God's viceroy, God's representative. It is because of this fact that to treat one such person as if he or she were less than this is veritably blasphemous. It is like spitting in the face of God. That is what filled some of us with such a passionate commitment to fight for justice and freedom . . . The Bible turned out to be the most subversive thing around in a situation of injustice and oppression. (Tutu, 1999, pp. 92–93)

Another connection of religion to war and peace is that religion offers stories, metaphors, and images that help people to understand what is happening to them. Some live under extreme circumstances, but all have at least everyday frustrations. These respond well to religious stories and imagery that allow people to gain some perspective that goes beyond their own limits in time and space. From individual predicaments to large-scale movements for social justice, for emotional nourishment, intellectual understanding, and gaining in willpower, these images connect current circumstances with those of other times and places.

The ancient Babylonian creation story has the god Marduk slaying Tianmut and dividing her body to make the earth and sky. The Hebrew story in Genesis, by contrast, starts with a process of creation that is quite orderly, logical, and *peaceful*. The difference between these two images for the nature of reality can be expected to have a psychological influence on subsequent perceptions and behavior. In psychology, the most extensive work on this point has been initiated by Carl Jung (pronounced "yoong"), with his concept of archetypes and the collective unconscious. Many other psychologists have also worked with how stories, images, and metaphors have meaning and help people interpret their circumstances.

COPING AND HEALING THROUGH ART

War

Stories and poetry of war have a long history—in fact, they are just about as old as history. Antiwar literary works also have a long history.

In the Greek tradition, the play by Aristophanes called *Lysistrata* was a comedy in which the women of Athens get together with the women of Sparta to go on a sex strike to stop their men from fighting. Several of the Hebrew prophets have negative remarks to make about war, and poetic images such as beating swords into ploughshares or the lion lying down with the lamb are still used.

The poetry of specific wars before the twentieth century has been almost entirely about the glories involved in that war. The poetry was often commissioned by the victors or otherwise intended to edify the rulers. It may have also helped people process their feelings about the war (Shay, 1994; 2002). Most importantly, the poetry that was published (and is therefore still available) was rarely written by combat veterans.

One exception is George Gasciogne, who died in 1577. He fought in the wars of Holland against Spain. He wrote a poem called *Dulce Bellem Inexpertis*, which gave some indication of Posttraumatic Stress Disorder ("The broken sleepes, the dreadfull dreames, the woe / Which wonne with warre and cannot from him goe"). He also comments bitterly in the poem that those who believe war to be sweet have never fought in one.

At around the beginning of the twentieth century, combat veterans translating their experiences into poetry became relatively common. Several instances can be found from the world wars. An explosion of such poetry occurred among veterans of the American war in Vietnam. Some of the poems mirrored the glories of past war poetry and involved bragging, fond memories of camaraderie, or sarcastic put-downs of the enemy. Much of it, however, was quite negative about the experience; during and after the American war in Vietnam, several books full of such negative poetry were published. These poems tended to focus on one of three broad themes: the hellishness of the war experiences, the absurdity of the war experiences or decisions that led to them, and various aspects of the psychological aftermath.

Paintings and drawings are another art form commonly used to help people cope with traumatic circumstances. There are famous painters such as Picasso who have offered classic pictures in this way. Children who witness war and its results are the most prolific picture drawers, using crayons, paints, pencils, or anything available to translate their experience to paper. Child's-eye view art tends to show simple themes untouched by all the rationalizations and euphemisms of adults. It can be quite blunt. Along with frequent spontaneous use of art by children, therapists often encourage this form of expression as part of a therapy program.

The relative disappearance of war songs is worthy of psychological consideration. Robust songs that motivate soldiers and make the general population feel a part of the effort have been common throughout history, up to World War II. There is a comparative dearth of such songs for the many wars that followed. Antiwar songs became more prominent during this period. While one could search and find the songs that are more pro-war, they are fairly scarce, certainly in comparison with what one finds in previous wars. LeShan (1992) suggests this is because the songs go with a shift to a mythic mode of thinking (see "Passions of War" in chapter 1) and the later wars never involved such a shift. Various other psychological theories could also be offered for this historical development.

By the time of the September 11 attacks of 2001, when the United States suffered a large-scale assault on its own soil, the songs that rallied people were once again robust. The two major ones, however, were "God Bless America" and "America the Beautiful." Both are peaceful and asking for divine intervention; they are lacking in the anger, hatred, or enemy images common to war songs. They celebrate togetherness of the in-group, but without a stated desire for aggression against the out-group. This remarkable development bears further psychological scrutiny.

Antiwar developments have grown over the course of time. Mark Twain in his cynicism on the human condition was particularly biting in his satire, as seen in both *The War Prayer* and his parody of *The Battle Hymn of the Republic*—"In a sordid slime harmonious / Greed was born in yonder ditch / With a longing in his bosom / And for others' goods an itch / As Christ died to make men holy / Let men die to make us rich / Our lust goes marching on" (Anderson, 1972). The nineteenth century saw an upsurge in antiwar literature, associated with the general social movements toward human betterment of the time. The twentieth century saw even more of a rise.

Movies that deal with the theme of war have seen a similar development over time. Early films tended to sanitize and glorify war, with later releases less likely to do so. Movies that are clearly opposed to war have become more frequent than they were in the early decades of the industry, and those that are not clearly opposed to war are at least more realistic about what war actually entails.

A peace studies course on war in literature could be very rich and much more detailed. The point here is the psychology of that literature: the storytelling and imagery can have psychological uses for perpetuating or opposing war, or for the psychological processing of the war's consequences.

Nuclear Anxieties

Unlike war, insights on the human mind to be gained from nuclear images are recent, limited to 1945 and later. Artistic imagery began at the beginning, with Robert Oppenheimer, the lead scientist involved in designing the atom bomb and regarded as its father. Upon seeing the first test, he associated it with the poetic image from the *Bhagavad Gita*: "If the radiance of a thousand suns were to burst at once into the sky, that would be like the splendor of the mighty one . . . I am Death, the Shatterer of Worlds."

In the realm of movies, there are those dealing with the theme of how terrible the aftermath of distressing scenarios would be, such as *On the Beach*. There are others that deal with the absurdity in exaggerated satire, such as *Dr. Strangelove, or How I Learned to Stop Worrying and Love the Bomb*, or in unexaggerated satire, such as *War Games*. In the realm of music, worries range from serious songs decrying nuclear weapons as an injustice, to jocular songs using humor to help defuse the tension, such as Tom Lehrer's 1959 song, "We Will All Go Together When We Go." Poetry followed similar lines; in the jocular category, there was as an anonymous limerick:

To crush the tiny atom
All mankind was intent.
Now any day
The atom may
Return the compliment.

There is also artwork suggesting that people were working through nuclear worries without an explicit anti-nuclear statement. In 1954, the movie *Godzilla: King of the Monsters* came out, the first scene of which was the destruction of Tokyo. This originated and was set in Japan, the location of the only two explosions of nuclear devices deliberately used against living people, just nine years previously. A scientist in the movie speculates that it is the explosion of the test hydrogen bombs that has brought Godzilla out, and no alternative theory is ever offered. The monster has radiation in its footsteps and atomic breath that burns. The nuclear connection is unambiguous.

Throughout the 1950s and early 1960s, there followed a range of movies with the theme of huge destructive monsters, from pterodactyls to giant turtles and praying mantises, and several more appearances of Godzilla. Many of the previews, designed to get people to attend the movies, stated explicitly that the hydrogen bombs were useless against these monsters.

Destructive invasions by Martians and other extraterrestrials was also a common and associated theme. In *The Day the Earth Stood Still*, this theme was turned around so that the extraterrestrials, in an effort to protect themselves, wanted to strong-arm humans into getting rid of the atomic weapons. The man representing races from outer space thus also represented the external view of ourselves, our ability to see things from the perspective of an outsider. In the much later *Superman IV: The Quest for Peace* from the 1980s, the all-American space alien, Superman, threw all nuclear weapons into the sun, to everyone's approval.

More recently, nuclear themes have mixed with other anxieties about technology run amok, a genre that essentially began with the classic *Frankenstein*. *Jurassic Park* had a picture of the father of the atomic bomb, Robert Oppenheimer, on a desk near the beginning of the movie, making a fairly explicit connection between the science of nuclear technology and the fictitious technology of cloning dinosaurs, which was about to wreak so much havoc throughout the film. In *Godzilla 2000*, a Japanese movie dubbed into other languages, the monster was endangering the computer network. This is a more recent technological anxiety, especially on people's minds that particular year. The final lines of the movie also took a turn of internal symbolism. The monster had just turned away from two scientists and a journalist, mid-rampage, after having looked at them carefully. With background music, the first scientist said, "We scientists produced this monster—Godzilla—and ever since, we tried to destroy him." The journalist said, "But then why—why does he keep protecting us?" The other scientist responds: "Maybe because Godzilla is inside each one of us." Thus, an action movie takes a psychological turn.

An interesting point about these symbolic expressions of nuclear anxiety in the monster movies is that the symbols are large animals—that is, predators. In the case of *Jurassic Park*, the motivation of the animals as being predators is unambiguous. Fear of large-animal predators has much more ancient roots in the human mind.

Quite a few of the later movies, from *War Games* to *Godzilla 2000*, and certainly *Dr. Strangelove*, also have more bits of humor. When art is a psychological coping mechanism for anxieties, it may be a logical outgrowth that the coping mechanism of humor is introduced as the themes develop over time and the initial fears settle down into chronic life situations.

The Poor and Oppressed

The literature of those suffering material deprivation is quite extensive. Most folk literature comes from this group. Music goes from old ballads to jazz, blues, and country music, from Southern Gospel to Negro spirituals and Black Gospel. Other art forms include folk stories, folk paintings, and artistically dramatic preaching or storytelling styles. The art that arises first from poor communities has been rich in meaning, expressiveness, and themes that serve as coping mechanisms for the problems of life.

Many of these problems expand beyond the poor. The poor themselves have also often advanced to greater material abundance and are accordingly no longer poor. For both reasons, the art forms have expanded beyond the poor to enrich entire cultures.

Shelby Steele commented on this:

The extreme experience of slavery—its commitment to broken-willed servitude—was so intense a crucible that it must have taken a kind of genius to survive it. In the jaws of slavery and segregation, blacks created a life-sustaining form of worship, rituals for every human initiation from childbirth to death, a rich folk mythology, a world-famous written literature, a complete cuisine, a truth-telling comic sensibility and, of course, some of the most glorious music the world has ever known. (Steele, 2001, p. 23)

One particular kind of literature is peculiar to the psychology of intense periods of oppression. When people are undergoing executions, torture, or massacres because of the nature of their group, and the dangers are acute, ever-present, and feared to come at arbitrary times, then apocalyptic literature often becomes very appealing to members of that group. This literature is characterized by heavy symbolism and cosmic themes, most especially of end times and ultimate resolutions of current conflicts. The symbols are sometimes necessary for members of the group to communicate their points without detection by the persecuting group, but they are also necessary for the grand and universal nature of the themes involved.

Examples of apocalyptic themes in ancient Hebrew literature include the last six chapters of the book of Daniel and the book of Ezekiel. In the early Christian literature, the bulk of the book of Revelation, the final book of the Christian Bible, is among the most famous examples of this kind of literature. Daniel is believed by many scholars to have been written at the time the Jews were under intense pressure from Antiochus, a king who was insisting the Jews abandon their own culture and religion in favor of Greek views. Ezekiel was written at another time when Judaism was under great persecution. Revelation was probably written in the 90s, by a man who identified himself as being exiled on a penal island for his beliefs.

The psychology of this literature may be helped by the understanding that realistic fear of being targets of violence at frequent and arbitrary times, along with memories of friends and loved ones who have already been such victims, was at the core of the symbolism. One of the major concerns at such a time is that members will be strongly tempted to leave the group. People might disavow their beliefs, their faith, or their group membership to avoid being tortured or killed; many did succumb to this temptation. A felt need to maintain the values and beliefs in the face of extreme pressure requires extreme counterpressure.

That counterpressure comes in the form of the cosmic themes, the grand symbols that make clear this is no ordinary, mundane conflict. The stakes are high. There are forces more vast and powerful than the everyday reality understood by the senses. While it may seem that offering a pinch of incense and saying "Caesar is Lord" is a small price to pay to avoid torture, apocalyptic literature treats it otherwise. That small act supports a system of vast structural violence, deception, and direct violence. That small act subverts the firm convictions needed by large numbers of people if violence is to be effectively opposed.

The apocalyptic literature becomes very popular among groups under great persecution because it bolsters their case. It adds to their fortitude in facing the violence aimed at them. With this imagery, they can believe they are not insignificant people facing impossible odds, as it would appear on the surface. Instead, they are crucial people in a cosmic drama that is bound to be resolved in their favor.

This writing comes about and gets into the conventional literature on the force of its popularity. When people who do not have the experience of such intense abuse read it, they tend to interpret it differently. Many see symbols of end times and try to find out what kind of current events might fit these symbols to see if end times are coming. They are practically always able to find current events that fit the symbols because they are designed to fit common dynamics of social and historical events. Their original psychological function, however, did not rely on treating the symbols as if they were magical predictions. They were not magic, but a way of turning the conflict of the time from one of apparent hopelessness to the utmost in hope.

As to the remainder of the literature of the poor and oppressed, some can have a markedly psychologically unhealthy aspect. The literature can, in turn, oppress others. The songs of "gangsta rap," for example, often have lyrics sung by Black men that are abusive of Black women. When asked if such women had not suffered enough bigotry, the answer given was that the singers were men who were reacting to their own oppression. The people who oppressed them include those who held lynchings in the South. The literature of the Ku Klux Klan is full of hatred. This is also the literature of the oppressed, however. Klansmen are generally poor people because they have been treated unjustly and are rightfully angry about it. In both cases, however—the "gangsta" rappers and the Klansmen—the frustration is aimed at innocent targets. Innocents become scapegoats because the deserving targets of their anger can and do strike back. It can be deadly to provoke them.

The task in this case becomes finding nonviolent alternatives for expressing the frustration. Some of these alternatives, from the civil rights revolution to unions, can have dangers of their own, but they have the strong advantage of being practical. Their targets are the actual causes of the frustrations, and they are dealing with these targets constructively.

Stories Promoting Peace

There are several questions that psychological research could answer in regard to nonviolent stories:

- What are the effects of stories that encourage nonviolent as opposed to violent problem solving?
- Can stories encourage more flexible thinking, more creativity in approaching problems? How do they affect people's sense of their ability to use nonviolence?
- Are there differences in impact of true stories and fictional stories?
- What kind of impact do adult stories have, and children's stories? Does the best use of various kinds of stories vary by developmental stages?

Disney movies are typical fare for children. Usually, there is a clearly identified villain who is then disposed of at the end by being killed—frequently by lengthy falling. Some have suggested that this is attractive because it is a symbolic way of getting rid of fears. However, it also fits an old mythological mode supporting violence as a way of dealing with dehumanized enemies. One exception among Disney films is *Pocahontas*, in which the heroine successfully uses courageous nonviolence to prevent violence. Another is *The Emperor's New Groove*, in which a peasant is offered the opportunity to avoid the use of violence himself, by allowing easily foreseen violence to solve his problems for him. He nevertheless follows his conscience, accepts danger to himself to protect the man who is causing his problem, and in the end his perseverance benefits him and everyone else. Would these kinds of plots be more likely to underlie the development of nonviolent personalities? If empirical studies find this, it may eventually have an influence on the artistic community, as well as a private-lifestyle impact on parents.

For adult literature, stories can also be used to explore social issues in depth. Issues of racism, foreign policy, military matters, the court and police systems, and a wide range of other peace and social justice issues have been dealt with through stories. Education about important historical events is also often done by turning those into movies, such as *Gandhi*, or into plays and books. When plays for the purpose of educating on an issue are done out in public without official sanction, this is called guerrilla theater or street theater.

Some forms of literature are more effective at inducing audiences to reflect more on the issues than others. The television miniseries *Roots*, by depicting a realistic history of American slavery and its aftermath from the viewpoint of one intergenerational family, had an impact so clear it was still documented in a television special on its twenty-fifth anniversary. It offered an education on American race issues that people were grateful to receive. On the other hand, there is question over the impact of depicting the aftermath of nuclear attack, as was done in a television movie called *The Day After*. Did it have the effect of causing people to be more supportive of nuclear disarmament, or did it instead make people more anxious about increasing nuclear arms on the idea this would insure their safety? Many people may not have taken it seriously at all. For many reasons psychologists can study, the film seemed to have minimal impact (Schofield & Pavelchak, 1985).

The techniques of psychological research can be used to ascertain the actual effect of works of art that are intended to cause reflection or changes in attitudes. In some cases, something may be more effective with one group, while something different is more effective with another. Doing the research rather than simply assuming the impact is what artists suppose can be an important contribution of peace psychology to activists.

CONCLUSION

In the introduction, we asked this as a basic question for peace psychology: "What causes violence, and what can be done to counter it?" Chapter 1 covered major psychological theories and evidence of what causes violence, while chapter 7 considered theories applied to specific issues. Countering these and causing people to be active in doing so was covered in chapter 3, with chapter 4 discussing how the dynamics of active nonviolence might work. Chapters 5 and 6 took common problem-solving approaches to countering and preventing violence, while chapter 8 finished with ongoing and chronic matters of lifestyle and culture.

Was the question thoroughly answered? Of course not; we do not yet have thorough answers. This book only covered major ideas about what is known at this point, and only in the field of psychology. On a subject that inspires so much passionate debate and reflection, many points that some would regard as crucial were undoubtedly left out. What is known so far is also probably a small portion of what can be learned, which is why areas needing research were mentioned constantly.

The book also dealt with general concepts, and used specifics mainly as examples. The reader is familiar with many important events of which the writer is utterly ignorant, because at the time of writing, the events have not yet happened. Applying concepts to new events, and modifying them accordingly, will be a continual task.

However, there is more to peace psychology than this question. Just as physical health is more than the absence of disease, peace is more than the absence of war or violence. Health professionals spend more time on studying disease and its prevention, and peace professionals spend more time studying violence and its prevention. Yet ordinary people can spend more time on diet, exercise, hygiene, and stress reduction than on medicine for their physical health. They can similarly spend more time cultivating peace-promoting practices and culture than on dealing with violence and conflict. Peace psychologists want to know how to be practical in preventing violence or ameliorating its effects, but it is also important to find out how to encourage or facilitate more ordinary people to cultivate the arts of peace promotion.

FURTHER READING

Community-Based Social Marketing

Fostering Sustainable Behavior: An Introduction to Community-Based Social Marketing. Official Web site: http://www.cbsm.com.

Communication Skills

Rosenberg, M. B. (1999). *Nonviolent communication: A language of compassion*. Del Mar, CA: PuddleDancerPress.
Web site for the Center for Nonviolent Communication: http://www.cnvc.org.

Child Rearing

Web site for Positive Discipline: http://www.positivediscipline.com. "Our mission is to create peace in the world through peace in homes and classrooms."

Entertainment

Bushman, B. J., & Anderson, C. A. (2001). Media violence and the American public: Scientific facts versus media misinformation. *American Psychologist, 56*, 477–489.

Vegetarianism

Web site for Physicians Committee for Responsible Medicine: http://www.pcrm.org.
Web site for Psychologists for the Ethical Treatment of Animals: http://www.psyeta.org.
Web site for Vegetarian Resource Group: http://vrg.org.

Jobs

Web site for the Graduation Pledge of Social and Environmental Responsibility: http:// www.manchester.edu / academic / programs / departments / peace__ studies/files/gpa.html.

Religion

The area of applying religion to nonviolence is extensive. Below is offered a sampling of books from different traditions, but this is not intended to be a summary of the best.

Buddhism

Thich, N. H. (1993). *Love in action: Writings on nonviolent social change*. Berkeley, CA: Parallax Press.

Christianity

Wink, W. (1998). *The powers that be: Theology for a new millennium.* New York: Doubleday.

Hinduism

Gandhi, M. (1957). *An autobiography: The story of my experiments with truth.* Boston: Beacon Press.

Islam

Easwaran, E. (1999). *Nonviolent soldier of Islam: Badshah Khan, a man to match his mountains.* Tomales, CA: Nilgiri Press.

Judaism

Wilcock, E. (1994). *Pacifism and the Jews.* Stroud, Gloucestershire: Hawthorn Press.

A Short Chronology of Peace Psychology

The discipline of psychology is generally accounted as beginning in 1879 with its first laboratory, yet has philosophical roots going back to ancient times. Similarly, the subdiscipline of peace psychology is probably best accounted as launched by the essay of William James in 1910, yet builds on long-standing musings about mental processes and behavior of war and peace from many religions and philosophies. More recently, influential seventeenth-century Czech education reformer Jan Amos Comenius proposed that the means to peace is education, which is international and universal. Early nineteenth-century Quaker writer Jonathan Dymond (1824) wrote a treatise on the causes and effects of war using reasoning that foreshadows many current psychological concepts. In 1905, Mark Twain wrote "The War Prayer," still used as a classic literary description of the psychology of war hysteria (Anderson, 1972).

1910   William James writes the classic essay, "The Moral Equivalent of War."

1912–1914 Maria Montessori publishes books on her teaching method, with many more throughout her life.

1924   Social psychologist Mary Parker Follet pioneers the concept of resolving conflicts by integrating instead of balancing interests.

1927   William McDougall, who had served in a British hospital during World War I and was thereby motivated to study peace strategies, publishes *Janus: The conquest of war. A psychological inquiry.*

1930   Ivan Pavlov, famous for experiments on conditioned responses, promotes a petition arguing "the present armament policies do not furnish any safety to the peoples of the world and in fact, lead all nations to economic disaster. That this policy makes a new war inevitable. That in the future every war will be a war of extermination. That the declaration of peace in behalf of governments remain futile as long as these governments keep on delaying disarmament, which should be the logical sequel to renouncing war" (in Nathan & Norden, 1968, p. 106).

1931   William McDougall predicts the coming of nuclear weapons: "if some physicist were to realize the brightest dream of this kind and teach us to unlock the energy within the atom, the whole race of man would live under the threat of sudden destruction, through the malevolence of some cynic, the inadvertence of some optimist, or the benevolence of some pessimist" (McDougall, 1931, pp. 44–45).

1936   The Society for the Psychological Study of Social Issues (SPSSI) is established, receives divisional status in the American Psychological Association (APA) in 1937, and is still going strong.

1945   A statement, "Human Nature and Peace: A Statement by Psychologists" is released to the press and public officials with 2,038 signatures.

1946   SPSSI issues report authored by David Krech, which opens: "Atomic energy has become a psychological problem." The report offered a six-point program, and was published in *The American Psychologist.* Features of it received widespread media attention and positive response.

1947   The British leave India after decades of successful nonviolent resistance. Experience now shows nonviolent action to be a plausible strategy in a real-world setting. A subsequent wave of movements gives peace psychologists ample material from which to build theory, concepts, and applications of psychological principles.

1948   Peace Studies as a scholarly focus of inquiry begins as a program at Manchester College under the guidance of Gladys Muir.

1952   The Research Exchange for the Prevention of War is founded, with psychologists being the majority. Using the term "prevention of war" instead of "peace" was due to the emerging atmosphere of McCarthyism, which continued to severely dampen peace psychology and the entire peace movement throughout the 1950s.

1957   The bulletin of the Research Exchange turns into *The Journal of Conflict Resolution,* an interdisciplinary journal in international relations. SPSSI takes over the remainder of the functions, so the Research Exchange is laid to rest.

1957–1960   Several trips by American psychologists to the Soviet Union occur, many sponsored by APA.

1959   APA authorizes a survey of seventy-five psychologists of various specialties who had been involved in peace issues on how psychologists might contribute to "maintenance of peace." The report is published in *The American Psychologist* and leads to an ad hoc committee that a year later becomes the standing Committee on Psychology in National and International Affairs (CPNIA).

1961   Psychologists for Peace is established in June, intended as a first step toward an international organization. Activities include a "walk for peace" in January 1962, a petition to President Kennedy on the Psychology of Negotiations signed by five hundred social scientists, and a workshop on the psychology of fallout shelters.

1961–1963   The Kennedy administration especially welcomes advice of academics, including psychologists. Senator Hubert Humphrey also wants to involve psychologists in foreign policy matters. This allows psychological knowledge of peace issues to flourish.

1961   On September 4, Ralph K. White gives a speech called "Mirror Images in the East-West Conflict." Senator Thomas J. Dodd puts the speech in the *Congressional Record,* refutes it, and wants White fired from his government post. APA comes to his defense.

1962   Charles Osgood presents his Graduated and Reciprocated Initiatives in Tension-reduction (GRIT) proposal in a book, *An Alternative to War or Surrender.* Osgood sent a copy of the book to President Kennedy and received a personal note from Kennedy's secretary saying the president had read it. Kennedy's later policies suggest he was influenced by it.

1964   The International Peace Research Association is founded.

1965   The first problem-solving workshops to find integrative solutions are held for representatives of governments, in this case the governments of Indonesia, Malaysia, and Singapore. Hostilities cease soon thereafter. Further development of the concept leads to training of diplomats in "second-track" diplomacy.

1968   Outraged by police brutality against antiwar protesters at the Democratic convention in Chicago, the APA votes to move its annual convention away from the city, where it had been set for the following year.

1970   Brazilian Paulo Friere publishes *Pedagogy of the Oppressed*, detailing the adult education method called "conscientization."

1971   The Stanford Prison Experiment, intended to be a simulated prison for two weeks, is shut down after six days due to excessive dehumanization.

1972   Richard Gregg publishes *The Psychology and Strategy of Gandhi's Nonviolent Resistance*. This introduces a psychological foundation for Gandhi's political concepts.

1972   Irving Lester Janis publishes *Victims of Groupthink: A Psychological Study of Foreign-Policy Decisions and Fiascoes*.

1973   Gene Sharp publishes a three-volume foundation work called *The Politics of Nonviolent Action*. The set covers political dynamics, history, and psychological components. It remains foundational.

1974   Stanley Milgram publishes *Obedience to Authority*, reporting experiments that showed an alarmingly high compliance rate with harmful orders from authority figures.

1980   The concept of Posttraumatic Stress Disorder is formally defined and replaces less precise terms such as battle fatigue. An explosion of research ensues.

1982   Psychologists for Social Responsibility (PsySR) is founded and focuses on preventing nuclear war. It currently remains one of the major grassroots networks of psychologists active in peace concerns.

1982   The APA Council of Representatives passes a resolution
              calling for a nuclear freeze, a return to a productive civilian
              economy, and encouraging members to be politically active
              in pursuit of these. APA's Board of Scientific Affairs objects
              strenuously, saying it is inappropriate for a scientific orga-
              nization to engage in social advocacy, but the resolution
              stands.

1984   On October 19, the United States Institute of Peace (USIP)
              is established, created by an act of Congress. Psychologists
              were active in lobbying for and running this government-
              sponsored peace academy.

1986   Ralph K. White edits and publishes *Psychology and the Pre-
              vention of Nuclear War*, sponsored by SPSSI.

1988   Division 48, the division for peace psychology in the APA,
              is established by vote of the association's council. It is still
              large and active.

1989   The first International Symposium on the Contributions of
              Psychology to Peace is held in Bulgaria and attracts peace
              psychologists from a variety of countries. Symposiums con-
              tinue to be held every other year in different countries.

1989   Prominent Salvadoran peace psychologist Ignacio Martín-
              Baró is one of six Jesuit priests, their housekeeper, and her
              daughter who are assassinated by a Salvadoran death
              squad on November 16. There were four memorial sessions
              the following year at the APA convention alone. Martín-
              Baró had been active in providing psychological healing
              services to the traumatized in El Salvador's war, in under-
              standing the subjective state of the population, and in pub-
              lic opinion polling of the population to find what was
              commonly thought. He was active in whatever ways psy-
              chology could be used to promote peace in the midst of a
              brutal war, and he became a victim of that war.

1990   Kulka and colleagues publish the primary report of the
              National Vietnam Veterans Readjustment Study, a large
              government-sponsored study with in-depth questions on
              postwar reactions. Posttraumatic Stress Disorder was a ma-
              jor focus of the study, and was shown to be prevalent in full
              and partial forms.

1994   UNESCO (United Nations Education. Scientific & Cultural
              Organization) commissions a background paper by the

Committee for the Psychological Study of Peace of the International Union of Psychological Science, highlighting the contributions psychology can make to peace and social justice.

1996–1998   In South Africa, the Truth and Reconciliation Commission holds hearings and investigations to deal positively with the aftermath of apartheid. Psychological principles underlie a societywide therapy that shows peaceful adjustments after massive violence in a real-world setting. Commission leader Desmond Tutu publishes a book reporting the experience in 1999 called *No Future without Forgiveness*.

2001   Christie and colleagues publish an anthology of peace psychology papers to be used as a reader in classes, entitled *Peace, Conflict, and Violence: Peace Psychology for the 21st Century*.

References

Adams, C. (1990). *The sexual politics of meat: A feminist-vegetarian critical theory*. New York: Continuum.

Adorno, T. W., Frenkel-Brunswick, E., Levinson, D., & Sanford, R. N. (1950). *The Authoritarian Personality*. New York: Harper & Brothers.

Allport, G. W. (1954). *The nature of prejudice*. Cambridge, MA: Addison-Wesley.

American Psychiatric Association. (1994). *Diagnostic and statistical manual of mental disorders* (4th ed.). Washington, DC: Author.

Anderson, C. A., Arlin, B. J., & Bartholow, B. D. (1998). Does the gun pull the trigger? Automatic priming effects of weapons pictures and weapon names. *Psychological Science, 9,* 308–314.

Anderson, F. (Ed.). (1972). *A pen warmed-up in hell: Mark Twain in protest*. San Francisco: Harper & Row.

Antonovsky, A. (1979). *Health, stress, and coping*. San Francisco: Jossey-Bass.

Antonovsky, A. (1993). Complexity, conflict, chaos, coherence, coercion and civility. *Social Science and Medicine, 37,* 969–974.

Archer, D. (1984). *Violence and crime in cross-national perspective*. New Haven, CT: Yale University Press.

Arendt, H. (1963). *Eichmann in Jerusalem: A report on the banality of evil*. New York: Viking Press.

Arendt, H. (1968). *Between past and future: Eight exercises in political thought* (enlarged ed.). New York: Viking Compass Edition.

Arendt, H. (1972). *Crises of the Republic*. New York: Harcourt Brace Jovanovich.

Arluke, A. (1991). Going into the closet with science: Information control among animal experimenters. *Journal of Contemporary Ethnography, 20,* 306–330.

Atholl, Justin. (1956). *The Reluctant Hangman: The Story of James Berry, Executioner 1884–1892.* Great Britain: The Anchor Press. Ltd., p. 158.

Austin, J. H. (1998). *Zen and the brain: Toward an understanding of meditation and consciousness.* Cambridge, MA: MIT Press.

Bandura, A., Barbanelli, C., Caprara, G. V., & Pastorelli, C. (1996). Mechanisms of moral disengagement in the exercise of moral agency. *Journal of Personality and Social Psychology, 71,* 364–374.

Batsche, G. M., & Knoff, H. M. (1994). Bullies and their victims: Understanding a pervasive problem in the schools. *School Psychology Review, 23,* 165–174.

Beardsworth, A., & Keil, T. (1992). The vegetarian option: Varieties, conversions, motives and careers. *The Sociological Review, 38,* 252–293.

Berkowitz, L., & LePage, A. (1967). Weapons as aggression-eliciting stimuli. *Journal of Personality and Social Psychology, 7,* 202–207.

Best, J. (2001). Social progress and social problems: Toward a sociology of gloom. *The Sociological Quarterly, 42,* 1–12.

Blass, T. (2000). *Obedience to authority: Current perspectives on the Milgram paradigm.* Mahwah, NJ: Lawrence Erlbaum Associates.

Bosch, J. A., DeGeus, E. J., Kelder, A., Veerman, E. C., Hoogstraten, J., & Amerongen, A. V. (2001). Differential effects of active vs. passive coping on secretory immunity. *Psychophysiology, 38,* 836–846.

Boulding, K. E. (1989). *Three faces of power.* Newbury Park, CA: Sage Publications.

Bourke, J. (1999). *An intimate history of killing: Face-to-face killing in twentieth-century warfare.* Great Britain: Granta Books.

Brennan, W. (1995). *Dehumanizing the vulnerable: When word games take lives.* Chicago, IL: Loyola University Press.

Bronfenbrenner, U. (1961). The mirror image in Soviet-American relations: A social psychologist's report. *Journal of Social Issues, 17,* 45–56.

Burton, J. W. (1969). *Conflict and communication: The use of controlled communication in international relations.* London: Macmillan.

Bushman, B. J., & Anderson, C. A. (2001). Media violence and the American public: Scientific facts versus media misinformation. *American Psychologist, 56,* 477–489.

Bushman, B. J., Baumeister, R. F., & Stack, A. D. (1999). Catharsis, Aggression, and Persuasive Influence: Self-fulfilling or self-defeating prophecies? *Journal of Personality and Social Psychology, 76,* 367–376.

Cabana, D. A. (1996). *Death at midnight: The confession of an executioner.* Boston: Northeastern University Press.

Cantril, H. (1950). *Tensions that cause wars.* Urbana: University of Illinois Press.

Carlson, M., Marcus-Newhall, A., & Miller, N. (1990). Effects of situational aggressive cues: A quantitative review. *Journal of Personality and Social Psychology, 58*, 622–633.

Christie, D. J., Wagner, R. V., & Winter, D. D. (2001). *Peace, conflict, and violence: Peace psychology for the 21st century.* Upper Saddle River, NJ: Prentice-Hall.

Christie, R., & Geis, F. (1970). *Studies in Machiavellianism.* New York: Academic Press.

Clark, K. B. (1955). *Prejudice and your child.* Boston: Beacon Press.

Clark, K. B., & Clark, M. P. (1947). Racial identification and preferences in Negro children. In T. M. Newcomb & E. L. Hartley (Eds.), *Readings in social psychology.* New York: Holt, pp. 169–178.

Cohen-Posey, K. (1995). *How to handle bullies, teasers and other meanies.* Highland City, FL: Rainbow Books, Inc.

Conway, L. G., Suedfeld, P., & Tetlock, P. E. (2001). Integrative complexity and political decisions that lead to war or peace. In D. J. Christie, R. V. Wagner, & D. D. Winter (Eds.), *Peace, conflict, and violence: Peace psychology for the 21st century.* Upper Saddle River, NJ: Prentice-Hall.

DeAngelis, T. (2001, November). Understanding and preventing hate crimes. *Monitor on Psychology, 32*, 60–63.

Dollard, J., Doob, L. W., Miller, N. E., Mowrer, O. H., & Sears, R. R. (1939). *Frustration and aggression.* New Haven, CT: Yale University Freer.

Dymond, J. (1824). *An inquiry into war.* Available at: http://www.qhpress.org/texts/dymond/index.html.

Eberstadt, N. (1991, Summer). Population change and national security. *Foreign Affairs, 70*, 115–131.

Ehrenreich, B. (1997). *Blood rites: The origins and passions of war.* New York: Henry Holt and Company.

Elliott, G. C. (1980). Components of pacifism: Conceptualization and measurement. *Journal of Conflict Resolution, 24*, 27–54.

Eron, L. D., Huesmann, R. L., Dubow, E., Romanoff, R., & Yarnel, P. W. (1987). Childhood aggression and its correlates over 22 years. In David H. Cravell, Ian M. Evans, & Clifford R. O'Donnell (Eds.), *Childhood aggression and violence.* New York: Plenum.

Etzioni, A. (1967). The Kennedy experiment. *Western Political Quarterly, 20*, 361–380.

Festinger, L. (1957). *A theory of cognitive dissonance.* Stanford, CA: Stanford University Press.

Fisher, R., & Ury, W. (1981). *Getting to yes: Negotiating agreement without giving in.* Boston: Houghton Mifflin.

Follett, M. P. (1924). *Creative experience,* New York: Longmans Green.

Forbes, H. D. (1997). *Ethnic conflict: Commerce, culture, and the Contact Hypothesis.* New Haven, CT: Yale University Press.

Friedman, M. J., Charney, D. S., & Deutch, A. Y. (Eds.). (1995). *Neurobio-*

logical and clinical consequences of stress. Philadelphia: Lippincott-Raven.

Friere, P. (1970). *Pedagogy of the oppressed.* New York: Seabury.

Galtung, J. (1969). Violence, peace, and peace research. *Journal of Peace Research, 6,* 167–191.

Geen, R. G., & Quanty, M. C. (1977). The catharsis of aggression: An evaluation of a hypothesis. In L. Berkowitz (Ed.), *Advances in experimental social psychology* (Vol. 10). New York: Academic Press, p. 1037.

Glad, B. (Ed.). (1990). *Psychological dimensions of war.* Newbury Park, CA: Sage Publications.

Goodwin, S. A., Operario, D., & Fiske, S. T. (1988). Situational power and interpersonal dominance facilitate bias and inequality. *Journal of Social Issues, 54,* 677–698.

Green, D. P., Abelson, R. P., & Garnett, M. (1999). The distinctive political views of hate-crime perpetrators and white supremacists. In D. A. Prentice & D. T. Miller, *Cultural divides: Understanding and overcoming group conflict.* New York: Russell Sage Foundation.

Green, D. P., Glaser, J., & Rich, A. (1998). From lynching to gay bashing: The elusive connection between economic conditions and hate crime. *Journal of Personality and Social Psychology, 75,* 82–92.

Green, D. P., Strolovitch, P. Z., & Wong, J. S. (1998). Defended neighborhoods, integration, and racially motivated crime. *American Journal of Sociology, 104,* 372–403.

Gregg, R. B. (1972). *The psychology and strategy of Gandhi's nonviolent resistance.* New York: Garland Publishing, Inc.

Grossman, D. (1995). *On killing: The psychological cost of learning to kill in war and society.* Boston: Little, Brown and Company.

Grossman, D., & Degaetano, G. (1999). *Stop teaching our kids to kill: A call to action against TV, movie and video game violence.* New York: Crown Publishers.

Hickey, J. E., & Scharf, P. L. (1980). *Toward a just correctional system: Experiments in implementing democracy in prisons.* San Francisco: Jossey-Bass Publishers.

Hovland, C. I., & Sears, R. R. (1940). Minor studies of aggression: correlations of lynchings with economic indices. *The Journal of Psychology, 9,* 301–310.

James, W. (1910/1971). *The moral equivalent of war, and other essays; and selections from some problems of philosophy.* New York: Harper & Row.

Janis, I. L. (1972). *Victims of groupthink: A psychological study of foreign-policy decisions and fiascoes.* Boston: Houghton Mifflin.

Johnson, E. C. (Ed.). (1960). *Jane Addams: A centennial reader.* New York: The Macmillan Company.

Joint Statement on the impact of entertainment violence on children: Congressional Public Health Summit. (2000, July 26). Retrieved December 4,

2000, from the World Wide Web: http://www.senate.gov/~brownback/violence1.pdf.

Joseph, J. M. (1993). Resiliency and its relationship to productivity and nonviolence. In V. K. Kool (Ed.), *Nonviolence: Social and psychological issues*. Lanham, MD: University Press of America.

Kaufman, J., & Zigler, E. (1987). Do abused children become abusive parents? *American Journal of Orthopsychiatry, 57,* 186–192.

Kelly, T. (1941/1992). *Testament of devotion*. San Francisco: HarperCollins Publishers.

Keniston, A. H. (1990). Dimensions of moral development among nonviolent individuals. In V. K. Kool (Ed.), *Perspectives on nonviolence*. New York: Springer-Verlag, pp. 86–89.

Kevorkian, J. (1991). *Prescription medicide: The goodness of planned death*. Buffalo, NY: Prometheus Books.

King, M. L., Jr. (1958). *Stride toward freedom*. New York: Harper & Row.

Kobasa, S. C. (1979). Stressful life events, personality and health: An inquiry into hardiness. *Journal of Personality and Social Psychology, 37,* 1–11.

Kohlberg, L. (1948). Bed for bananas: A first hand story of the S. S. Redemption and what happened afterwards in Cyprus and in Palestine. *Menorah Journal, 36,* 385–399.

Kohlberg, L. (1984). *The psychology of moral development: The nature and validity of moral stages*. San Francisco: Harper & Row.

Kool, V. K. (Ed.). *Nonviolence: Social and psychological issues*. Lanham, MD: University Press of America.

Kool, V. K, & Keyes, C. L. M. (1990). Explorations in the nonviolent personality. In V. K. Kool (Ed.), *Perspectives on nonviolence*. New York: Springer-Verlag, pp. 17–38.

Kool, V. K., & Sen, M. (1984). The nonviolence test. In D. M. Pestonjee (Ed.), *Second handbook of psychological and social instruments*. Ahemdebad: Indian Institute of Management, pp. 18–54.

Kostelny, K., & Garbarino, J. (2001). The war close to home: Children and violence in the United States. In D. J. Christie, R. V. Wagner, & D. D. Winter (Eds.). *Peace, conflict, and violence: Peace psychology for the 21st century*. Upper Saddle River, NJ: Prentice-Hall, pp. 110–119.

Kulka, R. A., Schlenger, W. E., Fairbank, J. A., Hough, R. L., Jordan, B. K., Marmar, C. R., & Weiss, D. S. (1990). *Trauma and the Vietnam War generation: Report on the findings from the National Vietnam Veterans Readjustment Study*. New York: Brunner/Mazel.

Lederach, J. P. (1995). *Preparing for peace: conflict transformation across cultures*. Syracuse, NY: Syracuse University Press.

Lehrer, T. (1959). We will all go together when we go. On *An evening wasted with Tom Lehrer* [recording]. Warner Bros. Records, Inc.

LeShan, L. (1992). *The psychology of war: Comprehending its mystique and its madness*. Chicago: Noble Press.

Liagin, E. (1996). *Excessive force: Power, politics and population control*. Washington, DC: Information Project for Africa.

Lifton, R. J. (1968/1982). *Death in life: Survivors of Hiroshima*. New York: Basic Books.

Lifton, R. J. (1986). *The Nazi doctors: Medical killing and the psychology of genocide*. New York: Basic Books.

Lifton, R. J., & Falk, R. (1982). *Indefensible weapons: The political and psychological case against nuclearism*. New York: Basic Books.

Linn, D., Linn, S. F., & Linn, M. (1997). *Don't forgive too soon: Extending the two hands that heal*. Mahwah, NJ: Paulist Press.

Linn, R. (1996). *Conscience at war—The Israeli soldier as a moral critic*. Albany: State University of New York Press.

Lockwood, R., & Ascione, R. R. (1998). *Cruelty to animals and interpersonal violence: Readings in research and application*. West Lafayette, IN: Purdue University Press.

Lockwood, R., & Church, A.(1996). Deadly serious: An FBI perspective on animal cruelty. *The Humane Society News, Fall*, 1–4.

MacNair, R. M. (1998). *Sense of Coherence and Machiavellian Personality*. Unpublished paper, University of Missouri at Kansas City.

MacNair, R. M. (2002). *Perpetration-Induced Traumatic Stress: The psychological consequences of killing*. Westport, CT: Praeger Publishers.

Mandel, D. R. (2001). Evil and the instigation of collective violence. *Analyses of Social Issues and Public Policy* (Vol. 2, No. 2). Available at: http://www.asap-spissi.org.

Mann, J. A. (1993). A social psychology of rules of war: A research strategy for studying civilian-based defense. In V. K. Kool (Ed.), *Nonviolence: Social and psychological issues*. Lanham, MD: University Press of America.

Mann, J. A., & Gaertner, S. L. (1991). Support for the use of force in war: The effect of procedural rule violations and group membership. *Journal of Applied Social Psychology, 21* (22), 1793–1809.

Mansfield, S. (1982). *The Gestalts of war: An inquiry into its origins and meanings as a social institution*. New York: The Dial Press.

Marmar, C. R., Weiss, D. S., Schlenger, W. E., Fairbank, J. A., Jordan, B. K., Kulka, R. A., & Hough, R. L. (1994). Peritraumatic dissociation and posttraumatic stress in male Vietnam theater veterans. *American Journal of Psychiatry, 151*, 902–907.

Mayton, D. M. (2001). Gandhi as peacebuilder: The social psychology of satyagraha. In D. J. Christie, R. V. Wagner, & D. D. Winter (Eds.), *Peace, conflict, and violence: Peace psychology for the 21st century*. Upper Saddle River, NJ: Prentice-Hall, pp. 307–313.

McClelland, D. C., & Cheriff, A. D. (1997). The immunoenhancing effects of humor on secretory IgA and resistance to respiratory infections. *Psychology and Health, 12,* 135–148

McClelland, D. C., & Krishnit, C. (1988). The effect of motivation on arousal through films on salivary immunoglobulin A. *Psychology and Health, 2,* 31–52.

McDougall, W. (1931). *World chaos: The responsibility of science.* London: Kegan Paul, Trench, Trubner.

Medved, M. (1995, October). Hollywood's 3 big lies. *Reader's Digest, 147* (882), 155–159.

Messina, V., & Burke, K. I. (1997). Position of the American Dietetic Association: Vegetarian diets. *Journal of the American Dietetic Association, 97,* 1317–1321. Also available on the World Wide Web: http://www.olympus.net/biz/messina/adapaper.htm.

Meyers, D. (2000). The friends, funds, and faith of happy people. *American Psychologist, 55,* 56–67.

Milgram, S. (1974). *Obedience to authority: An experimental view.* New York: Harper & Row.

Miller, C. (2001). Childhood animal cruelty and interpersonal violence. *Clinical Psychology Review, 21,* 735–749.

Moulton, P. P. (Ed.). (1971). *The journal and major essays of John Woolman.* Great Britain: Oxford University Press.

Mullen, T. (1989). *Laughing out loud, and other religious experiences.* Richmond, IN: Friends United Press.

Mulvey, E. P., & Cauffman, E. (2001). The inherent limits of predicting school violence. *American Psychologist, 56,* 797–802.

Nathan, O., & Norden, H. (Eds.). (1968). *Einstein on peace.* New York: Schocken.

Newberg, A., d'Aquili, E., & Rause, V. (2001). *Why God won't go away: Brain science and the biology of belief.* New York: Ballantine Books.

Ney, P. (2001). *Deeply damaged: An explanation for the profound problems arising from aborting babies and abusing children.* Victoria, B.C., Canada: Pioneer Publishing.

Nicholl, C. G. (1999). *Community policing, community justice, and restorative justice: Exploring the links for the delivery of a balanced approach to public safety.* Washington, DC: U.S. Department of Justice, Office of Community Oriented Policing Services.

Noonan, J. T. (1979). *A private choice.* New York: The Free Press.

Olweus, D. (1991). Bully/victim problems among school children: Basic facts and effects of a school based intervention program. In I. Rubin & D. Pepler (Eds.), *The development and treatment of childhood aggression.* Hillsdale, NJ: Earlbaum, pp. 411–447

Osgood, C. E. (1962). *An alternative to war or surrender.* Urbana: University of Illinois Press.

Paik, H., & Comstock, G. (1994). The effects of television violence on antisocial behavior: A meta-analysis. *Communication Research, 21,* 516–546.

Pelton, L. H. (1974). *The psychology of nonviolence.* New York: Pergamon.

Pettigrew, T. F., & Tropp, L. R. (2000). Does intergroup contact reduce prejudice?

Rabinowitz, E. (1963). Five years after. In M. Grodzins (Ed.), *The Atomic Age.* New York: Basic Books, pp. 156–162. Quote on page 156.

Recent meta-analytic findings. In S. Oskamp (Ed.), *Reducing prejudice and discrimination.* Mahwah, NJ: Lawrence Erlbaum Associates.

Roe, K. M. (1989). Private troubles and public issues: Providing abortion amid competing definitions. *Social Science and Medicine, 29,* 1191–1198.

Rouhana, N. N., & Kelman, H. C. (1994). Promoting joint thinking in international conflicts: An Israeli-Palestinian continuing workshop. *Journal of Social Issues, 50,* 157–178.

Ruby, C. L. (2001). Are terrorists mentally deranged? *Analyses of Social Issues and Public Policy* (Vol. 2, No. 1). Available at http://www.asap-spissi.org.

Sapolsky, R. M. (1994). *Why zebras don't get ulcers: A guide to stress, stress-related diseases, and coping.* New York: W. H. Freeman and Company.

Scanlon, D. (1959). The pioneers of international education—1817–1914. *Teacher's College Record, 4,* 214.

Schantz, C. U. (1987). Conflicts between children. *Child Development, 58,* 283–305.

Schlesinger, A. M. (1965). *A thousand days: John F. Kennedy in the White House.* Boston: Houghton Mifflin.

Schofield, J., & Pavelchak, M. A. (1985). *The Day After:* The impact of a media event. *The American Psychologist, 40,* 542–548.

Seligman, M. (1991). *Learned optimism.* New York: A. A. Knopf.

Shapiro, W. (2001, October 3). Groupthink a danger for White House war planners. *USA Today,* 7A.

Sharp, G. (1973). *The politics of nonviolent action* (Vols. 1–3). Boston: Extending Horizons Books.

Sharp, G. (1990). *Civilian-based defense: A post-military weapons system.* Princeton, NJ: Princeton University Press.

Shay, J. (1994). *Achilles in Vietnam: Combat trauma and the undoing of character.* Toronto: Maxwell MacMillan.

Shay, J. (2002). *Odysseus in America: Combat Trauma and the Trials of Homecoming.* New York: Scribner.

Sherif, M. (1966). *In common predicament: Social psychology of intergroup conflict and cooperation.* Boston: Houghton Mifflin.

Shils, E. (1956). *Tormented by secrecy: The background and consequences of American security policies.* Glencoe, IL: Free Press.

Silva, J. A., Derecho, D. V., Leong, G. B., Weinstock, R., & Ferrari, M. M.

(2001). A classification of psychological factors leading to violent behavior in Posttraumatic Stress Disorder. *Journal of Forensic Sciences, 46,* 309–316.

Solursh, L. (1988). Combat addiction: Post-Traumatic Stress Disorder re-explored. *Psychiatric Journal of the University of Ottawa, 13,* 17–20.

Southwick, S. M., Yehuda, R., & Morgan, C. A. (1995). Clinical studies of neurotransmitter alterations in Post-Traumatic Stress Disorder. In M. J. Friedman, D. S. Charney, &A. Y. Deutch (Eds.), *Neurobiological and clinical consequences of stress.* Philadelphia: Lippincott-Raven, pp. 335–350.

Steele, S. (2001, August 27). " . . . or a Childish Illusion of Justice?" *Newsweek,* 23.

Steinberg, L. D., Catalano, R., & Dooley, D. (1981). Economic antecedents of child abuse and neglect. *Child Development, 52,* 975–985.

Such-Baer, M. (1974). Professional staff reaction to abortion work. *Social Casework, July,* 435–441.

Surgeon General Reports. (2001). *Mental health: Culture, race, and ethnicity.* Retrieved from http://phs.os.dhhs.gov/library/mentalhealth/.

Surgeon General's Scientific Advisory Committee on Television and Social Behavior. (1972). *Television and growing up: The impact of televised violence.* Washington, DC: U.S. Government Printing Office.

Tint Alon, B. (2002). *Collective memory, cultural identity, and conflict resolution.* Dissertation in progress, University of Melbourne.

Turner, C. W., Simons, L. S., Berkowitz, L., & Farodi, A. (1977). The stimulating and inhibiting effects of weapons on aggressive behavior. *Aggressive Behavior, 3,* 355–378.

Tutu, D. M. (1999). *No future without forgiveness.* New York: Doubleday.

Vanderhaar, G. A. (n.d.). *Nonviolent response to assault. Solutions to violence: high school course.* Washington, DC: Center for Teaching Peace.

van der Kolk, B. A., Greenberg, M., Boyd, H., & Krystal, J. (1985). Inescapable shock, neurotransmitters, and addiction to trauma: Toward a psychobiology of post traumatic stress. *Biological Psychiatry, 20,* 314–325.

van der Kolk, B. A., McFarlane, A. C., & Weisaeth, L. (Eds.). (1996). *Traumatic stress: The effects of overwhelming experience on mind, body, and society.* New York: Guilford Press.

Wagner, R. V. (1993). The differential psychological effects of positive and negative approaches to peace. In V. K. Kool (Ed.), *Nonviolence: Social and psychological issues.* Lanham, MD: University Press of America.

Wagner, R. V. (2001). The differential psychological effects of positive and negative approaches to peace. In D. J. Christie, R. V. Wagner, & D. D. Winter (Eds.). *Peace, conflict, and violence: Peace psychology for the 21st century.* Upper Saddle River, NJ: Prentice-Hall, pp. 282–294.

Warren, R., & Kurlychek, M. B. (1981). Treatment of maladaptive anger and aggression: Catharsis vs. behavior therapy. *Corrective and Social Psychiatry and Journal of Behavior Technology, Methods, and Therapy, 27,* 135–139.

Widom, C. S. (1989). Does violence beget violence? A critical examination of the literature. *Psychological Bulletin, 106,* 3–28.

Wink, W. (1998). *The powers that be: Theology for a new millennium.* New York: Doubleday.

Wixen, B. (1973). *Children of the rich.* New York: Crown Publishers, Inc.

Wolf, R. S., & Pillemer, K. A. (1989). *Helping elderly victims: The reality of elder abuse.* New York: Columbia University Press.

World Health Organization. (1992). *International statistical classification of diseases and related health problems* (10th rev.). Geneva, Switzerland: Author.

Index

Abortion: back-alley butchers, 185–86; child abuse, 173–74; debate, 43, 114, 120; nuclear weapons reaction, 47; opponents' activities, 99, 141, 199; providers, 37, 59, 185

Abuse, 19, 32–33, 70, 77, 171. *See also* Child abuse; Family violence

Acceptance, 43, 44, 70–71

Active orientation, 72

Adams, Carol, 198

Addams, Jane, 35

Addiction to trauma, 38–39, 48–49, 82

Adolescents, 33

Adrenaline rush, 19, 38, 48

Aesop, 79

Afghanistan, 115

Africa, 117, 137. *See also* South Africa

African Americans, 3, 38, 149, 176, 200. *See also* Black people; Civil rights movement; *Roots*; Slavery

Agentic state, 11, 12

Agents provocateur, 53, 105, 135

Alcohol. *See* Substance abuse

Ali, Mohammed, 65

Allport, Gordon, 122

Al-Qaeda, 166

Alternative energy, 67, 100

Alternatives to Violence Program, 86, 181

Altruistic personality, 60–61

Analyze This, 26

Anger, 70–71, 88, 155, 167, 203

Anger management, 77, 174, 176

Anglo-Boer War, 36, 125

Animal Farm, 54

Animals: behavior, 23, 25; cruelty to, 2, 37, 179–80, 198–99; predators, 23–25, 205

Antisocial personality, 19

Antonovsky, Antonin, 68–69

Apartheid, 125, 137, 165, 201, 218

Apathy, 41, 45, 70, 104, 168

Apocalyptic literature, 206–7

Aquinas, Thomas, 70

Arabs, 74, 166

Archer, Dane, 50–51, 170–71

Arendt, Hannah, 14, 136

Argentina, 168

Aristophanes, 202

Aristotle, 26

Arms races, 163–64

Art, 79, 201–9

Ashoka, King, 73

Asian people, 101, 176

Assisted suicide. *See* Euthanasia
Atheists, 113–14, 120
Atom bomb. *See* Nuclear weapons
Attackers, 88–92, 154–58
Attribution theory, 89
Attributive projection, 119
Augustine, 168
Authoritarian personality, 16–17, 18,
    60, 71, 194
Authority: contact hypothesis, 122;
    destructive obedience, 9–13, 49, 58,
    216; institutional, 13–14;
    legitimation of violence, 51; moral
    development, 64; moral
    disengagement, 2; power, 134–38,
    157–58

Babies, 3, 24, 115, 153, 173–74, 285
Babylonian myth, 201
Back-alley butchers, 185–86
Backlash, 52, 104–5
Bandura, Albert, 1, 12
Bargaining, 70–71
Battle fatigue. *See* Posttraumatic
    Stress Disorder
Bay of Pigs, 14
Beliefs, 6–9, 69–74, 98, 163
Berlin blockade, 168
Berry, James, 36–37
Best, Joel, 150–51
Bhagavad Gita, 203–4
Bible, 73, 79, 112–13, 142, 201, 206–7
Bigotry, 141, 183, 207
Bin Laden, Osama, 167
Biology, 19, 38, 82–84, 112–13
Black people, 101, 122, 140, 152, 206,
    207. *See also* African Americans
Blaming the victim, 2, 6–7, 94, 165,
    173
Blood sacrifice, 24–25, 200
Blood sports, 37, 179
Bloodthirsty, 37
Blowback, 54, 106
Bombing, 4, 18, 52, 114, 177
Boulding, Kenneth, 134, 136
Boycott, 91, 96, 142, 164, 192
Brain, 38, 82–84
Brazil, 75

Brennan, William, 2–3
Brown v. Board of Education, 39
Buddhists/Buddhism, 24–25, 73, 84,
    210
Bullies, 154–58, 176–78
Burnout, 96, 100–103, 107, 148, 191,
    199
Bush, George W., 62, 169
Business, 20, 42, 78, 91, 104, 149, 199

Canada, 117
Cantril, Hadley, 67
Capital punishment. *See* Death
    penalty
Catharsis, 26–27
Catholics, 73–74, 76, 84, 120
Challenge, 68, 92
Changing the script, 156–57
Character education, 78
Child abuse, 3, 26, 173–74, 175
Children: art, 202, 208; burnout, 101;
    conflict skills, 116–17, 154–56;
    education for peace, 63, 74–82, 106;
    effect of violence on, 33–34, 39–41;
    learning violence, 179–80;
    protecting, 4, 20; rearing, 23, 60,
    194–95; unborn, 3, 115, 173–74, 185
Christians/Christianity, 24–25, 73, 201,
    211
Christmas Carol, A, 187
Chronic conflict, 118–25
Churchill, Winston, 50
Circular causation, 15–16, 48–50, 94,
    107, 135, 172
Civil disobedience, 139, 141, 142–43
Civilian-based defense, 144–45, 152,
    168
Civil liberties, 62–63
Civil rights movement, 63, 104, 135,
    139, 140, 200
Clark, Kenneth and Mamie, 39, 40
Classism, 113
Cocaine, 38–39, 82
Coercion, 186–87
Coffin, William Sloan, 4
Cognitive consistency, 91
Cognitive dissonance, 28, 41, 42–44,
    91

Cohen-Posey, Kate, 154
Cold War, 46, 48, 163, 166, 187
Combat fatigue. *See* Posttraumatic
    Stress Disorder
Comenius, Jan Amos, 74, 213
Commitment, 68, 72
Common ground, 115
Communication: skills, 76, 111,
    145–57; technology, 67, 136; uses,
    96, 126
Community-based social marketing,
    192–93
Community policing, 128
Comparison to worse conduct, 2
Compartmentalizing, 5, 49
Competition, 110
Complex PTSD, 32–33
Comprehensibility, 68
Confidence-building measures, 126,
    164
Conflict resolution, 109–31, 149, 174,
    193; education, 76
Connecting, as nonviolent defense,
    156–57
Conscience, 64, 91, 201, 208
Conscientious objection, 143–44
Conscientization, 75, 216
Consensus, 193–94
Conservatives, 78, 169
Consistent life ethic, 154, 186
Contact hypothesis, 122–23
Contagion, nonviolent, 88, 95, 151
Cooperation, 95, 121, 134–39. *See also*
    Conflict resolution; Noncooperation;
    Peace education
Corporate executive officers, 42
Corporations, 164, 187, 199
Coups d'etat, 67, 144, 152
Courage, 20, 61–62, 69–70, 77, 78, 88
Cowardice, 70, 71, 156, 168, 195
Creationism, 111–14
Creativity, 40, 79, 139, 191, 208
Creativity of the foreclosed option,
    99–100, 184
Crime, 170–81; nonviolent defense,
    156–58; PITS, 37; reductions with
    nonviolence, 51, 77, 95, 96;
    restorative justice, 127–28; violence,

19, 26, 40. *See also* Hate crime;
    Homicide rates
Cruelty to animals, 179–80, 198–99
Crusades, 113
Cuba, 14, 164
Cultural differences, 10, 76, 117,
    118–25
Culture of peace, 75, 79, 207–9
Cycles of violence, 8, 28, 48–50, 163
Cynicism, 17, 45, 47, 91, 200, 203, 214
Czechs, 74, 213

Darrow, Clarence, 50
Day After, The, 208–9
Day the Earth Stood Still, The, 204
Death penalty, 6, 37–38, 59, 114–15,
    170–71, 186
Debating, 114–16
Debs, Eugene V., 62
Deception, 13, 53, 105, 135, 151–52,
    156
Defense, 168–70; civilian-based,
    144–45, 152, 168; guns, 178–79;
    individual, 154–58; Marshall Plan,
    128–29, 169; nonviolence, 61, 62;
    predators, 24; violence, 54
Dehumanization, 2–3, 49, 84, 90, 100,
    165, 169, 208
De-legitimation of violence model, 51
Deming, Barbara, 71
Democracy, 40, 77, 78, 193–94
Demonizing, 2, 52, 76–77, 90, 103, 105
Demons, 24
Denial, 39, 41, 44, 70
Depression, 39, 41, 70–71, 97, 183
Desegregation, 39
Desensitization, 6, 179, 182, 196
Detachment, 32, 38, 47, 50, 66, 100
Deterrence: death penalty, 114,
    170–71; nonviolent, 144; retaliation,
    8; weapons, 163, 166, 179
Development education, 77
Devil's advocate, 60
Dickens, Charles, 187
Dictators, 18, 59, 73, 137, 164
Diet, 72, 99, 150, 197–98
Diffusion of responsibility, 44–45
Diplomacy, 109, 125–26, 168, 216

Direct violence, 31–39, 80–81. *See also individual types of violence*
Disabled people, 3, 99, 173, 182, 183–84, 186
Disarmament, 145, 208, 214
Discipline, 61, 74, 95, 174, 194–95
Disconnects, 1–8, 49, 156
Disney movies, 208
Disruptive stress hypothesis, 162
Dissociation, 37–38, 48, 49
Distancing, 3–5, 13, 37, 49, 84
Divergent thinking, 100
Diversity, 15, 120–23, 127
Divorce, 47, 96
Documenting, 77, 91, 144, 147
Dogmatism, 115, 200
Domestic violence. *See* Family violence
Doubling, 5, 49, 84
Draft, 65, 143–44
Dreams, 32, 34, 37, 38, 48
Dr. Strangelove, 204–5
Drug abuse. *See* Substance abuse
Drugs, 82, 83
Drug war, 172
Dunbar, Edward, 175
Durkheim, Emile, 50
Dymond, Jonathan, 213

Early warning system, 165
Eastern Europe, 137
Ecology: business, 67, 199; definition of peace, x, 80; meat production, 198; promoting, 77, 192–93
Economic conditions and violence, 26, 50, 163, 169, 175
Economic conversion, 129
Economic power, 134–35, 199
Economic sanctions, 92, 164–65
Ecumenism, 73
Education, 74–82, 121–22, 145–47
Effort justification, 28, 44, 84
Egalitarian personality, 60
Ehrenreich, Barbara, 23–25
Eichmann, Adolf, 14
Elder abuse, 173
Elders, 117, 174, 184
El Salvador, 217

Emotional numbing, 39, 41, 49, 173, 182, 185. *See also* Psychic numbing
Emotions, 19–28, 69–74. *See also individual emotions*
Empathy: absence, 18, 19, 177, 179; presence, 45, 61, 66, 76
Emperor's New Groove, The, 208
Employment, 129, 199
Environmental education, 77. *See also* Ecology
Erasmus, 50
Estrangement. *See* Detachment
Ethnic conflict, 74, 118–25, 200
Etzioni, Anotai, 164
Eugenics, 186
Euphemisms: absence, 84, 202; euthanasia, 183; genocide, 165, 182; moral disengagement mechanism, 1, 12, 46; post-trauma symptoms, 49
Europe, 20, 74, 117, 128, 137, 144
Euthanasia, 173, 182, 183–85, 186
Evolution, 23, 111–14
Executions. *See* Death penalty
Exercise, aerobic, 27, 72
Explanatory style, 97–99
Expressive violence, 27–28, 166–67, 174

Fables, 79
Factory farms, 180, 198
Families, 101, 106, 114, 124, 168, 171, 184, 208
Family violence, 26, 77, 81, 173–74, 175
Fanaticism, 167
Fear, 23, 39, 41, 66, 94, 121, 134–35, 138, 208
Federal Bureau of Investigation, 179
Female infanticide, 173
Feminist concerns, 154, 173–76, 183–88
Feminists for Life, 120
Feuds, 8, 28, 52, 88
Financial difficulties, 149
Flashbacks, 32, 35, 38, 48
Folk literature, 205–6
Follett, Mary Parker, 109–10, 213

Forgiveness, 70–71, 73, 74, 77, 127–28
Frankenstein, 205
Freud, Sigmund, 22–23, 26–27
Friere, Paulo, 75, 216
Frustration-aggression hypothesis, 25–26
Fundamental attribution error, 111, 119

Gabriel, Peter, 9
Galileo, 113
Galtung, Johan, 80
Gandhi, Mohandas: civil disobedience, 58, 140, 141; pacifism, 74, 142, 168; religion, 73; use of terms, 57, 135, 154
Gandhi movie, 197, 208
Gangs, 33, 39, 109, 172, 175
Gangsta rap, 207
Gas chambers, 4
Gasciogne, George, 202
Genocide, 15, 113, 165–66, 187
Genovese, Kitty, 44
Germany, 3, 9, 44, 128, 176, 183, 186
Gestalt analysis, 23
Goals, 51–55, 103–7, 137, 148
God, 4, 18, 21, 96, 113, 201, 203
Gods, 24, 112, 201
Godzilla, 204–5
Gorbachev, Mikhail, 163
Graduated and Reciprocated Initiatives in Tension-reduction, 164, 215
Great Britain, 36, 55, 58, 65, 107, 113, 137
Greed, 23, 91, 203
Gregg, Richard, 61–62, 88, 216
GRIT (Graduated and Reciprocated Initiatives in Tension-reduction), 164, 215
Grossman, Dave, 5–6, 156
Group decision making, 193–94
Group identification, 118–19, 164
Groupthink: causation, 14–15, 162; countering, 60; danger to goals, 52, 63, 169; nonviolent groups, 103; post-trauma symptoms, 49–50
Guerrillas, 50, 166

Guilt, 35, 40, 41, 71
Gulf War of 1991, 46
Gun violence, 178–79
Gypsies, 182

Habits: obedience, 138; optimism/ pessimism, 97; social referencing, 90; violence, 50, 155, 179, 184
Happiness, 42
Hardiness, 68
Hate crime, 26, 62, 174–76
Hatred: absence, 9, 63, 69, 104, 203; causing violence, 27–28, 127, 135, 167; countering, 77, 120–23; effect of violence, 52; literature, 107
Health, physical, x, 67–69, 70–71, 72, 97, 209
Hebrew literature, 201, 206
Hebrew prophets, 24, 73, 79, 200, 202, 213
Hindus, 73, 166, 211
Hiroshima, 34, 42, 46, 76
History vs. memory, 123–25
Hitler, Adolf, 19, 52
Hollywood, 26, 37, 63, 84
Homicide rates, 50–51, 54, 106, 170–71
Homosexual people, 120, 182
Honesty, 18, 25, 78, 117, 152
Hovland and Sears study, 26
Human rights education, 77
Humor: coping, 40, 103, 204, 205, 206; nonviolence, 96–97, 107, 143, 156, 191; physical health, 83
Hungary, 136
Hunger. *See* Poverty

Ideology, 6, 15, 128
Idolatry, 96, 200
Illusions, 46, 112
Imagination, 36, 42, 79, 88
India: Ashoka, 73; nonviolence campaign, 55, 58, 73, 107, 137, 141; violence, 104, 135, 197
Indonesia, 126, 216
Infanticide, 173
Inner peace, 70, 73, 78
Inquisition, 113
Instinct for violence, 7, 23, 69

Institutional peace, 74, 80
Institutional violence, 58–59, 65. *See also* Stanford Prison Experiment; Structural violence
Instrumental violence, 27–28, 166–67, 174
Integrative complexity, 72, 161–63
Integrative power, 134–35
Integrative solutions, 110, 125–26, 314
Intellectualizing, 5, 49
Intelligent design, 112, 114
Interdependency, 120–22
Interest-based approach, 110, 115
Intergenerational transmission, 173
Internalization, 61, 68, 72, 89, 98–99
International education, 76
International Peace Research Association, 80, 86, 214
Interpositioning, 144
Intimate violence. *See* Family violence
Intrusive imagery, 35–37, 42
Iraq, 164
Ireland, 74, 76
Islam, 24, 211. *See also* Muslims
Israel, 59, 65–66, 124, 141, 166
Italy, 74–75

James, Jesse and Frank, 50
James, William, ix, 19, 61–62, 213
Janis, Irving Lester, 14–15, 60, 216
Japan/Japanese, 62–63, 76, 128, 156, 176, 204
Jesus, 142
Jews: activists, 65, 73, 142–43, 211; dominated group, 143, 152; targeted by Nazis, 3, 4, 12, 14, 165, 176, 182; zealots, 166. *See also* Hebrew literature; Hebrew prophets
Jigsaw technique, 121–22, 123
Jokes, 18, 26, 69–70, 97, 157–58
Joseph, Joanne M., 69
Journalists, 45, 197, 205
Jungian psychology, 118, 201
Jurassic Park, 205
Justice: restorative, 127–28, 181; retaliatory, 7–8

Just war doctrine, 8, 105, 168–69
Just world view, 6–7, 69, 84, 93, 119
Juvenile offenders, 127

Kant, Immanuel, 65
Kelly, Thomas, 40
Kennedy, John F., 14, 164, 169, 215–26
Kierkegaard, Soren, 54
King, Martin Luther, Jr., 73, 96, 141
Kohlberg, Lawrence, 63–65, 78
Koran, 168
Korea, 76, 164
Korean-American war, 6, 22
Krech, David, 214
Khrushchev, Nikita, 164
Kübler-Ross, Elisabeth, 70
Ku Klux Klan, 166, 207

Latin America, 73, 76, 103, 117, 166
Lawrence, William, 59
Laws: object of protest, 89, 103, 141; against violence, 64, 174; for violence, 3, 12, 16, 43
Lederach, John Paul, 117–18
Legitimation of violence model, 51, 170
Lehrer, Tom, 204
LeShan, Lawrence, 20–22, 203
Liagin, Elizabeth, 187
Liberals, 78, 169
Lifton, Robert Jay, 4–5, 34, 46–47, 59
Lincoln, Abraham, 43
Linguistic war. *See* Semantic dehumanization
Linn, Dennis, Sheila, and Matthew, 70–71
Linn, Ruth, 65–66
Listening skills, 115, 193–94
Literature, 36, 201–9
Locus of control, 68, 72
London, 52, 126
Lorenz, Konrad, 23
Los Alamos, 47
Love, 75, 79, 96, 135
Lyman, Howard, 59

Lynching, 26, 150, 175, 207
Lysistrata, 202

Machiavelli, Niccolo, 17, 50
Machiavellian personality, 17–18, 60, 69
Machismo, 7, 69, 157
Malaysia, 126, 216
Manageability, 68
Mansfield, Sue, 23
Marriage, 47, 101
Marshall, George C., 128
Marshall Plan, 128–29, 169
Martín-Baró, Ignacio, 217
Martyrdom, 54–55, 106
Marx, Groucho, 96
Marx, Karl, 96
Maslach, Christina, 13–14, 100–101
Mayton, Dan, 89
McCartney, Paul, 197
McDougall, William, 213–14
McVeigh, Timothy, 18–19, 177
Meaning, 10, 20, 21, 49, 61, 68, 124, 205
Meat, 43, 99, 180, 197–98
Media, 26–27, 62–63, 67, 144, 145
Media violence, 6, 195–97
Medicine, 150, 181–88
Memory, 123–25
Men: draft resistance, 65, 143–44; gangsta rap, 207; homicide rates after war, 50–51; machismo, 7; meat consumption, 198; nuclear resistance, 59; obedience experiments, 10. *See also individual men's names*
Milgram, Stanley, 9, 10, 216
Milgram obedience experiments, 9–13; defiance, 58, 140; frustration, 26; genocide, 165; predispositions, 17, 65; sequential steps, 27, 179; structural violence, 41
Milosevic, Slobadan, 138, 165
Mirror image, 163, 215
Monolithic theory of power, 137–38
Montessori, Maria, 57, 74–75, 213

Montgomery bus boycott, 91, 96
Moral development, 33, 63–66, 78, 181
Moral disengagement, 1–2, 12, 46, 169, 173, 177, 182
Moral education, 78
Moral high ground, 53–54, 105
Moral jiu-jitsu, 57, 154
Moral obligation, 138
More, Sir Thomas, 50
Mothers, 68, 115, 117, 157
Movies, 83, 195–97, 203, 204–5. *See also titles of individual movies*
Muir, Gladys, 214
Mullen, Tom, 96–97
Multiple issue focus, 154
Murder simulation training devices, 6
Music, 9, 40, 165, 204, 205, 206
Muslims, 62–63, 73, 166, 176
Mutually Assured Destruction (MAD), 166
My Lai massacre, 65, 93
Mythic mode, 20–22, 72, 163, 203

Nader, Ralph, 62
Nagasaki, 47, 76
Narcissistic personality, 18–19
Native Americans, 3, 172, 208
Nazis, 6, 9, 15, 34, 37, 44, 113, 197. *See also Jews, targeted by Nazis*
Negative peace, 80
Neglect, 173, 183
Newcomers, 153–54
Nightmares, 32, 35, 37, 38
Noncooperation, 136–37, 155, 168
Nonlethal weapons, 66–67, 168
Nonparticipants, 44–46. *See also Observers of violence*
Nonviolence: causation, 57–86; defined, 57; education, 76; effects, 87–107; lifestyles, 78, 192–201; promoting with art, 79, 207–9; public policy, 125–29. *See also individual types of nonviolent action*
Nonviolent resistance, 55, 107, 133–59
Noonan, John, 43
North Korea, 164

Not Dead Yet, 183
Nuclear anxieties, 34, 203–5, 208
Nuclear energy, 44, 100
Nuclear weapons, 42, 44, 46–48, 59,
    163, 214. *See also* Hiroshima

Obedience, as basis for power,
    136–38. *See also* Milgram obedience
    experiments
Observers of violence, 44–46, 87, 88,
    92–94, 140, 154
Old-timers, 153–54
On the Beach, 204
Open-mindedness, 193
Operant conditioning, 5–6, 15, 66, 139
Oppenheimer, Robert, 47, 59, 203, 205
Oppression, 71, 75, 144, 201, 205–7.
    See also Structural violence
Optimism, 14, 45, 97–99, 107, 150, 191
Organizational power, 136
Orwell, George, 54
Osgood, Charles, 164, 215
Out-group homogeneity effect, 89–90,
    149
Oversimplified thinking, 49–50, 52,
    63, 73, 162, 169

Pacifism, 8, 24, 72, 168–69
Pacifists, 20, 69, 100
Palestinians, 124, 141, 166
Parables, 79, 153
Paradoxes, 150–51
Paranoia, 41, 151, 167
Parenting: encouraging peace, 106,
    116, 208; encouraging violence, 39,
    41, 177
Passive orientation, 72
Pathology view of war, 22–25
Pavlov, Ivan, 214
Peace, defined, x
Peace Brigades International, 144
Peacebuilding, 77, 81, 148
Peace education, 74–82
Peacemaking, ix, 81, 118
Peace movement, 59, 63, 186, 215
Peace psychology, defined, x
Peace Psychology Division of the

American Psychological
    Association, x, 217
Peace research, 80–84, 192–93, 216
Peace studies, 75, 79–80, 203, 214
Pearl Harbor, 62, 176
Pelton, Leroy, 91, 93
Perfectionism, 150
Perpetration-Induced Traumatic
    Stress, 34–37, 41, 55, 59, 83, 106,
    185
Personality: nonviolence, 60–61,
    68–69, 208; violence, 16–19, 32, 178
Persuasion, 79, 91, 134, 145–47
Pessimism, 97–99, 150–51
Philippines, 73, 137
Physical violence, 81
Picasso, Pablo, 202
Pluralistic-dependence theory of
    power, 137–38
Pocahontas, 208
Poetry, 36, 59, 79, 118, 201–2, 203–4
Poland, 73
Political prisoners, 92
Politics, 7, 47–48, 134–39. *See also*
    Public policy
Poor people, 75, 150, 172, 183, 187,
    200, 205–7. *See also* Poverty;
    Structural violence
Population control, 186–87
Positive discipline, 174, 195
Positive peace, 80
Posttrauma stress, 34, 106–7, 168, 171,
    202
Posttraumatic Stress Disorder, 31–33,
    45, 82–83, 174–75, 216, 217. *See also*
    Perpetration-Induced Traumatic
    Stress
Poverty: countering, 67, 75, 169, 186;
    effects, 33, 39–40, 45, 164–65. *See
    also* Poor people; Structural
    violence
Power theories, 134–39
Pragmatists, 153
Prayer, 78, 84, 86
Predators, 23–25, 205
Prejudice, 16, 18, 89–90, 119–20,
    120–23
Priming: catharsis, 27; cruelty to
    animals, 179; guns, 178–79

Prisons, 84, 106, 180–81. *See also* Stanford Prison Experiment
Progress, 62, 149–51
Pro-life Alliance of Gays and Lesbians, 120
Proliferation paradox, 151
Proportion paradox, 150
Protestants, 73–74, 76
Psychic numbing, 34, 46
Psychological violence, 81
Psychologists for Social Responsibility, x, 216
Psychology, defined, x
Psychopaths, 19
Psychosocial trauma, 40
Public health approach, 172
Public policy, 39, 65, 79, 111–14, 125–29, 161–89, 197
Purges, 3, 141
Purists, 153

Quakers, 40, 69, 75, 172, 213
Quantrill's guerrillas, 50

Racism, 91, 113, 174–76, 183, 186. *See also* Apartheid; Civil rights movement; Ethnic conflict; Segregation; Structural violence
Rape, 7
Realpolitik, 7, 69
Reconciliation, 70, 126–28. *See also* Forgiveness; Restorative justice; Truth and Reconciliation Commission
Reform, 74, 138, 153
Refuseniks, Israeli, 59
Relative deprivation, 119
Religion, 73–74, 200–201; ancient, 24–25; creation/evolution, 111–14; Machiavellians, 18. *See also individual religions, religious concepts, and religious literature*
Religious education, 78
Religious groups, 149, 210–11
Repetition compulsion, 48
Repression, 53, 92, 104–5
Republicans for Choice, 120
Resilience, 40, 67–69, 72, 97

Respectability, 153
Restorative justice, 127–28, 181
Retaliation, 7–8
Revenge, 7–8, 19, 27, 52, 174
Rich people, 42, 187
Rickover, Hyman B., 59
Rights-based approach, 110
Riots, 66, 104, 135, 168
Role expectations, 90–91
Role-playing, 66, 139
Root causes, 153, 170
Roots, 208

Sadists, 14, 19
Satyagraha, 57, 89, 135, 144
Saving Private Ryan, 37
Scapegoating, 2, 16, 49, 119, 165, 167, 207
Scarlet and the Black, The, 197
Schindler's List, 34, 197
School Peace League, 74
Schools of thought, 152–53
School violence, 53, 176–78
Secondary traumatization, 45
Second-track diplomacy, 126, 216
Secrecy, 47
Security, 7, 8, 67, 129
Segregation, 133, 137, 141, 206
Self-efficacy, 68, 72, 139, 158
Self-esteem, 40, 95, 113, 177
Self-fulfilling prophecy, 7, 147
Self-hatred, 20, 23, 99
Self-sacrifice, 19, 61–62, 78
Self-serving bias, 89
Seligman, Martin, 97–98
Semantic dehumanization, 2–3, 97
Sense of coherence, 68–69, 72
Sensory mode, 20–22
September 11 attacks, 62–63, 167–68, 176, 203
Sequential steps, 11–12, 165, 179
Serbia, 164–65
Sexism, 97, 150, 173
Sexual abuse, 7, 173
Sharp, Gene, 51, 92, 94–95, 137–39, 216
Shell shock. *See* Posttraumatic Stress Disorder

Sherif, Muzafer, 119, 120–21
Siege, 164
Sikhs, 73, 176
Singapore, 126, 216
Single issue focus, 154
Skinner, B. F., 5
Slaughterhouses, 37, 180, 197
Slavery, 3, 43, 142, 169, 176, 206, 208
Sleep disturbance, 37, 45, 48, 202
Slippery slope, 12, 165, 183
Slumlords, 40, 42
Social Darwinism, 113
Social identification, 118–19
Socialization, 138, 180, 194–95
Social movements, 59, 63, 67, 133–59, 201
Social referencing, 44–45, 90–91, 140
Sociopath, 19
Solar energy, 67
Soldier's heart. *See* Posttraumatic Stress Disorder
South Africa, 40, 125, 137, 165, 201
South African Truth and Reconciliation Commission, 45, 70, 125, 127, 218
South America. *See* Latin America
Soviet Union, 3, 46, 92, 113, 128, 162, 215
Spirituality, 73–74, 84
SPSSI (Society for the Psychological Study of Social Issues), 214
Stanford Prison Experiment, 13–14, 17, 41, 101, 180, 216
Star Trek, 99, 151
Steele, Shelby, 205–6
Stereotyping: causing problems, 16, 40, 73, 97, 113–14, 152, 169; countering 77, 90–91, 121–23
Stimson, Henry, 59
Stress: biology, 19, 83; coping, 67–69, 174; problems, 12, 28, 162, 180; reduction, 27, 66, 72–73, 74, 139. *See also* Burnout; Posttraumatic Stress Disorder
Structural violence, 39–44, 80. *See also* Ecology; Poor people; Poverty; Racism

Substance abuse, 31, 37, 40, 41, 45, 83, 172, 174
Suicide, 32, 39, 99, 183–85
Superman, 204
Survivor guilt, 35
Symbolic actions, 140–41
Systematic desensitization, 179

Technology: nonviolent, 66–67, 77, 136, 168; violent, 15–16, 24, 36, 47, 205
Teller, Edward, 42
Terrorism, 67, 166–68
Therapists, 45, 66, 154, 181–82
Therapy: preventing violence, 174, 181; promoting peace, 27, 70, 106–7, 167–68, 194, 202
Threat power, 134–35
Time distortion, 37–38
Tint Alon, Barbara, 123–25
Tobacco, 196–97
Tocqueville, Alexis de, 137
Tolerance for ambiguity, 71–72, 73, 74
Transarmament, 145
Truth and Reconciliation Commission, South African, 45, 70, 125, 127, 218
Tutu, Desmond, 40, 201. *See also* Truth and Reconciliation Commission
Twain, Mark, 4, 22, 203, 213

Unborn children, 3, 115, 173–74, 185
Unions, 207
United Nations, 75, 79, 127, 217
United States Department of Justice, 128
United States Federal Bureau of Investigation, 179
United States Surgeon General reports: hate crimes, 174–75; media violence, 196
Urgency, 45–46, 150, 153

Vegetarianism, 43, 59, 99, 197–98
Veterans, 34–36, 38–39, 48–51, 59, 202, 217
Video games, 6
Viet Cong, 4, 48–49, 65

Vietnam-American war, 4, 6, 22, 28, 46, 48, 202. *See also* My Lai massacre; Veterans
Vietnam Veterans Against the War, 59, 106
Violence: causation, 1–28, 82–84, 118–20; countering, 58–63, 154–58; definition, 1; effects, 31–55; public policy, 161–89. *See also* Cycles of violence; Direct violence; Expressive violence; Instrumental violence; Physical violence; Psychological violence; Structural violence; *and individual types of violence and violent events*
Violence prevention education, 77
Volunteers, 149, 198–99

Wagner, Richard, 148
War fever. *See* War hysteria
War Games, 47, 204–5
War hysteria, 20–22, 49–50, 52, 62–63, 72, 73, 163, 167, 213
War Prayer, 4, 22, 203, 213
War songs, 202–3
Watergate scandal, 48

White, Ralph K., 215, 217
White people, 40, 101, 122, 140–41, 172, 175
Wind energy, 67
Wink, Walter, 139, 142–43
Win-win solutions, 110, 193
Witness for Peace, 144
Wizard of Oz, 21–22
Women: assistance, 115, 185, 199; conflict handling, 117, 157–58, 202; dominated group, 3, 152, 183, 207; homicide rates after war, 50–51; meat consumption, 198; obedience experiments, 10; powerful group, 157–58; voting, 150. *See also individual women's names*
World Health Organization, 32
World War I, 20–21, 32, 35, 50, 62, 74, 129
World War II, 5, 32, 52, 62, 129, 202

Yugoslavia, 138

Zero-sum conflicts, 110
Zero-sum thinking, 119, 126
Zimbardo, Philip, 13, 17

About the Author

RACHEL M. MACNAIR is Director of the Institute for Integrated Social Analysis, a research organization which specializes in the connections between various social issues and violence. She is the author of *Perpetration-Induced Traumatic Stress: The Psychological Consequences of Killing* (Praeger, 2002).